THE FATHERS
OF THE CHURCH

A NEW TRANSLATION

VOLUME 70

THE FATHERS
OF THE CHURCH

A NEW TRANSLATION

SAINT AUGUSTINE

EIGHTY-THREE DIFFERENT QUESTIONS

Translated by

DAVID L. MOSHER

Scarborough College

University of Toronto

THE CATHOLIC UNIVERSITY OF AMERICA PRESS
Washington, D.C.

Nihil Obstat:
REVEREND HERMIGILD DRESSLER, O.F.M.
Censor Deputatus

Imprimatur:
✠ WILLIAM CARDINAL BAUM
Archbishop of Washington

April 22, 1977

The *nihil obstat* and *imprimatur* are official declarations that a book or pamphlet is free of doctrinal or moral error. No implication is contained therein that those who have granted the *nihil obstat* and the *imprimatur* agree with content, opinions, or statements expressed.

Library of Congress Cataloging in Publication Data

Augustine, Saint, Bishop of Hippo.
  Eighty-three different questions.

  (The Fathers of the Church; v. 70)
  Translation of: De diversis quaestionibus LXXXIII.
  Bibliography: p. xix-xx.
  Includes indexes.
    1. Theology—Miscellanea.   2. Philosophy—
Miscellanea.   I. Title.   II. Series: Fathers of the
Church; v. 70.
BR60.F3A8243 [BR65.A6544]   270s   [230'.14]   81-2546
ISBN 0-8132-0070-9   AACR2

CONTENTS

(only?)

PREFACE

Reading St. Augustine in Latin is a delightful task, not so much because of his grace of style as because of the majesty and rich nuance of the thoughts which he expresses in that language. If one is captivated by this aspect of his writings, then translating St. Augustine into some other language is an even more delightful task, because the translator must of necessity savor every word and phrase of the Latin Augustine before attempting to turn them into his own language. However, this is at the same time a difficult task, and a translator must often seek out others for advice in handling the myriad problems which any serious translation effort poses. In this regard, I am deeply grateful to E.A. Synan of the Pontifical Institute of Mediaeval Studies for many hours of his time. His assistance has been invaluable to me in all phases of this translation effort. I am also indebted to my colleague, Paul W. Gooch, of Scarborough College, the University of Toronto, who has read and commented on many things in the introduction, translation, and notes. However, the hardest work of all has been done by the editorial director and staff of the *Fathers of the Church* series. I owe a special word of thanks to the late Bernard M. Peebles, to Hermigild Dressler, O.F.M., and to the others who have worked diligently with them to try to remove the blemishes from my translation effort. However, for the blemishes that remain I take full responsibility.

Some financial support for this project came from the University of Toronto. I am grateful for summer grants in 1969 and 1970 which enabled me to indulge my interest in St. Augustine without at the same time having to work for a living.

Finally, my deep-felt thanks go to my understanding wife, Mary Elizabeth, who has suffered patiently St. Augustine's frequent intrusions into an otherwise happy marriage.

SELECT BIBLIOGRAPHY

Texts

Bardy, G. (et al. eds.), *Oeuvres de Saint Augustin*, Bibliothèque Augustinienne 10 (Paris: Desclée de Brouwer et Cie 1952) 52–378. The present translation is based on this text.

Caillau, D.A.B. (ed.) *Sancti Aurelii Augustini Hipponensis Episcopi Opera
Omnia* 38 (Paris: Parent-Desbarres 1840) 3–143.

Migne, J. P. (ed.), *Patrologiae Cursus Completus Series Latina* 40 (Paris: J. P.
Migne 1861) 11–100.

Mutzenbecher, A. (ed.), *Sancti Aurelii Augustini De diversis quaestionibus
octoginta tribus* Corpus Christianorum Series Latina 44A (Turnhout:
Brepols 1975).

Translations

Beckaert, J. A., "Quatre-vingt-trois questions différentes" *Bibliothèque
Augustinienne* 10 (Paris: Desclée de Brouwer et Cie 1952) 53–378. My
own translation effort owes much to this fine translation.

Perl, C. J., *Dreiundachtzig verschiedene Fragen* (Paderborn: Schöningh 1972).

Raulx, M. (ed.), *Oeuvres complètes de saint Augustin* 5 (Bar-le-Duc: L. Guérin
et Cie 1867) 428–891.

Other Works

Alfaric, P., *L'évolution intellectuelle de saint Augustin: Du manichéisme au
néoplatonisme* (Paris: E. Nourry 1918). The author argues the pro-
vocative thesis that St. Augustine's famous conversion was to
Neoplatonism rather than to Christianity.

Armstrong, A. H., *St. Augustine and Christian Platonism* (Villanova:
Villanova University Press 1967). An easy, readable introduction to
some interesting aspects of a very big problem.

Brown, P., *Augustine of Hippo: A Biography* (Berkeley: University of Cali-
fornia Press 1967). The best biography of Augustine available.

Cayré, F., *Initiation à la philosophie de saint Augustin* (Paris: Etudes augustiniennes 1947).

Flórez, R., "Sobre la mentalidad de Agustín en los primeros años de su
monacato. El 'Libro de las ochenta y tres cuestiones' " *La Ciudad de
Dios* 169 (1956) 464–77.

Gilson, E., *Introduction à l'étude de saint Augustin* 3d ed. (Paris: Librairie
philosophique J. Vrin 1949). English translation: L. Lynch, *The Christian Philosophy of Saint Augustine* (New York: Random House 1960). This
work is still the unsurpassed study of the theological and philosophical
views of St. Augustine.

Grandgeorge, L., *Saint Augustin et le néo-platonisme* (Paris: E. Leroux 1896).
A classic.

Harnack, A., *History of Dogma*. English translation from the 3d German
edition by N. Buchanan, 7 volumes in 4 (New York: Dover Publica-
tions 1961).

Hultgren, G., *Le commandement d'amour chez Augustin* (Paris: Libraire philosophique J. Vrin 1939). One of the definitive studies on the topic.

Markus, R., "Imago and Similitudo in Augustine" *Revue des études augustiniennes* 10 (1964) 125–43.

Marrou, H., *Saint Augustine and His Influence Through the Ages*. English translation by P. Hepburne-Scott (New York: Harper Torchbooks 1957).

————, *Saint Augustin et la fin de la culture antique* 4th ed. (Paris: E. De Boccard 1958). The definitive study. A superb and elegant piece of scholarship.

Mosher, D., "St. Augustine on Freedom" *Crux* 12.3 (1974–75) 18–29.

Myerhof, H., "On the Platonism of St. Augustine's *Quaestio de ideis*" *The New Scholasticism* 16 (1942) 16–45. A concise and well organized introduction to Augustine's Platonism through an analysis of Question 46 of DD 83.

Portalié, E., *A Guide to the Thought of St. Augustine*. With an introduction by V. Bourke. Translated by R. Bastian (Chicago: H. Regnery 1960).

Quasten, J., *Patrology* 3 vols. (Utrecht-Antwerp: Spectrum 1953–62). A very useful reference work.

Roche, W., "Measure, Number, and Weight in Saint Augustine" *The New Scholasticism* 15 (1941) 350–76.

Solignac, A., "Analyse et sources de la question 'De ideis' " *Augustinus Magister* 1 (Paris: Etudes augustiniennes 1954) 307–15.

Van Bavel, T., *Recherches sur la christologie de saint Augustin: l'humain et le divin dans le Christ d'après saint Augustin* (Fribourg Suisse: Editions universitaires 1954).

Wilmart, A., "Operum s. Augustini elenchus a Possidio eiusdem discipulo Calamensi episcopo digestus" *Miscellanea Agostiniana* 2 (Rome: Tipografia vaticana 1930–31) 149–233. This article contains an edition of the *Indiculus* of Possidius.

Wolfson, H., *The Philosophy of the Church Fathers: Faith, Trinity and Incarnation* 3d ed. (Cambridge, Mass.: Harvard University Press 1970).

Zimara, C., "Das Ineinanderspiel von Gottes Vorwissen und Wollen nach Augustinus" *Freiburger Zeitschrift fur Philosophie und Theologie* 6 (1959) 271–99, 361–94. For Question 46 of DD 83 see especially 275–84. This is an article which serious investigators of the topic cannot ignore.

ABBREVIATIONS

BA	*Bibliothèque Augustinienne*
C	*Confessiones*
CA	*Contra academicos*
CCSL	*Corpus Christianorum Series Latina*
CD	*Contra duas epistolas Pelagianorum ad Bonifatium Papam*
CI	*Contra Iulianum haeresis Pelagianorum defensorem*
CSEL	*Corpus scriptorum ecclesiasticorum latinorum*
CSIR	*Contra secundam Iuliani responsionem*
DAO	*De anima et eius origine*
DBe	*De beata vita*
DCa	*De catechizandis rudibus*
DCD	*De civitate Dei*
DCF	*Disputatio contra Fortunatum Manichaeum*
DCG	*De correptione et gratia*
DCnS	*De consensu evangelistarum*
DD83	*De diversis quaestionibus LXXXIII*
DDC	*De doctina christiana*
DDoP	*De dono perseuerantiae*
DDS	*De diversis quaestionibus ad Simplicianum*
DDu	*De duabus animabus contra Manichaeos*
DGA	*De gratia et libero arbitrio*
DGnI	*De Genesi ad litteram liber imperfectus*
DGnM	*De Genesi ad litteram contra Manichaeos*
DGrC	*De gratia Christi et peccato originali*
DGsP	*De gestis Pelagii*
DI	*De immortalitate animae*
DLA	*De libero arbitrio*
DME	*De moribus ecclesiae catholicae et de moribus Manichaeorum*
DNB	*De natura boni contra Manichaeos*
DNG	*De natura et gratia*
DO	*De ordine*
DPB	*De peccatorum meritis et remissione et de baptismo paruulorum*
DPI	*De perfectione iustitiae hominis*
DPS	*De praedestinatione sanctorum*
DQ	*De quantitate animae*
DSD	*De sermone Domini in monte*
DSL	*De spiritu et littera*
DT	*De trinitate*
DTC	*Dictionnaire de théologie catholique*
DUC	*De utilitate credendi*
DVR	*De uera religione*
E	*Epistulae* (E 28 = *Epistula* 28)
EnP	*Enarrationes in psalmos*

ER	*Epistulae ad Romanos incohata expositio*
ExG	*Expositio Epistulae ad Galatas*
ExR	*Expositio quarumdam propositionum ex Epistula ad Romanos*
FOTC	*The Fathers of the Church*
IE	*In Ioannis evangelium tractatus CXXIV*
NCE	*New Catholic Encyclopedia*
OED	*Oxford English Dictionary*
PG	*Patrologiae Cursus Completus Series Graeca*
PL	*Patrologiae Cursus Completus Series Latina*
R	*Retractationes*
S	*Sermones* (S 17 = *Sermo* 17)
So	*Soliloquia*

The abbreviations for the works of St. Augustine are taken, with some modifications from E. Portalié, *A Guide to the Thought of St. Augustine,* with an introduction by V. Bourke, translated by R. Bastian (Chicago: H. Regnery 1960), pp. 331-33. Throughout the footnotes, abbreviations have been used extensively. Refer to the select bibliography and to the list of abbreviations for full bibliographic form.

INTRODUCTION[1]

RARELY HAS A GREAT AND INFLUENTIAL THINKER taken pains to let others look at his previous literary career through his very own eyes. St. Augustine, however, has provided us with a rich opportunity to do just that. In his *Retractations*,[2] written a couple of years before his death in 430, St. Augustine reflects upon the merits and demerits of the numerous books, letters, and sermons which he had authored over a forty-year period. Frequently he also tells us why a particular work was written, when, and for whom.

Among the works discussed in this critical reassessment of his literary career is his *Eighty-three Different Questions*,[3] and he gives this work close scrutiny. His remarks clearly tell us when, why, how, and for whom the work was written, and they provide the most important material for determining the place of this work in Augustine's intellectual and spiritual development. He begins by saying:

> Among the things which we have written, there is also a work of a diffuse nature which, nonetheless, is thought of as a single book, and its title is *Eighty-three Different Ques-*

---

1 This introduction was submitted for publication in the Spring of 1973. It appears here in substantially the same form in which it was submitted. Whatever changes have been made are to be found primarily in the footnotes. In this regard, see below, n. 6.

2 PL 32.583–656. The Latin title of the work is *Retractationes*. See I. Bogan, trans., *St. Augustine: The Retractations*, FOTC 60 (Washington, D.C. 1968). I have followed Sister Bogan's translation of the Latin into English, because a *retractatio* is more than simply a retraction; it can also be a revision, a correction, a second though. This understanding of the term is more in keeping with the actual content of the *Retractationes*.

3 R 1.26 (PL 32.624–30). As for DD83 itself, it is found in PL 40.11–100. For other editions of the work, see select bibliography.

1

tions. However, the questions had been scattered through many leaves of paper, because, from the very beginning of my conversion and after our return to Africa, the questions were dictated, without any order having been preserved by me, in response to the brothers who were ever asking me things when they would see me unoccupied. When I became bishop, I ordered that the questions be gathered together and made up into a single book, and that numbers be added so that anyone could easily find what he wanted to read.[4]

St. Augustine then goes on to list the questions in the order in which they occur in the book itself and, where he deems appropriate, to provide certain explanations and corections. As G. Bardy points out,[5] all this—Augustine's initial care in bringing the scattered questions together into one volume and the space which he devotes to them in his *Retractations*—should convince us of the importance which St. Augustine himself attached to the *Questions* and should move us to give the work careful attention. In pursuing that end I shall, in this introduction, approximate St. Augustine's own procedure in the *Retractations* by considering first the usual queries: when, where, why, how, as well as some related questions, and then by going on to deal with the content of the *Eighty-three Different Questions.*

I. Literary Form and Chronology[6]

St. Augustine tells us that the various parts of the *Questions* were composed during the period between his return to North Africa from Italy (388) and his selection as bishop of Hippo (396),[7] a then flourishing North African coastal city

---

4 R 1.26 (PL 32.624).

5 G. Bardy, et al. eds., *Oeuvres de Saint Augustin*, Bibliothèque Augustinienne 10 (Paris 1952), pp. 11–50 (hereafter cited as BA 10). This introduction is a fine treatment of the literary problems, chronology, and doctrinal content of DD83.

6 Since the completion of this introduction in 1973, there has appeared A. Mutzenbecher's edition of DD83 in CCSL 44A (Turnhout 1975).

7 The date of 396 is Bardy's, BA 10, p. 12. Mutzenbecher, p. xxxiii, n. 2, places the date of Augustine's consecration as bishop somewhere between May 395 and 28 August 397. He also indicates some of the literature to be consulted in dealing with the problem.

several days' journey west of Carthage. During this time
Augustine was living in a sort of monastic community, first
located in his hometown of Thagaste and then at Hippo,
which he had organized upon his return to Africa. The
brothers of the community no doubt looked to Augustine for
moral, spiritual, and intellectual leadership, and hence they
pelted him with questions whenever they had the chance.
His responses were recorded and kept in the community's
library. After his election as cobishop of Hippo, St.
Augustine had the responses, then scattered among other
works, collected together into a single book. His language in
the *Retractations* makes it clear that someone else, and not St.
Augustine himself, was responsible for the actual work of
gathering together the various questions and their responses.
St. Augustine's further remarks in his *Retractations* about
QQ. 12 and 31[8] reinforce this point and identify the brothers
of the community as those responsible, presumably under
Augustine's guidance, for the collecting and editing, if any
were in fact done, of the *Eighty-three Different Questions*.

However, St. Augustine's account of when, where, why
and how the *Eighty-three Different Questions* came into being,
though an answer to those questions, raises a whole host of
others. Were the various questions grouped together in an
arbitrary manner, or was there a principle of organization,
sanctioned by Augustine, which guided the efforts of those
who compiled the book? If the latter, was the book organized
around one or several leading themes, or were the questions
compiled in the chronological order in which they had been
written? If the latter, did this of itself give sufficient unity to
the work to allow Augustine to speak of it as a "single book"
or must we speak of the work simply as an unstructured
grouping of questions and answers? If the latter, was there
nonetheless a literary genre which might justify Augustine's
looking at this loose grouping of questions and answers as
something which was still a literary unit? If there were such
a literary genre, was it Augustine's intent from the very
beginning to put together a "tolerable literary unit" of this
form? And finally, since the diverse questions which eventually constituted the *Eighty-three Different Questions* did in fact

8 See Q. 12, n. 1, and Q 31, n. 1.

lie in a dispersed condition for several years, did any of
them, separate from the others, ever circulate in a reading
public wider than the community of brothers at Thagaste
and then at Hippo?

Beginning with the last question, did any of the eighty-
three questions ever circulate independently of one another?
There is one important piece of prima facie evidence that
this may have been the case. Possidius, a disciple, friend,
and faithful biographer of St. Augustine, prepared shortly
after his death an *indiculus* or catalogue of Augustine's
works.[9] Dispersed throughout this catalogue, under the
various headings which Possidius used to organize it, one
finds all eighty-three questions of the *Eighty-three Different
Questions,* but one will find no separate work by that name.
What makes this piece of information even more important
is that Possidius in all probability employed Augustine's
own comprehensive catalogue of his writings, a catalogue
which is now lost.[10] Given this information, one could conclude that the individual questions were separately published and that Augustine had not from the start conceived
of uniting them together into one book, into a literary unit.

However, such a conclusion is not the only one warranted.
For it is open to dispute whether Possidius's *Indiculus* is
evidence for the independent circulation of the various questions. Possidius, in accord with his own scheme for catalogu-
ing Augustine's works, could have copied the titles of the
questions out of the *Retractations*, where Augustine lists them
under the general heading, *Eighty-three Different Questions.*[11]

---

9 For the *Indiculus* of Possidius, see A. Wilmart, "Operum s. Augustini
elenchus a Possidio eiusdem discipulo Calamensi episcopo digestus,"
Miscellanea Agostiniana 2 (Rome 1932), pp. 161–208.
10 St. Augustine himself mentions such a catalogue in R 2.41 (PL
32.647). On this point, see also Wilmart, p. 159, and Mutzenbecher,
pp. xxxix–x1.
11 It is also possible that Possidius copied the question titles from DD83
itself. But if that were the case, then how do we account for Possidius's
error in transcribing the title of Q. 46 as *De Iudaeis* ("On the Jews")
rather than *De Ideis* ("On the Ideas")? This is an error of transcription
which is, admittedly, easy to make. Nonetheless, if Possidius were
working with the actual text of DD83 itself, it seems unlikely that he
would have made such an error, since in all probability he would have
immediately noticed his error through an inspection of the contents of
Q. 46.

Or, more probably, the dispersed listing of the questions in Possidius may stem from the fact that St. Augustine "had retained some list representing the first, 'dispersed' state of these questions."[12] This list could have been separate from the catalogue in the library of the religious community at Hippo, or it could have been part of the catalogue itself. If the latter, then the list was probably composed of the original entries in the catalogue, entries made before Augustine had the various questions gathered into one book. Moreover, the very structure of Possidius's own catalogue could quite easily explain why the questions of the *Eighty-three Different Questions* are separately listed in it. For in respect to structure, Possidius's catalogue differs from St. Augustine's. Augustine, who probably kept much of the catalogue of his works himself, tells us in his *Retractations* that the catalogue was in three parts: books, letters, and sermons (*tractatus*).[13] Within these three divisions he seems to have observed a chronological order.[14] Possidius, however, composed his *Indiculus* for apologetic purposes, as is clear from the catalogue's various headings, e.g., "Against the Pagans," "Against the Manichaeans," "Against the Arians," and so on, and he lists the relevant books, letters, and sermons under each heading. Since the *Eighty-three Different Questions* is so diffuse a work in terms of topics dealt with, it could not be easily placed under any one of these apologetic rubrics. Hence it would be more suited to Possidius's purpose to distribute the contents of Augustine's work throughout the catalogue under the appropriate headings. All this, coupled with the additional fact that there is no evidence outside the *Indiculus* that the questions ever circulated separately, makes it probable that the questions did not in fact so circulate.[15]

This conclusion of itself does not tell us what St. Augustine's original intentions for the questions were, what

---

12 Wilmart, above, n. 10.
13 R, "Prologus," 1 (PL 32.583). Cf. R 2.41 (PL 32.647).
14 Wilmart, p. 158, and Mutzenbecher, p. xxxix. Cf. Augustine himself in R, "Prol.," 3 (PL 32.586).
15 Cf. Mutzenbecher, p. xxxix, n. 2.

unity, if any, there is to their collection, and to what literary genre the book of questions belongs. Still, however, the conclusion can be taken as a suggestion that Augustine from the beginning saw these various questions as something more than totally unrelated philosophical, theological, and exegetical reflections.

The suggestion contained in the above conclusion takes on more significance in light of the fact that the *Eighty-three Different Questions* is not the only work of its kind authored by St. Augustine. He wrote, beginning in 399, a work entitled *Questions on the Gospels of Matthew and Luke*. In the prologue to that work Augustine says some things quite germane to the issues raised about the form and composition of the *Eighty-three Different Questions*.

This work [*Questions on the Gospels*] has not been written as if we had undertaken it for the purpose of an orderly exposition of the gospel. Rather, its plan reflects the choice and time of the person with whom we were reading, who questioned me if anything seemed obscure to him. For that reason, many things—perhaps even rather obscure things—have been passed over, because he, having already learned them, was inquiring into what he did *not* know, and he did not want his rapid progress held up by what he had previously grasped, and grasped in such a way that he committed the material permanently and lastingly to memory through his unremitting zeal in listening to and handling it. Also, some things are not found here set forth in the same order in which they are reported in the gospel, because, on account of his haste, certain issues were considered later on when there was opportunity, and they were written down in the empty place which would immediately come after the order of questions already explained. When I learned of this, I acted, lest perhaps someone, seeking to read in this work something which had moved him in the gospel and had aroused him to investigation, be put off by the nuisance of this confused order (especially since I learned that those questions, which were dictated separately, as circumstances permitted, had been collected and gathered into one volume). In order to make his search easier [therefore], I prefixed the necessary titles to the questions, which were already numbered consecutively.[16]

As Bardy points out, everything said in this prologue of the *Questions on the Gospels* about the work's structure and mode of composition applies, mutatis mutandis, to the *Eighty-three Different Questions*.[17] The latter work is made up of pieces of varying length composed over a period of several years and in response to somewhat chance circumstances. Nonetheless, it is meant to be "a genuine book," and it is "published as such by St. Augustine, who deemed the reading of it useful for a wider circle than that of his habitual companions in Thagaste and in Hippo."[18]

Of added significance, however, is the fact that Augustine's two books of questions are not unique in ancient literature, and that they are representative of a clearly recognized literary genre. In fact, circumstances of roughly the same kind as those which generated Augustine's two books of questions were responsible in antiquity for a number of works characterized by the loosely structured question and answer form—works which were prior to Augustine's, and of which, in many cases, he probably had direct or indirect knowledge. Once again, appeal is made to Bardy's researches in this area.[19] It will be sufficient for our purposes simply to summarize the high points of his investigations.

Quite characteristic of the genre in question, but by no means the first works of this kind, are three works well-known in the late classical world: Plutarch's *Table-Talk,* Aulus Gellius's *Attic Nights,* and Macrobius's *Saturnalia*.[20] Even a casual inspection of these works will quickly reveal

---

16 *Quaestiones Euangeliorum ex Matthaeo et Luca, Prologus*, (PL 35.1321).
17 Bardy, BA 10, p. 15.
18 *Ibid.*
19 *Ibid.*, pp. 16–20.
20 Plutarch (ca.A.D. 46–after A.D. 120). See Plutarch, *Plutarch's Moralia,* vols. 8–9, *Table-Talk*, trans. P. Clement et al. (Cambridge, Mass. 1959–61). Aulus Gellius (ca.A.D. 123–after A.D. 169). See his *Attic Nights,* trans. J. Rolfe, 3 vols., rev. ed. (Cambridge, Mass. 1946–52). Macrobius (fl. ca. A.D. 400). See his *Saturnalia*, trans. P. Davies (New York 1969).

them to be collections of essays and conversations on the
most varied topics. In Plutarch's *Table-Talk*, a work portray-
ing a number of conversations around the banquet table,[21]
and a work which becomes practically a paradigm for many
subsequent works, the topics for discussion range over issues
such as the following: whether philosophy is a fitting topic
for conversation at a drinking party (1.1); whether the host
should arrange the placing of his guests or leave it to the
guests themselves (1.2); why horses bitten by wolves are said
to be mettlesome (2.8); concerning ivy, whether its nature is
hot or cold (3.2); why sailors draw water from .the Nile
before daybreak (8.5).[22] Although such topics appear quite
dilettantish, a deep concern for issues in the philsophy of
religion lies beneath the surface,[23] so that even here, in one
of the most famous works of the question and answer form,
Plutarch writes on matters of consequence. In the *Attic Nights*
of Aulus Gellius, we find topics of an equally wide-ranging
nature, but which, on the surface at least, are of a somewhat
more serious intent than those in Plutarch's work. For
example, Aulus Gellius speaks of the following: the story of
king Tarquin the Proud and the Sibylline Books (1.19); the
answer of the philosopher Taurus when asked whether a
wise man ever got angry (1.26); for what reason our
forefathers inserted the aspirate *h* in certain verbs and nouns
(2.3); on the function of the eye and the process of vision
(5.16); an incredible story about a dolphin which loved a boy
(6.8).[24]

The question and answer motif was also used for patently
philosophic purposes. Although the genre in this employ-
ment goes back probably to Aristotle, I mention only a
widely known commentator on Aristotle—Alexander of
Aphrodisias and his *Three Books of Scholastic Questions and Solutions on Physics.*[25]

---

21 The most famous work in antiquity to use this particular literary
   device was, of course, the *Symposium* of Plato.
22 Cf. the tables of contents in Plutarch, cited above, n. 20.
23 Cf. Bardy, BA 10, p. 18, n. 2, for some of the literature on this topic.
24 Cf. the table of contents in Aulus Gellius, cited above, n. 20, for these
   titles.
25 Alexander of Aphrodisias (fl. early 3rd cent. A.D.), *Phusikōn skholikōn
   aporiōn kai luseōn biblia tria*; see I. Bruns, ed., *Supplementum Aristotelicum*
   (Berlin 1892) 2.1.

With Philo of Alexandria, the famous representative of Alexandrian Judaism, the question and answer genre is turned to the exegesis of the Bible. He wrote two works of this kind, *Questions and Answers on Genesis* and *Questions and Answers on Exodus*.[26] Following his example, Christian expositors of the Bible, both orthodox and heretical, produced similar works. There are the *Antitheses* of Marcion,[27] the *Syllogisms* of Apelles,[28] the *Problems* of Tatian,[29] the *Solutions* of Rhodo,[30] the *Gospel Questions and Solutions* of Eusebius of Caesarea,[31] the *Questions on the Old and New Testament* of Ambrosiaster,[32] and the *Questions on the Hebrew Text of Genesis* of St. Jerome.[33]

Where then do we stand in regard to the questions raised at the very beginning of this section of the introduction?[34] Is the *Eighty-three Different Questions* a member of a clearly de-

26 Philo of Alexandria (ca. 30B.C.–A.D. 45), see Philo, *Philo Supplement 1: Questions and Answers on Genesis, Supplement 2: Questions and Answers on Exodus*, trans. R. Marcus (Cambridge, Mass. 1953).

27 Marcion of Sinope (2nd cent.), a Gnostic. The *Antitheses* is lost. Cf. E. Blackman, *Marcion and His Influence* (London 1948), pp. 6, 9, 49, 64f., 67, and 75; and J. Quasten, *Patrology*, 3 vols. (Utrecht-Antwerp 1953–62), 1. 268–72.

28 Apelles (2nd cent.), a former disciple of the Gnostic teacher Marcion. The *Syllogisms* is lost. Cf. A. Harnack, "Sieben neue Bruchstücke der Syllogismen des Apelles," *Texte und Untersuchungen* 6 (Leipzig 1890) pp. 111–20; and Quasten, 1. 272–74.

29 Tatian the Syrian (2nd cent.). The *Problems* is now lost. Cf. Quasten, 1. 220–28.

30 Rhodo (end of the 2nd cent.), a disciple of Tatian. The *Solutions* is now lost. Cf. G. Bardy, "Rhodon" DTC 13.2655–56.

31 Eusebius of Caesarea (ca. 263–339/40), bishop and early Christian historian. Cf. Quasten, 3.309–45, especially p. 337.

32 Ambrosiaster (4th cent.), a name assigned by the Renaissance scholar Erasmus to the otherwise unknown author of several important works. For his *Questions*, see A. Souter, ed., *Psuedo-Augustini Quaestiones Veteris et Novi Testamenti CXXVII* CSEL 50 (Leipzig 1908). Cf. NCE, s.v. "Ambrosiaster."

33 St. Jerome (c. 345–419/20), famous biblical scholar and reviser of the Latin Vulgate Bible. His *Questions* are printed in PL 23.983–1062. Cf. NCE, s.v. "Jerome."
For a comprehensive look at exegetical literature employing this question and answer technique up to St. Augustine, see G. Brady, "La littérature patristique des *Quaestiones et Responsiones* sur l'Ecriture sainte," *Revue biblique* 41 (1932), 210–36, 341–69, 515–37; 42 (1933), 14–30, 211–29, 328–52.

34 See above, pp. 2–4.

fined literary genre? The answer is yes. Was it Augustine's intent, in the period in which the questions were being composed, to put together a literary unit of this kind? The answer is a qualified yes. The answer is qualified by the consideration that Augustine might not have intended from the start to produce a book of this question and answer form. Rather, the idea might have occurred to him only after he saw how eagerly his brothers in the community received his responses to their questions. Moreover, he might not have been the first one who wanted eventually to collect the questions into a single volume; he might well have been goaded by insistent brothers. It cannot be claimed that this is what actually happened, but only that these two states of affairs are compatible with answering yes to the question posed, and that the evidence at our disposal warrants our saying at least that much. Since the question and answer genre was popular with the teachers of rhetoric among others, a career which St. Augustine had pursued until his conversion, it is possible that from the very first response he fully intended someday to pull together into one book the fruits of these discussions.

Two important questions about the organization of the contents of the *Eighty-three Different Questions* still remain unanswered. (1) Were the various questions grouped together in an arbitrary manner, or was there a principle of organization, sanctioned by Augustine, which guided the efforts of those who collated the questions to form a book? (2) If the latter, was the book organized around one or several leading themes, or do the questions simply occur according to the chronological order in which they had been written?

In answer to the first question, the grouping of the various questions was not arbitrary, but chronological. Moreover, this mode of organization is compatible with Augustine's remark in his *Retractations* that "the questions were dictated, *without any order having been preserved by me*, in response to the brothers who were ever asking me things when they would see me unoccupied."[35] Although this could be seen as a denial of *any* order, chronological or otherwise, in the

---

35 R 1.26 (PL 32.624), emphasis mine. See above, p. 2.

sequence of questions, it need not be so understood, for Augustine may simply be denying any *thematic* order to the sequence of questions and answers. This requires no forced interpretation of his language, for many who fill notebooks with reflections on varied topics would readily deny any order to these reflections, meaning by this, of course, not that the reflections do not succeed one another chronologically, but that there is no thematic arrangement to them. St. Augustine's denial is of the same character: he is denying that he has preserved any thematic order in the sequence of questions to which he responded. But, of course, the resulting "disorder" could be and, I suggest, was preserved in the chronological ordering of the questions asked and the answers given.

The above answer also serves as an answer to the last portion of the second question. But note well: although we claim the principle of organization to be a chronological one, this does not prevent our going on to claim, in answer to the first portion of the second question, that the book is organized around several leading themes as well. The two claims are compatible, and there should be no great mystery how this is possible. Bardy has provided the key which unlocks whatever mystery may surround it.

> There is. . . a certain order in the sequence of the *Questions*. If it is not clear whether the author has expressly desired this order, circumstances have in some way imposed it on him. For the first portion of his residence in Africa was filled with the Manichaean controversy. With the priesthood,[36] Holy Scripture assumed more and more a place in his life. Finally, the letters of Saint Paul became, for a time, the daily food of his spirituality. In their apparent disorder, the *Questions* trace approximately these steps.[37]

Bardy claims, in other words, that the order of the *Eighty-three Different Questions* generally follows the order of

---

36 St. Augustine, with great reluctance, was ordained a priest of the church at Hippo in 391. The religious community at Thagaste then moved to Hippo in order to join him.
37 Bardy, BA 10, p. 16.

Augustine's own preoccupations during the period from 388 to 396. Hence there are groups of questions which succeed one another in approximately the same order in time in which Augustine dealt with the problems raised in each of the groupings, and it is this broad chronicling of his concern with various philosophical, theological, and biblical themes which is the book's principle of organization. Should it be objected at this point that the *Eighty-three Different Questions* cannot properly be referred to as a broad chronicling of *Augustine's* concerns, because the questions raised in the work are those of the brothers in the religious community and not those of Augustine himself, one can respond that the objector overlooks the fact of Augustine's considerable moral, spiritual, and intellectual leadership in the little community. Accordingly, since Augustine's own interests and concerns in all likelihood became the predominant interests and concerns of the entire community, then to some significant degree the brothers' questions are his questions too and are therefore indicative of his own preoccupations during the period in which the questions were raised.

Bardy does not go beyond asserting the chronological ordering of several broad groups of questions. He does not claim that the questions *within* these groupings are so ordered, nor does he claim that all the questions in the first group are earlier than all the questions in the second group, and so on. Hence he does not claim that all eighty-three questions follow a strict chronological ordering. Nonetheless, I think it not unreasonable to suppose that the chronological order of the book extends beyond an overall chronological ordering for clusters of questions to the strict chronological ordering of all the questions in the book. For if Bardy is correct in his claim that there is a general chronological development in the *Eighty-three Different Questions,* and if it is independently known that, in his catalogue, St. Augustine's works were each listed chronologically,[38] then it is not unlikely that the chronological ordering of the *Eighty-three Different Questions* extends to each and every question, and

---

38 See above, n. 13.

that the brothers of Augustine's community simply assembled the questions in the order in which they appeared in the library catalogue.[39]

Is it therefore possible to date precisely each of the questions? Probably not. However, following the example of Bardy once again,[40] we can settle for the less ambitious task of trying to assign approximate dates to certain clusters of questions—clusters generated by the preoccupations which underlie them. In order to do this, we can investigate whether the preoccupations of these clusters correspond to preoccupations of Augustine which can be dated independently of the *Eighty-three Different Questions*. Employing this technique, we can, following Bardy, point to at least four groups of questions which can be assigned approximate dates. Group I consists of questions of a strictly philosophic character. Group II consists of more overtly theological questions aimed at Manichaean teachings. Group III consists of questions directed solely to the exegesis of Scripture. Group IV continues the preoccupations of Group III, but the questions here are concerned exclusively with the exegesis of passages from various letters of St. Paul.

---

39 In claiming that the contents of DD83 are arranged in a strictly chronological order, I do not pretend to advance an assured truth, but only a consistent hypothesis, and thus a possible explanation for the data at hand.

Mutzenbecher, pp. xxxviii–xliii, in agreement with Bardy, argues that the general ordering of the QQ. is chronological, although he does not go so far as to say that this extends to each and every Q. However, his arguments do not contradict my hypothesis, and, in fact, they lend considerable support to it. Not only does he note the chronological ordering of the catalogue of Augustine's works, but also, and more importantly, he argues that there are strong internal indications in DD83 itself which support some kind of chronological ordering of the work. In this regard he discusses Augustine's use of the Bible (pp. xl–xli) and the direction of certain doctrinal developments in the work (pp. xli–xlii). Under the latter heading, he deals with Augustine's christology, his doctrine of sin, and the emergence of new doctrinal themes. According to Mutzenbecher, the different stages of these developments can be dated by reference to other writings of Augustine. These dates indicate, in general, a chronological ordering of the contents of DD83.

40 Bardy, BA 10, pp. 20–36.

Group I consists of the following questions:
1. Is the Soul Self-existent?
2. On Free Choice
3. Is God Responsible for Human Perversity?
4. What is the Cause of Human Perversity?
5. Can an Animal without Reason be Happy?
6. On Evil
7. What does 'Soul' Properly Refer to in a Living Being?
8. Is the Soul Self-moving?
10. Does Body Come from God?
13. What Proof is There that Men are Superior to Animals?
15. On the Intellect
21. Is not God the Author of Evil?
22. That God is not Subject to Need
24. Do Sin and Right Conduct Result from a Free Choice of the Will?

The titles alone should be adequate for showing the philosophic character of the questions in this group. But furthermore, in the actual development of each of these questions, Augustine goes on to eschew any appeal to authority and to rely exclusively upon reason. This strong penchant for clearly philosophical issues, coupled with an almost exclusive appeal to reason, is characteristic of a significant part of his literary activity in the first few years following his conversion. In particular, however, the problems discussed in the questions of Group I are the very same problems which concerned him in his dialogue *On Free Choice*,[41] begun at Rome in 388 shortly before his return to Africa, and in a number of letters from the same period to his friend Nebridius.[42] Therefore these questions date from the time of his return to Africa in 388. If the individual questions in the *Eighty-three Different Questions* do follow a strict chronological

41 *On Free Choice* (DLA) (PL 32.1221–1310). See R. Russell, trans., *St. Augustine: The Free Choice of the Will*, FOTC 59 (Washington, D.C. 1968), pp. 63–241.
42 Cf. especially E 3, 5, 6, 7, 8, and 9 (PL 33.61–73).

sequence, then the *terminus ad quem* for Group I is probably 391.[43]

Group II consists of the following questions:
14. That the Body of Christ was not a Phantom
16. On the Son of God
18. On the Trinity
23. On the Father and the Son

These questions have a distinctly theological tone which sets them apart from the questions of Group I, for in Group II Augustine takes up christological and trinitarian issues. Nonetheless, in the actual development of each of the questions in the group, Augustine adopts the same technique employed in Group I. He turns to the philosopher and rhetorician's technique of syllogistic reasoning rather than to the text of Scripture in order to deal with the questions posed. Furthermore, though the questions of Group II have a theological flavor not found in the questions of Group I, the former do share another feature with many of the latter—they are directed against various teachings of Manichaean religion.[44] The polemical thrust of both groups is therefore of great importance in dating them, although of especial importance for Group II, in that the latter questions cannot easily be dated apart from their polemical thrust against Manichaeism. Augustine's literary concern with Manichaeism and its errors extends from 388 to 405, but especially is there a flurry of anti-Manichaean writing dating from his last months in Rome (388) to his first year or so in

---

43 Cf. Bardy, BA 10, pp. 20–22. The dates 388–91 are my own, although considerable borrowings from Bardy have aided me in arriving at them. In fact, unless otherwise noted, the responsibility rests squarely with me for all parts of the chronology developed in this introduction.
44 See, for example, Wilmart, pp. 165–66. Possidius lists QQ. 2, 6, 10, 21, 22, and 24 of Group I under the anti-Manichaean heading.
    Manichaeism was a religious movement founded by Mani (or Manes or Manichaeus), a Babylonian of Armenian ancestry who was born around A.D. 216. St. Augustine, although born into a Christian environment, became an adherent of the Manichaean religion at the age of nineteen, and remained one for about nine years, until his disillusionment with Manichaeism and eventual conversion to Christianity. Very briefly, Manichaeism can be described as "a complex dualistic religion essentially gnostic in character." For an elaboration of this remark, see NCE, s.v. "Manichaeism."

Hippo (391-92).[45] Therefore, given the similarity of Groups I and II in argumentative technique, and given the anti-Manichaean thrust of Group II, a thrust consonant with Augustine's known concerns in this period, we may suppose Group II to be a part of this flurry of anti-Manichaean writing. Consequently the questions in Group II date, at the earliest, from the time of St. Augustine's return to North Africa in 388. As in Group I, if the individual questions in the *Eighty-three Different Questions* do follow a strict chronological sequence, then the closing date for Group II is probably 391.[46] Hence Groups I and II are contemporaneous.

Group III consists of the following questions:

51. On Man Made in the Image and Likeness of God (Gn 1.26, 5.3)
52. On the Scripture: "I am sorry that I have made man" (Gn 6.6)
53. On the Gold and Silver Taken by the Israelites from the Egyptians (Ex 3.22, 12.35)
54. On the Scripture: "As for myself, it is good for me to cling to God" (Ps 72 [73]. 28)
55. On the Scripture: "There are sixty queens, eighty concubines, and young women without number" (Cant [Song] 6.7)
56. On the Forty-six Years for the Building of the Temple (Jn 2.20-21)
57. On the One Hundred and Fifty-three Fish (Jn 21.11)
58. On John the Baptist
59. On the Ten Virginis (Mt. 25.1-13)
60. "Concerning that day and hour no one knows, neither the angels in heaven nor the Son of Man—no one except the Father" (Mt 24.36)

45 Numbered among these writings are *The Magnitude of the Soul* (DQ), 388; *The Catholic and Manichaean Ways of Life* (DME), 388–90; *On Free Choice* (DLA), 388–394/95; *On Genesis against the Manichaeans* (DGnM), 389; *True Religion* (DVR), 390; *The Advantage of Believing* (DUC), 391; *On the Two Souls against the Manichaeans* (DDu), 392; and *Disputation against Fortunatus the Manichaean* (DCF), 28–29 August 392.
46 Cf. Bardy, BA 10, pp. 22–23. Mutzenbecher, p. xli, argues that Q. 18 (in Group II) was written in 390.

61. On the Gospel Story that the Lord Fed the Multitude on the Mountain with Five Loaves of Bread (Mt 14.15-21)
62. On the Gospel Passage: "that Jesus was baptizing more than John, although he himself baptized no one. Rather, his disciples [were baptizing]" (Jn 4.7)
63. On the Word (Jn 1.1)
64. On the Samaritan Woman (Jn 4.3-42)
65. On the Resurrection of Lazarus (Jn 11.44)

Although St. Augustine makes few references, direct or indirect, to Scripture in the questions through number 50, that is all changed beginning with Q. 51. He abruptly turns to Scripture problems with an enthusiasm that will carry him, without interruption, all the way through to Q. 76. It is reasonable to suppose, therefore, that this concern for Scripture approximately coincides with Augustine's ordination as a priest in 391, and accordingly I follow Bardy in adopting 391 as the *terminus a quo* for Group III. The closing date for the group would then be 394/5, which is the period wherein Augustine began to focus his Bible study almost exclusively on certain problems in St. Paul, problems which constitute the questions of Group IV.[47]

The abruptness with which Scripture problems come to the fore in the *Eighty-three Different Questions* must be evaluated with care. It does not of itself establish the initial date for the questions of this group, for Augustine was no stranger to the study of the Bible before his ordination in 391. As Bardy says, "well before his return to Africa, St. Augustine had frequented the Bible (St. Paul and the Psalms in particular), and the requirements of the Manichaean controversy had very quickly obliged him to study Genesis carefully, especially the accounts relative to the origin of the world."[48] Yet when one couples this abruptness with Augustine's lament and plea in a letter written in 391 to his aging bishop Valerius,[49] it seems reasonable to suppose that the time of the initial questions of Group III does approximately coin-

---

47 Cf. Bardy, BA 10, pp. 23-29, but especially p. 29.
48 *Ibid.*, p. 23.
49 E 21 3-6 (PL 33.88-90).

cide with Augustine's ordination in 391. For he tells his bishop that he is not sufficiently instructed in the Bible as a priest, and that he very much needs some time off in order to devote himself exclusively to the study of the Bible. However, the letter indicates that St. Augustine in the meantime, in the midst of his pastoral duties, is laboring to overcome this deficiency by studying Scripture with a previously unrealized intensity.

In Group IV St. Augustine focuses his Scripture study on St. Paul.

66. On the Text: "Or do you not know, brothers (for I speak to those who know the Law), that the Law is the master of a man as long as he lives?" to the Text: "He will bring even your mortal bodies to life through his Spirit living in you" (Rom 7.1-8.11)

67. On the Text: "For I do not consider the sufferings of this world to be worth much in comparison with the future glory which will be revealed in us," to the Text: "For we have been saved by hope" (Rom 8.18-24)

68. On the Scripture: "O man, who are you to answer back to God?" (Rom 9.20)

69. On the Scripture: "Then even the Son himself will be subject to him" (1 Cor 15.28)

70. On the Apostle's Claim: "Death has been swallowed up into victory. Where, O death, is your contending? Where, O death, is your sting? Now the sting of death is sin; but the power of sin, the Law" (1 Cor 15.54-56)

71. On the Scripture: "Bear one another's burdens, and in this way will you fulfill the law of Christ" (Gal 6.2)

73. On the Scripture: "And having been found in the [bodily] habit (habitus) of a man" (Phil 2.7)

74. On the Text in Paul's Letter to the Colossians: "in whom we have redemption and remission of sins; who is the image of the invisible God" (Col. 1.14-15).

75. On the Inheritance of God (Heb 9.17)

The order of the questions in Group IV follows both the order of the Pauline letters and the order of the chapters and verses within each letter. In this respect Group IV differs from Group III wherein the Scriptural ordering, except for the Old Testament references, is not at all preserved. Thus it seems that the questions of Group IV were written at a time when St. Augustine was involved in a systematic study of the Pauline letters. We know that he was involved in such study in the years 394-95, for Augustine composed the following treatises on Romans and Galatians during this period: *An Exposition of Certain Statements from the Letter to the Romans, An Exposition of the Letter to the Galatians,* and *An Incomplete Exposition of the Letter to the Romans.*[50] Hence we may reasonably conclude with Bardy that the questions of Group IV date from this same period.[51]

The above chronology still leaves three clusters of questions unaccounted for: QQ. 9, 11, 12, 17, 19, and 20; QQ. 25-50; and QQ. 72, 76-83. Bardy makes no explicit attempts to date these questions, presumably because they do not answer to clear preoccupations of St. Augustine which can be dated independently of the questions themselves. For example, QQ. 9, 11, 12, 17, 19, and 20 are not included among the questions of Group I, apparently because they do not correspond to any of the problems explicitly raised in St. Augustine's treatise, *On Free Choice,* and his letters to Nebridius. (It will be recalled that these treatises, whose dates we know, were used to determine the dates of the questions of Group I.) Furthermore, Q. 12, entitled "The Opinion of a Certain Wise Man," is not even written by Augustine himself, but is written by a certain Fonteius of Carthage.[52] Nor does Bardy include QQ. 9, 11, 12, 17, 19, and 20 among those of Group II, because the former are not explicitly anti-Manichaean. As for the other two clusters of questions, they present their own particular difficulties for the chronologist like Bardy who does not assert a strict chronological ordering of the contents of the *Eighty-three Different Questions.* For example, Q. 71, "Is Fear a Sin?" raises

---

50 *Expositio quarumdam propositionum ex Epistula ad Romanos* (ExR) (PL 35.2063-88), *Expositio Epistulae ad Galatas* (ExG) (PL 35.2105-48), and *Epistulae ad Romanos inchoata espositio* (ER) (PL 35.2087-2106).

51 Cf. Bardy, BA 10, pp. 30-36, but especially pp. 30-31. Mutzenbecher, (see above, n. 46) argues in particular that QQ. 66-88 (in Group IV) were written in 394/5.

52 R 1.26 (PL 32.624). The R passage is translated below in Q. 12, n.1.

issues which touch on concerns of Augustine in Q. 33, "On
Fear" and in Q. 34, "Must Nothing Else be Loved but
Freedom from Fear?" Although Q. 71 comes much later in
the text than QQ. 33 and 34, one might argue that there is
reason to suppose the questions contemporaneous, whatever
be the actual time of their composition. Again, in Q. 81,
"On Quadragesima and Quinguagesima," St. Augustine
indulges in the same numerological speculation that
characterizes several questions in Group III, which was
assigned the dates 391-94/5. Similar remarks can be made
about the other questions in the group consisting of QQ. 72,
76-83.

However, if the hypothesis of a strict chronological ordering of the questions is correct, then there is little trouble in
filling in the approximate dates for the remaining questions.
QQ. 9, 11, 12, 17, 19, and 20 would share the same dates as
Groups I and II, viz., 388-91. QQ. 25-50 would come in the
year 391. Although this means that St. Augustine would
have had to compose twenty-six questions in the period of a
year or less, thus spending more effort on the *Eighty-three Different Questions* than in any other comparable period of time
during its composition, this need not be taken as evidence
against the hypothesis of a strict chronological ordering in
the treatise. For the questions dealt with are consonant with
the interests of a man who is rapidly being drawn into the
full life of the Church, i.e., into its letters, language, liturgy,
concerns, problems, and so on. Furthermore, St. Augustine
was easily capable of the literary output represented in QQ.
25-50, as can be seen by even a brief glance at a
chronological listing of his writings[53] and, as well, at the
relatively few pages which these questions actually take up in
the *Eighty-three Different Questions*. Finally, QQ. 72, 76-83
would fall into the period from 394 until his consecration as
bishop.

---

53 See the list of St. Augustine's works adapted by J. O'Meara in H.
   Marrou, *Saint Augustine and His Influence Through the Ages* (New York
   1957), pp. 183–86.

II. Doctrinal Content

If the piecemeal nature of the *Eighty-three Different Questions* makes it difficult to come to grips with the literary character and chronology of the work, it makes it even more difficult to grasp its doctrinal content in a systematic fashion. Still, the latter task is not impossible, and it is to this task that I now turn. In pursuing this objective, I shall first establish an appropriate doctrinal framework for any subsequent discussion of the substance of the book, and then I shall say something about the character and mood of the work. The realization of these two aims, viz., the doctrinal framework and the chracter and mood of the work, will at the same time constitute an introduction, albeit sketchy, to the teachings of the *Eighty-three Different Questions.*

The doctrinal content of St. Augustine's treatise is primarily of a philosophical, theological, and exegetical nature. In fact, if one examines the content of the work closely, one will see that the various questions seem to bunch up into fairly separate clusters of questions, each cluster being devoted more to one of the topics previously noted than to the other two. According to A. Solignac, in a study of Q. 46 published some years ago, this clustering gives rise to a "global order" in the work consisting of four series of questions: the first series (QQ. 1-15) deals with philosophical problems about the soul; the second (QQ. 17-28), with problems of generally speculative theological nature; the third (QQ. 30-40), with certain problems in moral philosophy; and the fourth (QQ. 51-83), with problems of biblical exegesis.[54] Thus the first and third series are devoted to philosophical themes, while the second is given over to speculative theological issues, and the fourth, to problems of Bible interpretation.

Nonetheless, this four-part arrangement of the questions—an arrangement drawn from the order of the questions themselves—is not wholly satisfactory, as Solignac himself would be the first to admit.[55] For one thing, the four

54 Cf. A. Solignac, "Analyse et sources de la Question 'De Ideis,' " *Augustinus Magister* 1 (Paris 1954), p. 307.
55 *Ibid.*

groupings leave a number of questions unaccounted for, especially Q. 46 which is of the highest importance in understanding Augustine's philosophical and theological views. For another thing, the very fact of the groupings could give rise to the mistaken impression that St. Augustine treated philosophical, theological, and exegetical questions in strict isolation from one another. However, nothing could be farther from the truth, for often all three concerns are intermingled in one and the same question. Furthermore, in all of his writings St. Augustine self-consciously allowed a great deal more overlap between philosophy and theology, with its attendant exegetical concerns, than many medieval and most post-medieval thinkers would countenance.

For this reason, while the natural division of the *Eighty-three Different Questions* into the above four series of questions may be of value for an understanding of the work, a more worthwhile approach to an organized understanding of it is obtained by grouping the questions around certain leading themes which correspond to those developed by Augustine in the works published during the period in which the *Eighty-three Different Questions* itself was being composed. In those early works, in accord with a program detailed in other places but succinctly stated in his *Soliloquies,* Augustine consistently focused on God and the soul and the themes generated by such concerns.[56] Thus, in regard to God, he develops in the *Eighty-three Different Questions* the following themes:

1. God's knowledge (Q. 17)
2. God's freedom (QQ. 22, 28)
3. God's providence (QQ. 27, 79, 82)
4. God's transcendence in relation to space (Q. 20)
5. The Trinity (QQ. 16, 18, 23, 37, 43, 50, 51.4, 60, 63, 69, 74)
6. Christology (QQ. 11, 14, 25, 42, 44, 73, 80)

---

56 *Ibid.* Cf. Augustine's *Soliloquies* (So), a work written in 386/87. "*Augustine:* Look, I've finished praying to God. *Reason:* Then what do you desire to know? *A: God and soul*—that's what I desire to know. *R:* Nothing more? *A:* Nothing at all" (emphasis mine). The passage is found in So 1.2.7 (PL 32.872). See T. Gilligan, *St. Augustine: Soliloquies,* FOTC 5 (New York 1948), pp. 333–426.

7. Creatures in relation to God (QQ. 5, 19, 28, 41, 46.2, 54, 81)

On the other hand, in regard to the soul, Augustine develops the following themes:

1. The nature of the soul (QQ. 1, 7, 8, 38, 40)
2. The superiority of reason (QQ. 5, 7, 9, 13, 30, 45.1, 46.2, 51.2, 54)
3. The need to turn from the sensible world to the spiritual world (QQ. 9, 12, 46.2)
4. Free will (QQ. 2, 3, 4, 6, 21, 24)
5. Knowledge and truth (QQ. 9, 39, 46.2, 47, 48, 78)
6. Love (QQ. 30, 34, 35, 36)
7. Happiness (QQ. 5, 35)
8. Virtues and passions (QQ. 31, 33, 77)[57]

Two features of these lists require attention: (1) many of the questions are repeated in the lists, and (2) less than half the questions on Bible exegesis appear in the lists. The first feature has been nicely accounted for in the following way:

None [of the questions]...is systematic to the point of referring only to an object rigorously circumscribed or to an isolated point of view. The mind of St. Augustine is open, synthetic, intuitive in regard to the relations of thought with all of its sources and all of its possibilities. Moreover, the exposition is always of extreme compactness, and ordinarily it hints at directions for investigation in addition to or as a consequence of those already chosen.[58]

This feature serves, then, to reinforce my own earlier suggestion that St. Augustine does not treat philosophical, theological, and exegetical questions in strict isolation from one another. Although this suggestion is weakened by and hence must take into account the second above-noted feature, still, fully thirteen questions numbered among the exegetical group (QQ. 51, 54, 60, 63, 69, 73, 74, and 77-82) are found in the two lists above.

Nonetheless, the second feature requires serious atten-

---

57 These two lists are taken, with some significant modifications, from Solignac, pp. 307-8. The modifications have been made in the light of my own investigations and those of J. Beckaert in BA 10, pp. 697-701, n. 1.

58 Bardy, BA 10, p. 701.

tion, for twenty questions making up almost one quarter of the total number of questions and almost one half of the physical bulk of the book are so far unaccounted for. Numbered among these exegetical questions are three important discussions of central chapters from St. Paul's letter to the Romans (QQ. 66-68). The issues raised in these chapters are issues whose immense importance for Christian faith was quickly grasped by Augustine, and they are issues which, having attracted an ever increasing amount of his time and talent, received his unreserved attention in that body of later writings called the anti-Pelagian writings.[59] Hence these considerations require that, in addition to using God and the soul as focal points around which to organize the contents of the *Eighty-three Different Questions*, the Bible be used as well. This gives rise to a third list of themes, themes which focus on the contents of the Bible itself:

1. Problems in the letters of St. Paul (QQ. 66-76, 82)[60]
2. Problems in the Gospel of St. John (QQ. 56, 57, 62-65)
3. Problems in the Old Testament (QQ. 49, 51-53, 79)
4. Numerological speculations (QQ. 55-59, 61, 64, 81)
5. The Trinity (QQ. 51.4, 63, 69, 74)
6. Christology (Q. 73)
7. Sacraments (Q. 62)
8. Marriage (Q. 83)

---

59 Here follows a list of a number of these writings together with their date of composition: *The Deserts and Remission of Sins and the Baptism of Infants* (DPB), 411-12; *The Spirit and the Letter* (DSL), 412; *Nature and Grace* (DNG), 413-15; *The Perfection of Man's Righteousness* (DPI), 415-16; *The Doings of Pelagius* (DGsP), 417; *The Grace of Christ and Original Sin* (DGrC), 418; *Against the Two Letters of the Pelagians* (CD), 420-21; *Against Julian* (CI) 13 June 421; *Grace and Free Choice* (DGA), 426-27; *Admonition and Grace* (DCG), 426-27; *The Predestination of the Saints* (DPS), 428-29; and *The Gift of Perseverence* (DDoP), 428-29.

60 Q. 76 contains a discussion of Jas 2.20: "Would you like to know, you empty-headed man, that faith without works is useless?" However, I include Q. 76 among the Pauline questions for the following reason. In discussing Jas 2.20, St. Augustine seems more concerned to specify the content of St. Paul's own teachings rather than to deal with St. James per se. Since the two Apostles appear to disagree over the respective roles of faith and works in effecting salvation, it is not surprising that Augustine, while immersed with his community in a study of the Pauline letters, should be called upon by his brothers to explain this apparent discrepancy.

The role played by the Bible in the *Eighty-three Different Questions* raises some interesting questions. In the light of Augustine's announced program in the *Soliloquies* to know only God and the soul, and in the light of the inadequacy of this program for organizing all the contents of the questions, what does the addition of the Bible as a third and necessary structural element in the work tell us about Augustine's intellectual and religious development from the time of his conversion in 386 to the early years of his priesthood? Does the addition of the Bible themes signal an important change in Augustine's understanding of what is needed for knowing God and the soul? The response to these questions is yes, but there is not space in this brief introduction to justify this answer. In the meantime, however, let it be carefully noted that the questions raised are substantive questions about *St. Augustine himself*. They are not questions which have been generated by some arbitrary interpretative scheme—God and the soul—which has, with only partial success, been imposed on the *Eighty-three Different Question*. For an attempt to understand the work in terms of the God and soul motif is authorized not only by the young Augustine's program in the *Soliloquies*, as mentioned above, but also by the actual content of many of the writings dating from the period 386-91. It is these writings, together with the *Soliloquies*, which provide the proper context for understanding what Augustine had in mind when he expressed his intentions to know only God and the soul.

Having established an appropriate doctrinal framework for the *Eighty-three Different Questions*, I turn now to an examination of those features of the work which serve to define its mood and character. While these features cannot, of course, be adequately seen apart from the doctrinal content which gives expression to them, nonetheless, a brief sketch of them now will give the reader some useful perspectives from which to approach that content in detail at some other time. There are six important features: (1) the strongly dialectical character of the *Eighty-three Different Questions* on the one hand, (2) its strong reliance on the authority of Scripture on the other, (3) its Pythagorean concerns, (4) its heavy Platonic and Neoplatonic flavor, (5) its optimism, and

(6) its dynamic character imparting a sense of movement and development in the work.[61]

The first three characteristics are unevenly represented in the work, the first being seen primarily in the earlier questions, the second, in the later questions, and the third, in a number of the late middle questions. On the other hand, the last three characteristics are more evenly and widely represented in the *Eighty-three Different Questions.* Moreover, while the first five characteristics can be readily seen in a single reading of the book, the sixth feature comes to light only after persistent digging. What this digging turns up is a work which is dynamic rather than static in character, for it discloses a document which is a running account, as it were, not only of Augustine's changing concerns as he turns from a life of religious seclusion to one of priestly involvement, but also of various substantive changes in his outlook and thinking. In particular, some of the important changes in Augustine which unfold in the pages of the questions concern: (a) his understanding of the role of the Bible in the quest to know only God and the soul; (b) his assessment of the ability of man, and particularly the wise man (*sapiens*), to achieve a proper knowledge of God and the soul; and (c) his understanding of man as a being created in the image of God.[62] These three changes cannot be documented in this introduction. Rather, we must now turn to the first five of the six characteristics listed above.

The dialectical character of the questions has already been noted in Section I of the introduction.[63] There it was pointed out that, in the questions making up Groups I and II,

---

61 Cf. Solignac, pp. 308–9, for a discussion of characteristics (1), (3), and (4). Mutzenbecher, pp. xxx–xxxi, rightly emphasizes yet another feature of DD83, viz., its polemical character.

62 To this list of changes one should also add St. Augustine's developing views on christology (see Mutzenbecher, pp. xli–xlii). A study of change (b) is really a study of Augustine's doctrine of sin and grace. For this, see Bardy, BA 10, pp. 36 ff. For change (c), consult the fascinating study by R. Markus, "*Imago* and *Similitudo* in Augustine," *Revue des études augustiniennes* 10 (1964), 125–43.

63 See above, pp. 15–16. On the meaning of the term dialectic (*dialectica*) in Augustine, see H. Marrou, *Saint Augustin et la fin de la culture antique* (Paris 1958), p. 195 (hereafter cited as *Saint Augustin et la fin*), for a brief discussion and a list of pertinent texts. Marrou notes that dialectic has a two-fold meaning in St. Augustine: on the one hand it refers to the

Augustine turned to the philosopher and rhetorician's technique of syllogistic reasoning rather than to the text of Scripture in order to deal with the questions posed. However, the use of dialectic is not limited to the questions of Groups I and II, for few questions in the first forty-five or so of the eighty-three questions are without some kind of syllogistic foray. An inventory of these forays would include QQ. 5, 17, and 22, which can reasonably be construed as categorical syllogisms. A clear example of such a syllogism is Q. 5. In answer to the question whether animals lacking reason can be happy, Augustine says: "An animal which lacks reason lacks knowledge. But no animal which lacks knowledge can be happy. It therefore does not belong to animals lacking reason to be happy."[64]

Again, the inventory would include QQ. 1, 2, 3, 10, 15, 16, 18, 19, 20, 21, 22, and 28, in which one finds what Solignac describes as "more or less regular sorites," i.e., arguments composed of several categorical syllogisms which are so ordered that the conclusion of every syllogism but the last serves as a premise for the next syllogism. Likewise, one must not overlook QQ. 14, 34, and 41, which contain hypothetical syllogisms. A clear instance of Augustine's use of this kind of syllogism is Q. 14. In answer to the question whether the body of Christ was a phantom, he says: "If the body of Christ was a phantom, Christ was a deceiver; and if he was a deceiver, he is not the Truth. However, Christ is the Truth. Therefore his body was not a phantom."[65] Finally, QQ. 4 and 6 contain instances of disjunctive syllogisms.

However, lest the reader be left with a distorted picture, it must be quickly added that the dialectical character of the questions is dominant only in the first forty-five or so questions. In fact, in order adequately to understand Augustine's development, it is important to go on to the second characteristic of the *Eighty-three Different Questions* and to note

---

science of logic in the rigorous Stoic sense of the term, and on the other it refers to "the art of convincing or confounding an adversary" in Aristotle's sense of the term. In DD83, Augustine's use of dialectic is more Stoic than Aristotelian in character.

64 See below, p. 39.
65 See below, p. 44.

that dialectic is in the background in the latter portion of the work, while the authority of the Bible is in the foreground. The development signalled here appears to be this: the more Augustine came to appreciate both the authority of the Bible in the life of the Church and the teachings of the Bible on God and man, the less he relied on dialiectic as a means of satisfying his thirst to know God and the soul.[66] Expressed in another way, the development recorded in the pages of the *Eighty-three Different Questions* issued from the fact that Augustine the Christian was in the process of discovering the wealth of Scripture—a wealth which, as a new convert, he had believed was there but which he was only now, in the years 391-95, eagerly appropriating for himself out of a new realization of its value. Hence the importance of dialectic was not so much reduced in Augustine's eyes. Rather, dialectic became overshadowed by the importance of the Bible for spiritual development. What is significant about the *Eighty-three Different Questions* in this regard is that within its pages it has captured this important change as it is happening.

A third feature of the *Eighty-three Different Questions* is its Pythagorean concerns. Like the Pythagorean philosophers of the ancient Greek world, St. Augustine had an abiding fascination for numbers. With these philosophers he shared two important convictions: (1) that numbers (or at least the laws governing them) are objective, timeless, and un-changeable features of the universe which are of fundamental importance not only for the actual structuring and ordering of the universe, but also for the understanding of it; and (2) that numbers have special symbolic meanings which, for Augustine at least, somehow derive from their privileged metaphysical status. The first view I will call "number metaphysics," the second, "number mysticism." The latter

---

66 But see Marrou, *Saint Augustin et la fin,* pp. 315–27. In these fascinating pages Marrou documents the crucial role played by dialectic in the last six books of St. Augustine's great work, *The Trinity* (DT), a work written in his mature years as a bishop. I accept Marrou's conclusions, and hence nothing in the above exposition should be seen as a challenge to those conclusions. In my remarks, I seek only to emphasize that St. Augustine came to esteem the importance of the Bible more, not that he came to esteem dialectic less.

view enjoyed widespread popularity at all levels of late classical and of patristic culture, while the former view enjoyed the attention of a much smaller and more cultivated circle who, like Augustine, had been directly or, more probably, indirectly influenced by Pythagorean thought. Although there seems to be no internal logical connection between number metaphysics and number mysticism such that the former strictly entails the latter, nonetheless, the Pythagoreans and St. Augustine enthusiastically endorsed both views. However, in the *Eighty-three Different Questions* it is only problems of number mysticism which for the most part bother Augustine, and hence the Pythagorean concerns of the work are primarily of this sort. The development and application of his number metaphysics must be sought for elsewhere.[67]

This number mysticism is clearly seen in at least eight questions (QQ. 55-59, 61, 64, and 81), wherein St. Augustine discusses, sometimes in great detail, the symbolic meanings of various numbers in Scripture. The most elaborate example of this number mysticism is Q. 57: "On the One Hundred and Fifty-three Fish."[68] Intrigued by the problem of the number 153 mentioned in Jn 21.11, Augustine conducts a detailed investigation into the symbolic meanings of the numbers which generate 153. His general conclusion is that this number signifies the perfected and holy Church of God. Further examples of St. Augustine's number mysticism could be adduced, but, since his most significant and lasting contributions to western civilization are to be found elsewhere, no more will be said on this topic.

As for the Platonic and Neoplatonic character of the *Eighty-three Different Questions*, it is unmistakable. At any number of places in the work Augustine voices themes and arguments drawn from Plato and even more so from those philosophers of late antiquity whom Augustine himself called

---

67 For appropriate texts from Augustine's writings, together with a commentary, see W. Roche, "Measure, Number, and Weight in Saint Augustine," *The New Scholasticism* 15 (1941), 350-76.
68 See below, pp. 99-103.

Platonici, i.e., Platonists,[69] but whom modern historians of philosophy have chosen to call "Neoplatonists."[70] These philosophers, some pagan, some Christian, who viewed themselves as the legitimate spiritual heirs of Plato in regard to both doctrine and lifestyle, played a significant role in the intellectual life of the late Roman Empire in general and of Augustine in particular. In fact, so great was their influence on the thinking of the young Augustine, and so manifest is this influence in the works especially of the period 386-90, that some biographers and historians have claimed that his famous conversion, described in the eighth book of his *Con-*

---

69 Cf. DCD 8.12 (PL 41.237) where St. Augustine says: "nonetheless, the noblest philosophers of more recent times who have chosen to follow Plato did not want to be called Peripatetics or Academics, but *Platonists*" (emphasis mine). He then goes on to mention explicitly Plotinus, Iamblichus, Porphyry, and Apuleius. See below, n. 70, for a brief list of reference works which would be useful in identifying these thinkers.

70 Platonism and Neoplationism are enormously complex and rich traditions which give rise to all sorts of puzzles, not the least of which concerns the precise relation between the two traditions, the latter being obviously dependent on the former. Furthermore, as traditions they are distinct from the philosophy of Plato which is preserved in part, if not in full, in the writings of Plato. Hence we are confronted with the even more intricate puzzle of the relationship of the philosophy of Plato to Platonism and Neoplatonism, both of which claim Plato as their progenitor. For an overview of all this, consult D. Rees, "Platonism and the Platonic Tradition," *The Encyclopedia of Philosophy*, vol. 6, ed. P. Edwards (New York 1967) pp. 333-41, and the highly readable and sympathetic treatment by A. Taylor, *Platonism and Its Influence* (Boston 1924). For a brief but interesting discussion on the problem of the relation of the philosophy of Plato to Platonism, see H. Myerhoff, "On the Platonism of St. Augustine's *Quaestio de Ideis,*" *The New Scholasticism* 16 (1942), pp. 16-18. For Neoplatonism, two classic works are the following: C. Bigg, *Neoplatonism* (London 1895) and T. Whittaker, *The Neo-Platonists* (2nd ed., Cambridge 1901). For a discussion of the manner in which Plato was read by the Neoplatonists—a manner which may account for some of their more noteworthy departures from Plato—see R. Hathaway, "The Neoplatonist Interpretation of Plato: Remarks on its Decisive Characteristics," *Journal of the History of Philosophy* 7 (1969), 19-26. As for the influence of Neoplatonism on St. Augustine, the literature here is vast. A classic work is that of L. Grandgeorge, *Saint Augustin et le néo-platonisme* (Paris 1896). A more accessible and readable, but less detailed, treatment of the problem is found in the recent work of A. Armstrong and R. Markus, *Christian Faith and Greek Philosophy* (London 1960).

fessions, was a conversion to Neoplatonism rather than to Christianity.[71] While this is a one-sided exaggeration of a complex event in the life of a complex man, the exaggeration provoked a lengthy controversy whose lasting result has been a more widespread appreciation of the depth of Neoplatonic influence on St. Augustine.

In his *Eighty-three Different Questions* this influence finds expression in the following themes:

1. The intimate connection between knowledge and happiness (QQ. 5, 35)
2. The opposition of the sensible to the intelligible (QQ. 6, 9)
3. The depreciation of knowledge acquired by the senses (QQ. 9, 54, 81)
4. The distinction between belief and knowledge (QQ. 48, 54, 81)
5. The self-moved soul (Q. 8)
6. The purification of the soul by flight from the sensible world (QQ. 9, 12, 29)
7. The Ideas (or Forms) and participation (QQ. 1, 6, 21, 23, 24, 35.2, 46, 54, 78, 81.2)
8. The goodness and beauty of beings drawn from form (QQ. 6, 10, 21, 24, 45, 51.2)
9. God's freedom from envy (Q. 50)
10. The privative nature of evil (QQ. 6, 21, 66.5)
11. Immutability and eternity, mutability and time (Q. 19)[72]

While it is true that St. Augustine, years later in his *Retractations,*[73] sought to soften some of this Platonism by qualifying his depreciation of the body in Q. 9 and his moral intellectualism in Q. 35, nonetheless, the majority of the themes listed above became permanent and welcome features of his worldview. Once these chords were struck, they continued to be replayed by him throughout the remainder

---

71 The work which argues this view most forcefully was that of P. Alfaric, *L'évolution intellectuelle de saint Augustin: Du Manichéisme au Néoplatonisme* (Paris 1918).
72 For this list of Platonic and Neoplatonic themes, I owe much to the investigations of Solignac, p. 308.
73 For these references, see below, Q. 9, n. 1, and Q. 35, n. 1.

of his life. This feature of the *Eighty-three Different Questions*, i.e., the influence of Platonism and Neoplatonism on St. Augustine, is worthy of careful examination if for no other reason than to show us how a sensitive, thoughtful practitioner of Christian faith sought to interact with the great intellectual currents of his time.

A fifth important characteristic of the questions is their optimism about man.[74] This optimism stems, among other things, from Augustine's cautious confidence, but confidence nonetheless, in the *sapiens*, the wise man,[75] and in that wise man's ability to live victoriously here and now among the common adversities of the human condition. This confidence is most evident in the earlier, nonexegetical questions. However, even in those questions on St. Paul's letter to the Romans (QQ. 66-68), where issues of human sin and divine grace come to the fore, Augustine views man and his abilities in a way which can only be called optimistic in contrast to his later anti-Pelagian teachings which obliterate all human initiative in deference to divine grace.

Who is this wise man who is the subject, whether expressed or unexpressed, of many of the earlier questions? He is none other than the man who has made philosophy, i.e., the love for wisdom, his vocation, and who has arranged his life-style to suit the demands of that quest for wisdom. He is the man who has turned his back on earthly pursuits, whatever they be, who has retired to a life away from the hustle and bustle of worldly ambition and the cares of this world, who has given himself over to a life of rigorous intellectual, moral, and religious discipline, and who has done all this with a view to attuning himself to that transcendent and incorporeal realm which is the true home of the soul and the abode of wisdom. In short, he is the man who has been con-

---

74 Cf. QQ. 2-4, 12, 24, 25, 36, and 44. Also, cf. R. Flórez, "Sobre la mentalidad de Augustín en los primeros años de su monacato. El 'Libro de las ochenta y tres cuestiones'," *La Ciudad de Dios* 169 (1956), 467-68, 471-73.
75 The term *wise man* is specifically mentioned in QQ. 3, 12, and 36.4.

verted to philsophy and to all that such a conversion entailed
for Augustine and his contemporaries.[76]

Augustine's conception of the wise man, a conception
rooted deeply in the cultivated circle of which he was a part,
takes on more reality and meaning if we glance for a
moment at some of those dialogues composed by Augustine
in the year following his conversion to the Christian faith in
386.[77] What we see is Augustine himself struggling to
become a concrete embodiment of the wise man described
above. We find him eagerly pursuing the contemplative
philosophic life, having recently resigned not only his position as a professor of rhetoric in Milan, but also all aspira-
tions to whatever imperial office he might have obtained by
such a position. We see him engaged in prayer and in study
and conversation of a sort designed to further his quest for a
wisdom which is not simply an impersonal body of knowledge, but God himself. More particularly, we see him
engaged in formulating a program designed to lead him and
others of like concern to the soul's one true abode, the
transcendent and intelligible reality which is God. We see
him employing this program not only to exercise his mind
for its ascent to God, but also to furnish it with the truths
which are the very stairsteps for that ascent.[78] Finally, we see
him expressing the view that the wise man, through
philosophy, can attain salvation (although admitting that
this very rarely happens),[79] and that he can, in this life, obtain genuine and lasting happiness.[80]

On the other hand, the wise man of the *Eighty-three Different Questions* is more restrained and cautious, as I have
indicated earlier. Augustine no longer speaks of the wise
man's ability to find happiness in this life, let alone of the

---

76 On the "conversion to philosophy and to all that such a conversion entailed," see Marrou, *Saint Augustin et la fin,* pp. 161–86.
77 See especially his *Answer to Sceptics* (CA), *The Happy Life* (DBe), *Divine
   Providence and the Problem of Evil* (DO), and *Soliloquies* (So), all translated
   in the FOTC 5.
78 For this, see the excellent discussion of Marrou, *Saint Augustin et la fin,*
   pp. 277–327.
79 DO 2.5.16 (PL 32.1002). Also, cf. 2.11.30 (PL 32.1009) and CA 1.1.3
   (PL 32.907).
80 Contrast DBe 4.25 (PL 32.971) with R 1.2 (PL 32.588).

remote possibility of his achieving salvation through philosophy. However, the earlier questions seem to be stamped with an attitude which, as one has said, "insists upon the possibilities of the mind's mastery over the passions."[81] In QQ. 2, 4, and in 24 especially Augustine speaks of a free choice of the will which appears to be fully capable of issuing in either right action or sin.

> That which merits punishment is sin, and that which merits reward is right conduct. And neither sin nor right conduct can be justly charged to anyone who has done nothing of his own will. Accordingly sin and right conduct result from a free choice of the will.[82]

This view of the will's power is both consonant with and reinforced by Augustine's portrayal of Christ as the perfect moral example whose deeds the wise man is called upon to emulate (QQ. 25, 36.2, and 44). Hence it lies within the wise man's power, following Christ's example, to face with equanimity not only death, but also the cruelest forms of death (Q. 25).

A fuller treatment of Augustine's optimism about man in the *Eighty-three Different Questions* must take into account QQ. 66 and 68, where Augustine began to wrestle with the issues of sin and grace with an intensity that would only increase in the years to follow.[83] However, that is a topic for another time and another place.

---

81 Flórez, p. 468.
82 See below, Q. 24. Cf. DLA 1.10.20 (PL: 32.1232–33).
83 For an excellent account of the development of the notion of the wise man up to and including Augustine's most mature thought on the matter, see P. Brown, *Augustine of Hippo: A Biography* (Berkeley 1967) pp. 146–57.

EIGHTY-THREE
DIFFERENT QUESTIONS
(De diversis quaestionibus LXXXIII)

1. IS THE SOUL SELF-EXISTENT?

Everything true is true by truth, and every soul is a soul in virtue of that by which it is a true soul. Accordingly every soul is dependent upon truth for its very existence as a soul. Now the soul is one thing, truth another. For truth is never susceptible of falsehood, whereas the soul is often mistaken and deceived. Therefore, since the soul is dependent upon truth for its existence, the soul is not self-existent. But truth is God. Therefore God is the author of the soul's existence.

2. ON FREE CHOICE[1]

Nothing which comes into being can be equal to that which brings it into being. Otherwise one necessarily does away with justice, which must render to each its due. Therefore, when God made man, although he made him very good, nevertheless he did not make him what he himself is. But that man is better who is good freely and willingly than the man who is good by necessity. Accordingly free will[2] was a fitting and appropriate gift for man.

3. IS GOD RESPONSIBLE FOR HUMAN PERVERSITY?

No wise man is responsible for human perversity, because the blame for this is not small. Rather [the blame] is so great

---

1 *libero arbitrio.*
2 *uoluntas libera.* However, in the following QQ. *uoluntas* is sometimes translated "choice." Where this happens, the occurrence is footnoted. (See my article, "St. Augustine on Freedom," *Crux* 12.3 (1974–75), especially pp. 19–21, for a discussion of some of the nuances of *arbitrium* and *uoluntas.*)

37

that it cannot be charged to any wise man. But God far excells every wise man. Much less, therefore, is God responsible for man's perversity, for God's will is far more excellent
than the wise man's. Now the phrase *is responsible for* means
"wills." Therefore it is a moral failing of the will which is
responsible for human perversity. If this moral failing is not
at all the result of God's will, as reason teaches, then we
must look for its source.

4. WHAT IS THE CAUSE OF HUMAN PERVERSITY?

The cause of man's perversity is either man himself, or
something else, or nothing. If [it is] nothing, there is no
cause. However, if the sentence *the cause is nothing* is
understood to mean "man is made from nothing or from
those things drawn from nothing," on the contrary the cause
will be found to be man himself, because the stuff of which
he is made is nothing.

If there is some other cause than this, is it God or any
other man? Or is the cause something which is neither God
nor man?

It certainly is not God, for God is the cause of good. If
therefore man is the cause, he is such either by force or by
persuasion. But certainly he is not such by force, lest he be
more powerful than God. For indeed God has so excellently
fashioned man that, should he will to retain this excellence,
no one could forcefully hinder him. But if we concede that
man's perversity is due to the persuasion of another man, we
will again have to inquire into the cause of perversity, and
this time the perversity of the persuader (since it is impossible for one responsible for such things not to be evil).

There remains an I-know-not-what which is neither God
nor man; but nevertheless this, whatever it is, either compels
or persuades. If it compels, we repeat the above answer. But
if it, whatever it is, persuades, then, since persuasion does
not compel against one's will, the cause of a man's corruption is referred back to the will of the same man, whether he
be corrupted by the persuasion of someone else or of no one.

5. CAN AN ANIMAL WITHOUT REASON BE HAPPY?

An animal which lacks reason lacks knowledge. But no animal which lacks knowledge can be happy. It therefore does not belong to animals lacking reason to be happy.[1]

6. ON EVIL

Everything which is, is either corporeal or incorporeal. The corporeal is embraced by sensible form,[1] and the incorporeal, by intelligible form. Accordingly everything which exists is not without some form. But where there is form there necessarily is measure,[2] and measure is something good. Absolute evil, therefore, has no measure, for it lacks all good whatever. It thus does not exist, for it is embraced by no form, and the whole meaning of evil is derived from the privation of form.

---

1 It does not follow from this that animals are therefore *unhappy*. Rather, Augustine's point is that both happiness and unhappiness are possible only for rational beings, whereas nonrational beings are incapable of such states.

---

1 The word *form* translates the Latin term *species*. For this translation and a study of the term *species,* see the extremely useful article of W. Roche, "Measure, Number, and Weight in Saint Augustine," *The New Scholasticism,* 15 (1941), 350–76. Also, see below, Q. 46.2, for St. Augustine's own remarks on this term.

2 The word *measure* translates the Latin term *modus,* an Augustinian notion difficult to encompass in an equivalent English word. Roche, p. 353, remarks: "we may regard 'modus' on the side of the creature as equivalent to the principle of existence or subsistence of things, which is set off from their species and order as a separate principle. Or 'modus' may be regarded as qualitative to denote intrinsic limitation in virtue of which a being is determined to a form. This notion of 'modus' is equivalent to capacity for determination to a form, or it may be conceived as arising out of the comparison of forms, since every form as such is that which it is, and is distinct from all others."

7. WHAT DOES 'SOUL' PROPERLY REFER TO IN A LIVING BEING[1]

In speaking of soul,[2] one sometimes understands it to involve mind,[3] as when we say that a man consists of a soul and a body. At other times, mind is excluded from the meaning of the term. But when mind is excluded from its meaning, soul is understood in relation to those activities which we have in common with the lower animals. For animals lack reason, which is always a feature of mind.

8. IS THE SOUL SELF-MOVING?

One is aware that the soul moves of itself when one is aware of the will within oneself. For if we will, no one else wills for us. And this movement of the soul is spontaneous, for this has been granted to the soul by God. But this movement is not from place to place as is that of the body, for movement from place to place is proper to the body. And though it is, nevertheless, by the will, i.e., by that movement which is not in place, that the soul moves its own body from place to place, it does not follow from this that the soul itself also moves from place to place. Thus we see that something is moved by a hinge through a considerable distance, and yet the hinge itself is not moved in place.

9. CAN TRUTH BE PERCEIVED BY THE BODILY SENSES?

Everything which the bodily sense touches and which is called sensible is constantly changing.[1] Thus, when the hairs

---

1 Cf. DT 15.1.1 (PL 42.1057). See below, Q. 27, n. 2.
2 *anima.*
3 *mente.*

---

1 Concerning this Q., Augustine says in R 1.26 (PL 32.624): "I have said: 'Everything which the bodily sense touches and which is called

on our head grow, or the body declines into old age or
blooms out into youth, this happens continually, and there is
never any letup in the process. But what does not remain
stable cannot be perceived, for that is perceived which is
grasped by knowledge, but that cannot be grasped which
changes without ceasing. Therefore truth in any genuine
sense is not something to be expected from the bodily senses.

However, lest anyone say that there are some sensible
things which remain forever in the same state, and lest he
bring up for us the issue of the sun and the stars—an issue
susceptible of no easy solution,[2] this much, to be sure, no
one can help but admit: there is no sensible object which is
not similar to the false so as to be indistinguishable from it.
For (omitting other considerations), in regard to all the
things that we sense through the body, even when they are
not present to the senses, we nevertheless experience their
images (whether in sleep or in hallucinatory madness) as if
they were immediately present. In such experiences we cannot at all tell whether we are aware of the sensible objects by
the senses themselves or whether they are the images of sensible objects. If, therefore, there are false images[3] of sensible
objects, and if they cannot be distinguished by the senses
themselves, and if nothing can be perceived except what is
distinguished from the false, then there is no criterion for
truth resident in the senses.

---

sensible is constantly changing.' Without doubt this is indeed *not* true
of the incorruptible bodies of the resurrection. But in our present state
none of our bodily senses has any contact with the incorruptible and
immutable unless, of course, something such be divinely revealed to
it.''

2 St. Augustine is referring here to a problem of great concern in
classical and medieval times. The problem concerns the makeup of the
heavenly bodies and whether they are subject to generation and
destruction and to quantitative and qualitative change. Aristotle had
set the stage for the controversy by arguing in his *On the Heavens* 1.2-3
(268b11-270b31) that the heavenly bodies are composed of a special
material unknown on earth and that they are not subject to generation
and destruction and to quantitative and qualitative change, although
subject to a circular movement.

3 For Augustine, an image is false when it is the ground for a mistaken
judgment.

Accordingly it is in our own greatest interest that we are admonished to turn away from this world, which is clearly corporeal and sensible, and to turn with all haste to God, i.e., Truth,[4] which is grasped by the intellect and the inner mind, which ever abides and exists always the same, which presents no false image from which it cannot be distinguised.

10. DOES BODY COME FROM GOD?

Everything good comes from God. Everything that has form is good insofar as it has form, and everything which form embraces has form. Now all body in order to be body is embraced by some form. Therefore all body comes from God.[1]

11. WHY WAS CHRIST BORN OF A WOMAN?[1]

When God sets free, he does not free a part, but he frees the whole of that which chances to be in danger. Therefore the Wisdom and Power of God, who is called the only be-gotten Son, has declared mankind's deliverance through the assumption of human nature. But mankind's deliverance had to be evidenced among both sexes. Therefore, since it was needful to become a man, which is the more honorable sex, it reasonably followed that the deliverance of the female sex be seen by that man's birth from a woman.

---

4 The word *truth* is often used by Augustine as a proper name for God. Hence, both here and elsewhere, the word is capitalized when it is employed (or seems to be employed) in this manner.

---

1 It is not completely clear whether St. Augustine is here speaking of body in general, i.e., extension, or of the human body in particular in contrast to the soul. If the latter, then the title of this Q. would be more suitably translated, "Does the Body Come from God?"

---

1 Origen (ca. 185–253), one of the most important of the Alexandrian Christians, had already addressed himself to this question. See his *Contra Celsum (Against Celsus)* 6.73 (PG 11.1407 ff.).

12. THE OPINION OF A CERTAIN WISE MAN[1]

"Come now, O wretched mortals," he says, "take heed
that the wicked spirit may never foul this habitation, and
that, intermingled with the senses, it may not pollute the
sanctity of the soul and becloud the light of the mind. This
evil thing creeps stealthily through all the entrances of sense:
it gives itself over to forms, it adapts itself to colors, it sticks
to sounds, it lurks hidden in anger and in the deception of
speech, it appends itself to odors, it infuses tastes, by the tur-
bulent overflow of passion it darkens the senses with
darksome affections, it fills with certain obscuring mists the
paths of the understanding, through all of which the mind's
ray normally diffuses the light of reason."

"In fact, since it consists of heavenly light, [that] ray mir-
rors the divine presence, for in it God, in it the blameless
will, in it the merit of virtuous action all shine forth. God is
everywhere present, and he is simultaneously present to
each of us in the very moment when the undiminished purity
of our mind has recognized itself to be in his presence. For
just as defective vision does not recognize the presence of
whatever it cannot see (for in vain does the image of things
present impinge on the eyes if their powers are impaired), so
also God, who is nowhere absent, is present in vain to de-
filed souls, since the mind in its blindness cannot see him."

13. WHAT PROOF IS THERE THAT MEN
ARE SUPERIOR TO ANIMALS?

Among the many ways in which it can be shown that man

---

1 Cf. R 1.26 (PL 32.624): "it is not mine, but because I was responsible
for making it known to certain brothers who were at that time ques-
tioning me very closely on these topics and were pleased with it, they
wanted me to write it among our *Questions*. Its author is a certain
Fonteius of Carthage, and it is entitled *On the Need for Purifying the Mind
in Order to See God.* He wrote it while yet a pagan, but he died a baptized
Christian."

is superior to animals by virtue of his reason, this is clear to all: animals can be domesticated and tamed by men, but men not at all by animals.

14. THAT THE BODY OF CHRIST WAS NOT A PHANTOM

If the body of Christ was a phantom, Christ was a deceiver; and if he was a deceiver, he is not Truth. However, Christ is Truth. Therefore his body was not a phantom.[1]

15. ON THE INTELLECT

Everything which understands itself comprehends itself. But what comprehends itself is limited with respect to itself. Now the intellect understands itself. Therefore it is limited in respect to itself. Nor does it wish to be without limits, although it could be, since it wishes to be known to itself, for it loves itself.[1]

---

1 Augustine is here referring to the Manichaean view which denied the reality of Christ's body, substituting for it only the appearance of a body, i.e., a phantom body. See NCE, s.v. "Jesus Christ, II (in Dogmatic Theology)." The Manichaean view was itself rooted in an even older heresy called Docetism, which maintained that Christ in his earthly career only "seemed" or "appeared" to be man. Docetism takes its name from a Greek word *(dokein)* which means "to seem," "to appear." See NCE, s.v. "Docetism."

An early North African critic of the view which Augustine seeks to refute in this Q. is Tertullian (ca. 155–after 220). See his *Adversus Marcionem (Against Marcion)* 3.8 (PL 2.359-60).

1 St. Augustine does not mean that the intellect in question need be limited with respect to its *substance,* otherwise God would be finite. Rather, he means that any intellect which knows itself fully and completely is limited in respect to itself in the sense that it knows all that it can possibly know about itself. Therefore, in this sense, even God's knowledge of himself, and hence his intellect, is "limited," for God's self-knowledge does not exceed the limits of his being, even though his being is infinite. Cf. DCD 12.18 (PL 41.367-68).

16. ON THE SON OF GOD

God is the cause of all that exists. But because he is the cause of all things, he is also the cause of his own Wisdom, and God is never without his Wisdom. Therefore, the cause of his own eternal[1] Wisdom is eternal as well, nor is he prior in time to his Wisdom. So then if it is in God's very nature to be the eternal Father, and if there was never a time when he was not the Father, then he has never existed without the Son.

17. ON GOD'S KNOWLEDGE

Everything past no longer exists, everything future does not yet exist, therefore nothing past and nothing future exists. But in God's sight there is nothing which does not exist. Therefore, in God's sight, [nothing exists] as past or future, but everything is now.

---

1 In Latin, *sempiternae*. St. Augustine does not make the linguistic distinction between eternal *(aeternum)* and sempiternal *(sempiternum)* which Boethius will make later on in a passage well-known to medieval philosophers, though Augustine promotes the same doctrine as does Boethius. In his *De Trinitate (On the Trinity)* 4 (PL 64.1253), Boethius states: "But the expression 'God is ever' denotes a single Present, summing up His continual presence in all the past, in all the present—however that term may be used—and in all the future. Philosophers say that 'ever' may be applied to the life of the heavens and other immortal bodies. But as applied to God it has a different meaning. He is ever, because 'ever' is with Him a term of present time, and there is this great difference between 'now,' which is our present, and the divine present. Our present connotes changing time and sempiternity; God's present, abiding, unmoved, and immoveable, connotes eternity. Add *semper* to *eternity* and you get the constant, incessant and thereby perpetual course of our present time, that is to say, sempiternity." (The translation is that of H. Stewart and E. Rand, *Boethius: The Theological Tractates, The Consolation of Philosophy* [Cambridge, Mass. 1962], pp. 21 and 23. The Latin text of the *Loeb* volume differs slightly from the PL text.) Cf. also Boethius, *De consolatione philosophiae* 5, *prosa* 6 (PL 63.858–59).

18. ON THE TRINITY[1]

For every existing thing there is something responsible for its existing, something responsible for its distinguishing marks, and something responsible for its coherence.[2] Accordingly if any created thing exists in some sense, differs in practically all respects from what is absolutely indeterminate, i.e., nothing, and possesses a coherent structure, it requires a threefold cause: that by which it exists, that by which it is this particular thing, that by which it is internally consistent. But the cause, i.e., the author, of every created thing we call God. Therefore it is fitting that he be a trinity such that perfect reason cannot find anything more excellent, intelligent, and blessed. For this reason also, in

---

1 This Q. is somewhat obscure. In order to understand what St. Augustine is saying, we must first note the important parallels in the passage, for they help to unlock its meaning. (1) There are the "elements" of any existing thing: (1a) that responsible for its existing, (1b) that responsible for its distinguishing marks, (1c) that responsible for its coherence. (2) There is the threefold cause: (2a) that by which something exists, (2b) that by which something is this particular thing, (2c) that by which something is internally consistent. (3) There are the attributes of the Trinity: (3a) excellence (the Father), (3b) intelligence (the Son), (3c) blessedness (the Holy Spirit). (4) Finally there are the fundamental questions in the search for truth: (4a) Does something exist? (4b) Is it this or that? (4c) Should it be approved or disapproved? These parallels clearly show that St. Augustine is already interested in the question of vestigial traces of the Trinity in the created order—a question which will draw much of his attention in the latter part of his later work DT. In the present work, one may also compare Q. 38, "On the Structure of the Soul."

However, a recognition of this Augustinian concern does not automatically clear up all of the connections noted above. Of particular difficulty is the relation of (1c) and (2c) to (3c) and (4c). The connection is more clearly seen when one understands that for St. Augustine a thing's worth or perfection is partly a function of the relative absence or presence of structure in the thing. The more structured or internally coherent an entity is within its own kind, the more it realizes the purpose for which it was made. The more it realizes this, the greater worth it has and the more susceptible it is of "approval." On the level of the rational soul, another element as well comes up for consideration, the element of happiness or blessedness. The more the rational soul comes into line with its divinely ordained purpose, viz., to know God and to enjoy him, the happier it becomes.

2 For these elements in any existing thing, see also E 11.3 (PL 33.76).

the search for truth, there can be no more than three kinds of question: Does a thing exist at all? Is it this particular thing or something else? Should it be approved or disapproved?[3]

19. ON GOD AND THE CREATED

What is unchangeable is eternal, for it always exists in the same state. But what is changeable is subject to time, for it does not always exist in the same state and accordingly is not correctly said to be eternal. For what changes does not remain, and what does not remain is not eternal. Now between the immortal and the eternal there is this difference. Everything eternal is immortal, but not everything immortal is with sufficient accuracy called eternal. For although something may live forever, still, if it is subject to change, it is not properly called eternal, since it does not always exist in the same state. However, it can be called immortal because it lives forever. But sometimes what is immortal is also called eternal. However, what is both subject to change and said to live by the presence of a soul, although it is not a soul, cannot at all be understood to be even immortal, much less eternal. For in that which is properly called eternal there is nothing past as if it has already transpired, nor anything future as if it does not yet exist, but whatever is simply is.

20. ON THE PLACE OF GOD

God is not anywhere. For what is somewhere is contained in a place, and what is contained in a place is body. But God is not body, so he is not anywhere. Nevertheless, since he is and yet is not in a place, all things are in him rather than he himself being anywhere. Still, they are not in God as if he himself were a place, for place is in space which is occupied by the length, breadth, and height of a body. But God is not

---

3 For these three questions, see also C 10.40.65 (PL 32.807).

of this character. Therefore all things are in him, and he is not a place. Nonetheless, the temple of God, through a misuse of the term, is called the place of God, not because he is contained in it, but because he is present there. But in the understanding of this nothing excels the soul which is pure.

21. *IS NOT GOD THE AUTHOR OF EVIL?*[1]

Whoever is the author of all things which are and whose goodness is responsible for the existence of all that exists cannot have anything at all to do with nonbeing. Now everything which lacks anything lacks in relation to being and tends toward nonbeing. However, to be and to lack in nothing is good, whereas evil is a lacking. But he on whom nonbeing has no claim is not the cause of [this] lacking (*causa deficiendi*), i.e., of the tending toward nonbeing, because he is, if I may say so, the cause of being (*causa essendi*). Therefore he is the cause only of good, and for that reason he is the highest good. Consequently he who is the author of all things which are is not the author of evil, because to the degree that things are, to that degree are they good.

---

1 Cf. R 1.26 (PL 32.625): "care must be taken that one not misunderstand my claim that 'God is not the author of evil because he is the author of all things which are, and because to the degree that things are, to that degree are they good.' Let no one think on this account that the punishment of the wicked, which is obviously an evil to those who are punished, does not come from him. But I have spoken thus in the same way in which it was said: 'God has not made death' (Wis 1.13), although it was elsewhere written: 'Death and life are from the Lord God' (Ecclus [Sir] 11.14). Therefore the punishment of the wicked, which is from God, is indeed evil to the wicked; but it is counted among the good works of God, because it is just that the wicked be punished, and, of course, everything which is just is good." The Latin wording of the last sentence in Q. 21 differs from the Latin wording of that sentence as quoted by St. Augustine in R. There is thus a corresponding difference in the English translation.

22. THAT GOD IS NOT SUBJECT TO NEED

Where there is no want, there is no need; and where there is no deficiency, there is no want. But there is no deficiency in God. Therefore there is no need.

23. ON THE FATHER AND THE SON

Everything chaste is chaste by chastity, and everything eternal is eternal by eternity, and everything beautiful, beautiful by beauty, and everything good, good by goodness. As well, therefore, everything wise is wise by wisdom, and everything alike, alike by likeness. Now there are two ways in which a thing is said to be chaste by chastity: first, [when] the chaste thing produces chastity so that it is chaste by that chastity which it produces and for which it is the generative principle and cause of existence; or, second, when by participation in chastity everything is chaste which can at some time not be chaste.

And furthermore, the other examples must be understood in this way. For it is the claim of either knowledge or belief that the soul acquires eternity, but it does so by participation in eternity. But God is not eternal in this fashion. He is eternal because he is the author of eternity itself. This may also be seen in the case of both beauty and goodness. Accordingly, when God is said to be wise, and when he is called wise by that wisdom which it is preposterous to believe that he ever lacked or could lack, he is called wise not by participation in wisdom, as is the soul, which can both be and not be wise. Rather, God is called wise because he has himself begotten that wisdom by which he is called wise.[1]

---

1 Cf. R 1.26 (PL 32.625): "I have said: . . . because he has himself begotten that wisdom by which he is called wise.' We have handled this issue more ably in a later book, *On the Trinity*." Cf. DT 6.2.3 (PL 42.924–26). Also, compare this Q. with DGnI 16.57–58 (PL 34. 242), which dates from the same period.

Again, those things which by participation are either chaste or eternal or beautiful or good or wise admit of the possibility of being neither chaste nor eternal nor beautiful nor good nor wise. But as for chastity, eternity, beauty, goodness, and wisdom themselves, they in no way admit either or perishing or, so to speak, of a temporal character, deformity, or malice.

Therefore even those things which are alike by participation admit of unlikeness, but likeness itself cannot in any manner and to any degree be unlike. It therefore results that when the Son is called the likeness of the Father (because by participation in the Son whatever things are alike are alike either to one another or to God, for the Son is the first species by which, so to speak, all things are specified, and the form by which all things are formed), he can in no respect be unlike the Father. He is therefore the same as the Father, but with the result that he is the Son and the latter is the Father. That is, the Son is the likeness, the Father, that of whom he is the likeness; the Son is substance, and the Father is substance, from which results one substance. For if there is not one substance, likeness admits of a likeness—a possibility which the most exacting reason denies.

24. DO SIN AND RIGHT CONDUCT RESULT FROM A FREE CHOICE OF THE WILL?[1]

Whatever happens by chance happens without design. Whatever happens without design does not happen due to Providence. If therefore some things in the world happen by chance, then not all the world is governed by Providence. If

---

1 In R 1.25 (PL 32.625) Augustine makes a further comment on the issue whether sin and right conduct result from a free choice of the will. "It is unmistakably true that this is absolutely the case," he says. "But to be free to act rightly is a result of being set free by the grace of God." (See the article referred to in Q. 2, n. 2.)

not all the world is governed by Providence, there is therefore some nature and substance which does not belong to the workings of Providence. But everything which is, insofar as it is, is good. For that is supremely good in whose participation other things are good. And everything which is subject to change is good insofar as it exists, though not in and by itself, but by participation in the unchangeable good. In its turn, that good whose participation renders good whatever other things exist is good not by any thing other than itself; and this good we also call Divine Providence. Therefore nothing happens in the world by chance.

This having been established, it seems to follow that whatever is done in the world is done partly by divine agency and partly by our will. For God is by far incomparably better and more just than any man, no matter how good and just. And the just ruler and governor of all things allows no punishment to be inflicted undeservedly on anyone, nor any reward to be given undeservedly to anyone. That which merits punishment is sin, and that which merits reward is right conduct. And neither sin nor right conduct can be justly charged to anyone who has done nothing of his own will. Accordingly sin and right conduct result from a free choice of the will.

25. ON THE CROSS OF CHRIST

The Wisdom of God became man in order to show us how to live virtuously. Part of living the virtuous life involves not fearing those things which ought not to be feared. But death is not to be feared. Therefore it was necessary to show this by the death of that Man whom the Wisdom of God became.

However, there are men who, although they do not fear death itself, are nevertheless terrified of some one kind of death. But even here, just as death itself is not to be feared, so no kind of death is to be feared by the man whose life is good and upright. No less, therefore, had this also to be shown by that Man's cross. For among all the ways of dying, none was more accursed and terrible than that one.

26. ON THE DIVERSITY OF SINS

There are sins of weakness, others, of ignorance, others, of malice. Weakness is the opposite of strength, ignorance is the opposite of wisdom, and malice is the opposite of goodness. Consequently whoever knows what is the strength and wisdom of God can judge which are the pardonable sins. And whoever knows what is the goodness of God can appreciate which sins are due some kind of punishment both in this world and in the one to come. Once these matters have been adequately treated, one can plausibly determine those who are not to be compelled to a penance full of sorrow and mourning, although they acknowledge their sins, and those for whom no salvation whatever is to be hoped except they offer in sacrifice to God a spirit broken through penance.[1]

27. ON PROVIDENCE

Through an evil man Divine Providence can both punish and succor. For the impiety of the Jews was the Jews' downfall and yet provided salvation for the Gentiles. Again, Divine Providence through a good man can both condemn and help, as the Apostle says: "To some we are the scent of life unto life, but to others we are the scent of death unto death."[1] But every tribulation is either a punishment of the impious or a testing of the just (hence the word *tribulation* is derived from *tribula* ["threshing sledge"], an instrument which cuts up the chaff as well as separates the grain from the chaff). Further, peace and quiet from disruptive times can both profit the good and corrupt the evil. Therefore Divine Providence governs and tempers all these things in proportion to the worth of souls. But, nevertheless, the good do not choose for themselves the beneficial ministry of tribulation, nor do the evil love peace. For that reason the

---

1 Cf. Ps 50(51).19

1 2 Cor 2.16.

evil also, as unknowing agents, receive the recompense, not of the justice which belongs to God, but the recompense of their own evil wills. Likewise, neither is there charged to the good the harm which is done to someone in their desire to do good. Rather, the good soul[2] is rewarded on the basis of its good will. So too the remainder of creation, either openly or hidden from view, hinders or helps in proportion to the worth of rational souls.[3] For since the highest God governs well all that he has made, there is nothing disordered and nothing unjust in the world, whether we know this or not. But the sinful soul, for its part, suffers misfortune. Still, because it is deservedly in the state befitting such a being, and because it suffers that which it is reasonable for such a being to suffer, the sinful soul does not mar by its deformity any of God's sovereign rule. Accordingly, since we do not know everything which the Divine Order does on our behalf, in respect to the goodwill alone do we act in conformity to the law. In other respects, however, we are acted upon in conformity to the law, since the law itself remains unchangeable and directs all changeable things by a supremely beautiful government. Therefore, "glory to God on high, and on earth peace to men of good will."[4]

---

2 *bono animo*. St. Augustine uses two words in this Q. which I translate indifferently here by the word *soul*. The words are *animus* and *anima*, which at times appear to have fairly distinct but related meanings in St. Augustine's thought. When a distinction is made, *anima* generally refers to the animating principle common to *all* physical life, man included. The term *animus*, however, refers specifically to the kind of *anima* or life-principle possessed by man, viz., a *rational* life-principle. (Cf. Gilson, *Introduction a l'étude de Saint Augustin* [Paris 1949], p. 56, n. 1, and his numerous references to appropriate texts from Augustine.) However, Augustine recognizes that even the term *anima* by itself can bear these two meanings. CF. Q. 7, "What does 'Soul' properly Refer to in a Living Being?"

Although *anima* and *animus* in Q. 27 can probably be translated by *soul* and *mind* respectively, nonetheless, I have here translated the two terms by the word *soul,* principally because the meanings of the two Latin words are more closely related than they are distinct, and because the English term *soul* better captures that common meaning than does *mind*. Furthermore, I shall continue to translate both *anima* and *animus* by *soul* unless the passage in question clearly calls for a distinction to be made.

3 *animarum rationalium*. See above, n. 2.

4 Lk 2.14.

28. WHY DID GOD WANT TO MAKE THE WORLD?

To inquire into why God wanted to make the world is to
inquire into the cause of God's will. But every cause is productive of some result, everything productive of some result
is greater than that which is produced, and nothing is
greater than God's will. Therefore [God's will] has no cause
to be sought after.

29. IS THERE AN 'ABOVE' AND A 'BELOW' IN THE UNIVERSE?

"Set your mind on the things which are above."[1] We are
bidden to set our minds on those things which are above,
viz., spiritual things, which must not be understood to exist
above in respect to the places and parts of this world, but by
virtue of their excellence, lest we fix our mind[2] on a part of
this world when we ought to divest ourselves of the whole
thing.

However, among the parts of this world, there is an
'above' as well as a 'below.' On the other hand, the world as
a whole has neither an above nor a below, for it consists of
body, because everything which can be seen consists of
body, and nothing in body taken as a whole is above or
below. Indeed, since there seem to be six kinds of rectilinear,
i.e., noncircular, motion—forward and backward, right-
hand and left-hand, upward and downward—there is absolutely no reason why, in respect to body as a whole, there
should be anything in front and in back, to the right and to
the left, but yet there should be above and below.

Nonetheless, those who consider this matter are fooled
because of the tough resistance offered by the senses and
habit. For to effect the rotation of our body through the wish
that the head point downward is not as easy for us as to turn

1 Col 3.2.
2 *animum*.

from right to left or from front to back.[3] Accordingly, to be able to see this, words must be set aside, and the mind[4] must activate its own special resources.

30. HAS EVERYTHING BEEN CREATED FOR MAN'S USE?

There is the same difference between the terms *honorable*[1] and *useful* as between the terms *enjoyable* and *useful*. For although it can be maintained (though requiring some subtlety) that everything honorable is useful and everything useful is honorable, nevertheless, since the term *honorable* more appropriately and usually means "that which is sought for its own sake," and the term *useful*, "that which is directed to something else," we now speak in terms of this distinction, while safeguarding, of course, the fact that the word *honorable* and the word *useful* are in no way opposed to one another. For these two terms are sometimes thought to be mutually exclusive, but this is an uninformed opinion of the crowd. Therefore we are said to enjoy that from which we derive pleasure. We use that which we order toward something else from which we expect to derive pleasure.

---

3 Augustine apparently means that the relativity of right and left and back and front is easily discerned, because we can easily turn our bodies in these directions and discover that the left is now the right, the right is now the left, and so on. However, because we rarely, if ever, are turned upside down onto our heads, we fail to notice the same relativity in up and down, and thus assume that they are absolute.

4 *animo.*

---

1 The word *honorable* translates the Latin term *honestum*. An English word which adequately translates the Latin is as hard to come by as an adequate English word for the equivalent Greek term *kalon*. H. Hubbell, in his translation of Cicero, *De inuentione,* The Loeb Classical Library (Cambridge, Mass. 1960), p. 326, note, remarks that *honestum* "denotes 'honour' in a broad sense; 'moral beauty' might be a more exact rendering." See below, Q. 31.

Consequently every human perversion (also called vice) consists in the desire to use what ought to be enjoyed and to enjoy what ought to be used. In turn, good order (also called virtue) consists in the desire to enjoy what ought to be enjoyed and to use what ought to be used. Now honorable things are to be enjoyed, but useful things are to be used.

I mean by *honor* the intelligible beauty which properly we call spiritual, whereas by *usefulness* I mean Divine Providence. Accordingly, though there are many visible beautiful things which are not appropriately called honorable, nevertheless, Beauty itself, by which whatever is beautiful is beautiful, is not at all visible. Again, many useful things are visible. But Usefulness itself, by which whatever is useful is useful to us, and which we call by the name *Divine Providence*, is not visible. Note well, however, that all corporeal beings are comprehended by the term *visible*. Therefore it is invisible beautiful things, i.e., honorable things, that should be enjoyed. But whether all should be is another question, although perhaps only things which ought to be enjoyed may properly be called honorable.

All useful things, however, ought to be used according as there is need for each of them. And indeed, it is not so very absurd to think of animals as enjoying nourishment and all the bodily pleasures. However, only a living being possessed of reason can use anything. For the knowledge of that to which each thing must be ordered is not given to beings lacking reason, nor is it given to simple, dull rational beings. Nor can anyone use that which is to be ordered to an end of which he has no knowledge, and no one can know this except he who is wise. Accordingly those who do not use things well are usually and more correctly called *abusers*. For what is badly used benefits no one, and what is of no benefit obviously is not useful. But whatever is useful is useful by being used. Thus no one uses anything except what is useful. Therefore he does not use anything who uses it badly.

Accordingly the perfect reason of man, which is called virtue, uses first of all itself to understand God, in order that it may enjoy him by whom also it has been made. It uses, moreover, other rational living beings for fellowship and nonrational living beings for [a display of] its eminence. It also directs its life to this end—the enjoyment of God, for thus is it happy. Therefore perfect reason uses even itself and indeed ushers in misery through pride if it is directed to itself and not to God. It also uses certain bodies which it must make alive for its own benefit. It uses its own body in this way—accepting or rejecting some things to achieve health, suffering others to achieve patience, regulating others to achieve justice, examining others to achieve some evidence of the truth. It uses also those things from which it abstains to achieve moderation. Thus reason uses everything, both sensible and nonsensible, and there is no third kind of being.

Moreover, reason judges everything that it uses. God alone it does not judge, because God is the standard according to which it judges other things.[2] Nor does perfect reason use God, but it enjoys him. For God must not be ordered to anything else, because everything which must be ordered to another is inferior to that to which it is ordered. Nor is anything higher than God—not in terms of place but in terms of the excellence of its nature. Therefore everything which is made is made for man's use, because reason, which is given to man, uses all things by judging all things.

Moreover, before the Fall man was not in fact using those things which must [now] be endured nor after the Fall does he use them. [Rather, man uses them] only after he has been converted and has become a friend of God (as much as is possible now even before the death of the body), because he has become of his own volition a servant.

---

2 *quia secundum Deum de caeteris iudicat.*

31. CICERO'S OPINION ON THE DIVISION
AND DEFINITION OF THE VIRTUES OF THE SOUL[1]

(1) Virtue is a habit of the soul conformable to the ways of nature and to reason. Therefore, when all the parts of virtue are known, we will have considered the full nature of honor, simply understood.[2] Accordingly virtue has four parts: prudence, justice, courage, and moderation.

Prudence is the knowledge of things good, evil, and indifferent. The parts of prudence are memory, intelligence, and foresight. Memory is that by which the soul recalls those things which have been. Intelligence is that by which the soul observes those things which are. Foresight is that by which a future event is seen before it has happened.

Justice is a habit of the soul which, with proper regard for the common welfare, renders to each man his own desert. It proceeded originally from nature, then certain things passed over into custom by reason of their usefulness, then afterwards a respect for law and religion sanctioned the very things that proceeded from nature and were approved by custom.

There is a law rooted in nature. Opinion has not begotten it; rather, a certain innate force has implanted it, [and it finds expression in such things] as religion, duty, gratitude, revenge, reverence, and truthfulness. Religion involves the service and ritual veneration of a certain kind of higher nature called divine. Duty is that whereby kindly service and attentive care are offered to blood relations and to country.

---

1 Q. 31 is an almost literal quotation of Cicero, *De inuent.* 2.53.159–55.167. Concerning this Q., St. Augustine writes in R 1.26 (PL 32.625): "it is not mine, but Cicero's. But since I was also responsible for making this known to the brothers, they have written it among those things which they were collecting, since they wanted to know how Cicero divided and defined the virtues."

2 Cicero is trying to provide a complete analysis of the term *honestum*, which is translated here by the word *honorable*. See above, Q. 30, n. 1. The class of the honorable, Cicero says, has two divisions, one simple and the other complex. Everything in the simple division is embraced by one term, *virtue*. Cf. *De inuent.* 2.53.159. It is at this point that Augustine's Q. 31 picks up Cicero's discussion.

Gratitude is that quality wherein is contained, in the case of friendship, a memory of the same, and, in the case of services, a desire to provide remuneration for the same. Revenge is that whereby violence or assault and absolutely everything which would injure may be repulsed by defending or by avenging oneself. Reverence is that quality whereby we deem worthy of honor and some kind of veneration men who excel in some merit. Truthfulness is that quality whereby one speaks of things present, past, and future without alteration of fact.

There is a law grounded in custom. It is either that which, drawn only slightly from nature, usage has nourished and made stronger (e.g., religion or any of those mentioned earlier which we see to be derived from nature and strengthened through custom), or that which time has brought into common usage through public approval. Of this kind are the contract, equity, and judgment. A contract is an agreement among several individuals. Equity involves the fair treatment of all. A judgment is a decision already settled upon by the official determination of one or several persons.

There is a law based on statutes. It is that which is contained in a written document promulgated for public compliance.

Courage is the considered undertaking of dangers and bearing of hardships. Its parts are highmindedness, confidence, patience, and perseverance.

Highmindedness is the pursuit and management of great and lofty things with a certain noble and splendid resolve of mind. Confidence is that quality whereby the soul itself, in things great and honorable, has placed with assured hope great trust in itself. Patience is the voluntary and sustained suffering of arduous and difficult things for an honorable or useful purpose. Perseverance is unwavering and unbroken persistence in a well thought-out plan.

Moderation is the firm and measured control of reason in respect to lust and other improper impulses of the soul. Its parts are continence, forbearance, and modesty. Continence is that quality whereby desire is controlled by the guidance of counsel. Forbearance is that quality whereby souls rashly enticed and agitated into the hatred of another are held in check by kindness. Modesty is that quality whereby an honorable sense of decency procures a manifest and enduring reputation.

(2) All of these things just discussed are to be sought strictly for their own sake, without any advantage being attached to them. The demonstration of this is not part of our purpose, and it conflicts with the brevity of our instruction.

However, those things to be avoided for their own sake are not only those opposed to the above qualities (e.g., cowardice is the opposite of courage, and injustice, the opposite of justice), but also those things which appear to be related and connected to them but are actually very much different. Diffidence is opposed to confidence, and therefore diffidence is a vice. Temerity is not thus opposed. Rather, it borders upon and is related to confidence, and yet it is a vice. Thus for each and every virtue a related vice will be found either already called by a specific name (as temerity and obstinacy border upon confidence and perseverance respectively, and superstition comes close to religion) or without any specific name. All of these likewise we shall class as things to be avoided, just as we did with the opposites of good qualities.

Enough has been said of this kind of honor which is sought wholly for its own sake. Now it seems that we should speak of that kind to which usefulness is coupled, and which nonetheless we call honorable.

(3) Accordingly there are many things which draw us both by their intrinsic value and by their consequences as well. Of this kind are glory, rank, influence, and friendship.

Glory is the widespread and praiseworthy reputation of a person. Rank is the distinguished authority that a person has—an authority worthy of veneration, honor, and reverence. Influence consists in power or grandeur or the great abundance of some resource. Friendship is the disinterested desire for good for that person whom one loves, together with a reciprocal desire on his part. Since here we are speaking of issues relating to public life, we associate with friendship its benefits so that it may appear worthy to be sought for the sake of these as well. We do this in order that they perhaps will not criticize us who thought that we were speaking of every kind of friendship. In fact, there are those who think that friendship should be sought strictly for its usefulness, others, for its own sake, and others, both for its own sake and for its usefulness. Which of these conceptions may be chosen as most accurate will be considered in another place.[3]

32. CAN SOMEONE UNDERSTAND SOMETHING BETTER THAN SOMEONE ELSE, AND THEREFORE CAN THERE BE AN ENDLESS ADVANCE IN THE UNDERSTANDING OF THE THING?

Whoever understands a thing to be other than it really is makes a mistake, and everyone who is mistaken does not understand that about which he is mistaken. Accordingly whoever understands a thing to be other than it really is does not really understand it. Therefore nothing can be understood except as it really is. But as for ourselves, when we understand something not as it really is, it is not understood at all, because it is understood to be other than it really is. For this reason, there should be no doubt that there is a total understanding which admits of no higher degree, and that, consequently, there is no endless advance in the understanding of anything nor the possibility of one understanding it better than another.

---

3 I must here acknowledge my indebtedness to Hubbell's English translation of Cicero's *De inuent.* (Cf. Hubbell, pp. 327–35).

33. ON FEAR[1]

Unquestionably the only cause for fear lies in the fact that what is loved[2] might be lost, once acquired, or might not be acquired, once hoped for. Therefore, for each one who has loved and possessed freedom from fear, what fear is there that he can lose this freedom? For we fear losing many things which we love and possess, and so we fearfully stand guard over them; but no one can preserve freedom from fear by being fearful. Again, as for the person who loves freedom from fear, but does not yet possess it and hopes that he will have it, it is not necessary for him to fear that he not get it, for by this fear nothing other than fear itself is feared. But all fear flees something, and nothing flees itself. Therefore fear is not feared. However, if someone thinks it incorrect to say that fear fears something for the reason that fear fears by the soul and not by fear itself, then let him consider this point easily grasped: there is no fear except of a future and imminent evil. But it is necessary for the one who fears that he flee something; and so whoever fears fear is, to be sure, in a most absurd position, because he has in fleeing the very thing which he flees. For, since one fears only the happening of something evil, to fear that fear will happen is nothing else but to embrace what you reject. Now if this is contradictory, as it is, there is absolutely no way for him to fear who loves nothing other than freedom from fear. And for this reason no one can love this by itself and not have it.

However, whether this condition alone ought to be loved is another question. Now as for the one who is not terrorized by fear, he is not ravaged by covetousness, nor is he tormented by grief, nor is he agitated by exultant and empty

1 *Metu.* St. Augustine seems to gather in under this term that whole range of feelings running from apprehension to terror.
2 This word, in the present context, might also be translated "to like," "to find pleasure in," "to delight in," or "to be fond of." I have preferred the translation "to love" because this English term best preserves the full nuance of St. Augustine's own use of *amo.* See below, Q. 35; and cf. G. Hultgren, *Le commandement d'amour chez Augustin* (Paris 1939), the whole of Part I, and Gilson, pp. 170 ff.

delight. For if he covets, since covetousness is nothing else but the love of transient things, it is necessary to fear lest either he lose them, once acquired, or not get them. But he does not fear, therefore he does covet. Again, if he is tormented by mental anguish, it is necessary that he also be vexed by fear, because anguish results from present evils whose imminence occasions fear. But he is free of fear, therefore, of anguish also. Again, if he is frivolously joyful, he is joyful over those things which he can lose. For this reason, it is necessary to fear lest he lose them. But he has no fear whatever, so he does not rejoice frivolously at all.

34. MUST NOTHING ELSE BE LOVED BUT FREEDOM FROM FEAR?

If freedom from fear is a vice, then it must not be loved. But no one who is completely happy is fearful, and everyone who is completely happy is without vice. Accordingly it is not a vice not to be afraid. Now presumptuousness is a vice. Therefore not everyone who does not fear is presumptuous, although everyone who is presumptuous does not fear. Again, there are no corpses which fear. For this reason, since the absence of fear is common to the completely happy person, to the presumptuous person, and to the corpse, but the perfectly happy man possesses that quality by the serenity of his mind, the presumptuous man by his foolhardiness, and the corpse by its complete lifelessness, it follows that neither must freedom from fear not be loved (because we desire to be happy), nor must it alone be loved (because we do not want to be presumptuous and devoid of life).

35. WHAT OUGHT TO BE LOVED?[1]

(1) Since lifeless things do not fear, nor would we be persuaded to deprive ourselves of life so that we could be free of

---

1 Cf. R 1.26 (PL 32.625): "I do not completely approve of my claim that 'that should be loved which is possessed in the knowing of it.' For

fear, a life without fear ought to be loved. But, on the other hand, since life free of fear is not even desirable if it lacks a capacity for reason,[2] life without fear but possessed of this capacity ought to be loved.

Is that the only thing to be loved? Or is love itself also to be loved? Of course [it is to be loved], because without it those other things are not loved.[3] But if love is loved for the sake of the other things which ought to be loved, it is a mistake to say that it ought to be loved. For to love is nothing other than to desire something for its own sake. Accordingly love ought not to be sought for itself, should it, when unmistakable misery follows on the loss of what is loved? Then again, since love is a kind of motion, and since there is no motion except it be toward something, when we seek what ought to be loved we are looking for something to which this

---

neither did they *not* possess God to whom it was said: 'Do you not know that you are the temple of God and that the Spirit of God dwells in you?' (1 Cor 3.16), and, nonetheless, they did *not* know him (or rather, they did not know him as he *ought* to be known). Again, I said: 'Therefore no one knows the happy life and is wretched.' Instead of 'knows the happy life,' I meant to say, 'knows the happy life as it *ought* to be known.' For who is wholly ignorant of that life when indeed, among those who at least have the use of reason, they know that they want to be happy?''

2 The phrase *capacity for reason* translates the Latin term *intelligentia*. For the appropriateness of this translation in this context, cf. Hultgren, p. 128.

3 This sentence should not be taken to signify St. Augustine's view in this Q. He is not saying that love ought to be loved for its own sake, but rather, the opposite. This is clear from the question which follows a little later: ''love ought not to be sought for itself, should it, when unmistakable misery follows on the loss of what is loved?'' The question is so constructed in Latin that it expects a negative reply.

Why then does Augustine appear to endorse the view that love ought to be loved for its own sake? Because he is ever the debater ready for disputation, and the footnoted sentence falls in the middle of one such imaginary interchange. If the following contrivance be permitted, the point becomes clear.

Augustine: Is that the only thing to be loved? Or is love itself also to be loved?

Opponent: Of course [it is to be loved], because without it those other things are not loved.

Augustine: But if love is loved for the sake of the other things which ought to be loved, . . . , etc.

See below, Q. 77, which is an incomplete report of an actual debate.

motion ought to direct us. For this reason, if love ought to be loved, surely not every kind of love ought to be. For there is a base love by means of which the soul chases after things inferior to itself, and this love is more properly called *covetousness,* that is to say, "the root of all evils."[4]

Accordingly that should not be loved which can be taken away from a love persisting and delighting in its object. Therefore, what kind of object should a love love, unless it be that kind of object which cannot be absent while being loved? That object is what is possessed in the knowing of it.[5] But as for gold and any material thing possessing them is not the same as knowing them; so they should not be loved. Moreover something can be loved and not had, not only of those things which should not be loved, e.g., something of physical beauty, but also of those things which should be loved, e.g., the happy life. On the other hand, something can be had and not loved, e.g., impediments. One therefore rightly asks of that whose possession consists in the knowing of it: could anyone not love it when he has it, i.e., knows it? Yet we see people who are learning mathematics, for example. Their only reason is to use this science to become wealthy or to please men. When they have learned the science, they direct it toward the very end which they had proposed to themselves while learning it. Since this is so, and since to possess any science is no different from knowing it, it is possible for each to have something whose possession lies in the knowing of it, even though he does not love it.

However, as for a good which is not loved, no one can possess it or have it perfectly. For who can know to what extent something is good when he does not enjoy it? But he does not enjoy it if he does not love it, nor therefore does he who does not love it possess what is to be loved, even if he who does not possess it could love it. Therefore no one knows the happy life and is wretched, because if it should be loved (and it should be), then to know the happy life is the same as to possess it.

---

4 1 Tm 6.10.
5 See n. 1 above.

(2) Since these things are so, what else is it to live happily but to possess an eternal object through knowing it? For the eternal is that in which alone one can rightly place his confidence, it is that which cannot be taken away from the one who loves it, and it is that very thing which one possesses solely by knowing it. For of all things, the most excellent is what is eternal, and therefore we cannot possess it except by that part of ourselves in which lies our excellence, i.e., by our mind. But whatever is possessed by the mind is had by knowing, and no good is completely known which is not completely loved. Nor is it the case, since the mind alone can know, that thus it alone can love. For love is a kind of desire, and we see that desire is also present in other parts of the soul. If this desire is in accord with the mind and reason, it will be possible for the mind to contemplate what is eternal in great peace and tranquillity. Therefore the soul ought to love with its other parts as well this magnificent object which must be known by the mind. And since that which is loved necessarily affects with itself that which loves, it follows that what is eternal, loved in this way, affects the soul with eternity. Wherefore, strictly speaking, it is eternal life which is the happy life. However, what else but God is that eternal object which affects the soul with eternity?

Now the love of those things worthy to be loved is better termed "disinterested love" *(charitas vel dilectio).*[6] For this

---

6 Cf. Gilson, p. 177, n. 2. *Charitas* or *dilectio* mean the same thing in this context, so I have translated them by one and the same phrase, viz., *disinterested love.* It is worth noting that there is a general problem here which any translator of Latin must face. Latin, like Greek, has a number of words to handle a variety of experiences, emotions, and concepts which, in general, are designated by the one English word *love.* St. Augustine makes use of the three words *amor, charitas,* and *dilectio. Amor* and *charitas* could be straightforwardly translated "love" and "charity" respectively, though there are problems with the latter. *Dilectio* is also ordinarily translated "love." But what is one to do with *dilectio* when it occurs in a context in which the English word *love* has been preempted for *amor,* as has happened in translating this Q. and the next? My general rule, Q. 36 being the exception, is to translate all three Latin words by the same English word *love.* I do not, except as noted in the text or footnotes, use *charity* to translate *charitas,* because this translation cannot do as successful and sustained a job as the word *love.* Futhermore, although he has used *amor* and the *amare* almost

reason, one ought to reflect carefully with all the power of one's thought on that most salutary precept: "You shall love[7] the Lord your God with all your heart and with all your soul and with all your mind";[8] and again, on that which the Lord Jesus says: "This is eternal life, that they know you the only true God and whom you have sent, Jesus Christ."[9]

36. ON NOURISHING CHARITY

(1) *Charity* denotes that whereby one loves those things whose worth, in comparison to the lover itself, must not be thought to be of lesser value, those things being the eternal and what can love the eternal. Therefore in its consummate and purest sense *charity* is used only of the love of God and of the soul by which he is loved (and this is also appropriately called *dilectio*[1]).

However, when God is loved more than the soul so that a man prefers to belong to him rather than to himself, then is

---

exclusively up to this point, Augustine gradually abandons them in subsequent QQ., except perhaps in those cases where he is discussing a love which is less than the disinterested and self-giving love encompassed by the terms *charitas* and *dilectio*. (But see below, Q. 78, n. 6, and DCD 14.7.) For example, the later QQ. dealing with problems of Biblical exegesis rarely use the words *amor* and *amare*. This is probably explained by the influence of the Old Latin Bible, which seems to use *charitas* and *dilectio* and their associated verbs almost exclusively.

7 *diliges.*
8 Mt 22.37.
9 Jn 17.3.

---

1 Cf. R 1.26 (PL 32.625-26): "I have said: 'Therefore, in its consummate and purest sense the term *charity* is used only of the love of God and of the soul by which he is loved.' If this is true, how does the Apostle say: 'No one has ever hated his own flesh' (Eph 5.29)? And with this in mind he admonishes husbands to love *(diligantur)* their wives. But for that reason it was said: 'charity is also correctly called love *(dilectio)*,' since the flesh is indeed loved *(diligitur)*, nonetheless, not in its own right, but for the sake of the soul to whose use it is subject. For although the flesh *seems* to be loved *(diligi)* for its own sake when we do not wish it to be ugly, one must refer its beauty to something else, viz., to that by which all beauty exists." For the word *dilectio* and its verb complement *diligo*, see above, Q. 35, n. 6.

it that we are genuinely mindful in the highest degree of the soul and consequently also of the body; for we are not solicitous of the body because of the promptings of some desire, but we take only what is at hand and what is offered.

However, the poison of charity is the hope of getting and holding onto temporal things. The nourishment of charity is the lessening of covetousness, the perfection of charity, the absence of covetousness. The lessening of fear is the sign of its progress, the absence of fear, the sign of its perfection. For "the root of all evils is covetousness,"[2] and, "love[3] made perfect casts out fear."[4] Accordingly whoever wants to nourish charity in himself, let him pursue the lessening of covetous desires (covetousness being the love of getting and holding onto temporal things).

The lessening of covetousness begins with the fear of God who alone cannot be feared apart from love. For one strives toward wisdom, and nothing is truer than the saying: "The fear of the Lord is the beginning of wisdom."[5] In fact, there is no one who does not flee pain more than he seeks pleasure, since indeed we see that even the fiercest beasts are frightened away from the greatest pleasures through dread of pain. When this becomes habitual in them, they are said to be broken and tamed. Consequently, since man possesses a reason which, in the service of covetousness through a deplorable perversion, suggests that transgressions can be hidden and carefully prepares the cleverest devices for hiding secret sins, and all for the purpose of not fearing [the judgement of] men, then it follows that men not yet enticed by the beauty of virtue are more difficult to tame than wild animals. [This is so] unless they be deterred from sinning by the punishments most truly proclaimed by holy and divine men, and unless they agree that they cannot conceal from God what they conceal from men. But in order that God be feared, one must be persuaded that the universe is ruled by Divine Providence. But one must be persuaded not so much

2 1 Tm 6.10.
3 *dilectio.*
4 1 Jn 4.18.
5 Ecclus (Sir) 1.16.

by reasoned arguments, since one who can appreciate them
can already perceive the beauty of virtue, as by examples
either recent, if there be any, or from history, and especially
that history which through the watchcare of Divine Providence has received in the Old and New Testaments the most
excellent weight of religious authority. However, one must
treat simultaneously the two issues of punishment for sin
and reward for right conduct.

(2) Now, however, as soon as a habitual avoidance of sin
has shown the supposedly burdensome to be easy, there is
need to begin tasting the sweetness of piety and commending
the beauty of virtue so that the freedom of charity might
stand out in comparison with the bondage of fear. Then,
after the faithful have received the rites of regeneration (and
these should be deeply moving), they must be clearly shown
the difference between two men: the old and the new, the
outer and the inner, the earthly and the heavenly, i.e., the
difference between the one who pursues carnal and temporal
goods and the one who pursues spiritual and eternal goods.
The faithful must also be warned not to expect from God
perishable and transient benefits whose abundance even impious men can enjoy, but rather, lasting and eternal benefits
whose acceptance requires a complete disdain of all things
deemed good and evil in this world. Here one must point out
that most extraordinary and unique example of the Lord's
Man[6] who, when he had shown by a great variety of

---

6 *Dominici hominis.* This curious and difficult phrase is found in two other
places in DD83, viz., in QQ. 57.3 and 75.2. The phrase could be
translated "God-man" or even "Christ-man." (For the latter, see G.
Lampe, ed., *A Patristic Greek Lexicon* (Oxford, 1961), p. 142b, *s.v.*
"anthrōpos," I.4.) However, in the light of van Bavel's brief discussion
of the phrase, it seems better to translate it "Lord's Man." (See T.
van Bavel, *Recherches sur la christologie de Saint Augustin: l'humain et le divin
dans le Christ d'après Saint Augustin* (Fribourg 1954), pp. 15–16. Van
Bavel himself translates the expression thus: *l'homme seigneurial.*)
    Many years after composing this Q., St. Augustine expresses some
second thoughts about his use of *homo Dominicus.* These thoughts are
found in R 1.19.8 (PL 32.616–17), where he is reassessing his use of the
phrase in DSD 2.6.20 (PL 34.1278). However, his remarks are equally
applicable to his use of it here and elsewhere in DD83. Augustine says:
"Again in the second book I say: 'No one will be permitted ignorance
of the kingdom of God when his only begotten shall come from heaven

miracles how great is his power over things, spurned those things which the ignorant esteem as great goods and, as well, endured those things which they think to be great evils. Lest one be less bold to undertake that way of life and discipline the more one honors it, there is need to show from that Man's promises and exhortations and from his imitators — a multitude of apostles, martyrs, and innumerable saints — why that way of life and discipline are not to be despaired of.

(3) But where the enticements of carnal pleasures have been overcome, one must be careful that the desire of pleasing men does not slip in and take their place, i.e., the desire of pleasing men either through extraordinary deeds, or through difficult self-control and patience, or through some kind of largesse under the heading of knowledge or eloquence.[7] The desire for honor is also in this class. Against these things one must bring up everything written about the praiseworthiness of charity and the emptiness of boasting. One must teach the need of shame in wanting to please those whom you do not want to imitate. For either they are not good men, and there is nothing worthwhile in the praise of the wicked, or they are good men, and it is necessary to imitate them. But the good are good by virtue, and virtue does not desire what is in the power of other men. Therefore one who imitates good men desires the praise of no man; one who imitates the wicked is not worthy of praise. But if you want to please men on this account, that you might help

---

not only in an intelligible way, but also in a visible way in the Lord's Man ''in order to judge the living and the dead'' (2 Tim. 4.1).' But I do not know whether he can rightly be called the Lord's Man, he who is the 'mediator between God and men, the man Christ Jesus' (1 Tim. 2.5), [since he is plainly the Lord]. Moreover, who in his holy family cannot be called the Lord's man? Indeed, I should mention that I have seen this expression in certain Catholic commentators on the divine Scriptures. However, wherever I have used this expression, I wish that I had not. For I saw afterwards that the expression should not be used, although there is possibly some rationale in defense of it.'' (The bracketed phrase may not belong in the text. Cf. the edition and apparatus for line 10 in CSEL 36, p. 94.)

7 The latter part of this sentence could possibly be translated as follows: ''either through extraordinary deeds, or through difficult self-control and patience, or through some kind of largesse, or under the heading of knowledge or eloquence.''

them to love[8] God, you no longer desire the praise of men, but something else. However, one who desires to please still needs to have fear: first, that he not be counted by God among the hypocrites because of secret sinning; second, if he desires to please through good deeds, that he not lose what God is going to give through chasing after this reward.

(4) Once this kind of covetousness is overcome, there is need to watch out for pride. For it is difficult for him who no longer desires to please men and who considers himself to be fully virtuous to think the company of men worthwhile. Consequently fear is still necessary that even that which he seems to have may not be taken from him,[9] and that with hands and feet bound he may not be cast into outer darkness.[10] For this reason, the fear of God is not only the beginning of the wise man's wisdom, but the completion of it as well. And the [wise man] is he who loves[11] God supremely and his neighbor as himself. As for the dangers and difficulties to be feared in this journey and the remedies to be used, that is another question.

37. ON THE FOREVER BORN[1]

He who is forever born is superior to one who is forever in the process of birth, because the one who is forever in the process of birth has not yet been born, and neither has he

---

8 *diligendum.*
9 Mt 25.29.
10 Mt 22.13.
11 *diligit.*

---

1 Although Possidius, St. Augustine's friend and biographer, states in his *Indiculus* that this Q. is an anti-Arian piece (see Wilmart, p. 173), the content of the Q. is not directly concerned with the basic heretical teaching of Arius. Indeed Arius, an Alexandrian priest from Libya who died in 336, denied the eternal preexistence of the Son with the Father, maintaining instead that the Son is a created being, albeit the first among such beings. Hence talk about the Son being "forever born" or "forever in the process of birth" has no *direct* connection with his views, since he would deny that either expression is correct. (For more on Arius, see Quasten, *Patrology* 3.7-13).

ever been born nor will he ever be born if he is forever in the
process of birth. For it is one thing to be in the process of
birth, it is another to have been born. Consequently one
never becomes a son if one is never born. But the Son,
because born, is forever the Son. Therefore he is forever
born.

38. ON THE STRUCTURE OF THE SOUL[1]

Although nature, learning, and habit differ, they are
understood [to exist] in a soul which is one without distinction of nature. Again, native endowment, courage, and
tranquillity differ, yet similarly they belong to one and the
same substance. The soul, furthermore, is a substance other
than God, although made by him. And God himself is that
most sacred Trinity, known by name to many but in reality

However, this Q. may have an *indirect* relation to the Arian controversy which would allow us to view it as anti-Arian. For Augustine
is arguing here in Q. 37 that the expression *semper natus* is to be preferred to the expression *semper nascitur*. The reason for this preference
seems to be the following: if the Son were truly he who is "forever in
the process of birth," then he would never be a son, whereas if he were
truly "forever born," then he is both a son and forever a son. Furthermore Augustine's interest in this terminological dispute might very
well have been aroused by criticism of Catholic trinitarian teaching by
Arians who had seized on Origen's expression *semper nascitur* (found in
St. Jerome's Latin translation of one of Origen's homilies on Jeremias
[see *In Ieremiam homiliae* 9.4 (PG 13.358)], which Jerome translated in
the early 380's) in order to show the alleged incoherence of orthodox
belief. Augustine's argument on behalf of the Son being "forever
born" would therefore be a response to just such a criticism.

---

1 St. Augustine is here once again interested in the issue of the vestiges
  of the divine Trinity in the created order. (See above, Q. 18, "On the
  Trinity,"   and n. 1.) In particular, he has an interest in certain
  "trinitarian" features of the life of the mind or soul, an interest whose
  rationale and whose detailed expression are found in Books 9 and 10 of
  DT (PL 42.959–84). But here he speaks first of the triad of nature
  (*natura*), learning (*disciplina*) and habit (*usus*) in one and the same soul,
  and then of native endowment (*ingenium*), courage (*uirtus*), and tranquillity (*tranquillitas*). He then goes on to mention explicitly the Trinity.
  And, as well, each Scripture verse of the three which he cites at the end
  of the Q. is understood to refer to one of the persons of the Trinity.

to few. [For these reasons,] one should investigate with great attentiveness the following sayings of the Lord Jesus: "No one comes to me except the Father draw him";[2] "No one comes to the Father except through me";[3] and, "He himself will lead you into all truth."[4]

39. ON THE SOURCES OF NOURISHMENT[1]

What is it that takes the thing which it changes? The animal eating food. What is it that is taken and changed? Food. What is it that is taken and not changed? Light by the eyes and sound by the ears. However, the soul gets these things through the body; but what is it that the soul gets through itself and changes within itself? Another soul which it assimilates to itself by receiving it into its friendship. And what is it that the soul gets through itself and does not change? The truth. For this reason, one should come to understand the meaning of both the statement to Peter: "Kill and eat,"[2] and the statement in the gospel: "And the life was the light of men."[3]

40. SINCE THE NATURE OF SOULS IS THE SAME, WHY ARE THE CHOICES[1] OF MEN DIFFERENT?

Diverse sense impressions give rise to diverse desires in souls; diverse desires, to diverse means of getting; diverse means of getting, to diverse habits; and diverse habits, to diverse choices. Now the order of things produces the differ-

---

2 Jn 6.44.
3 Jn 14.6.
4 Jn 16.13.

---

1 See below, Q. 73.1.
2 Acts 10.13.
3 Jn 1.4.

---

1 *uoluntates*. Throughout this Q. *uoluntas* is consistently translated "choice." See above, Q. 2, n. 2.

ing sense impressions—a hidden order, to be sure, but nonetheless, a true and determinate order submitted to Divine
Providence. Therefore one should not think, because there
are differing choices, that the natures of souls are different,
since even the choice of one soul varies with the changing of
time. Indeed, at one time the soul longs to be rich; at
another time, contemptuous of riches, it desires to be wise.
Even in the desire for temporal things, at one time the
business world pleases a given man, at another time a
military career pleases him.

41. SINCE GOD HAS MADE EVERYTHING, WHY DID HE NOT MAKE EVERYTHING EQUAL?

Because there would not be everything if everything were
equal. For there would not be the many kinds of things
which make up the universe in its hierarchy of created things
from the first and second levels of created things right down
to the last. This kind of universe is what is meant by the
word *everything*.

42. HOW WAS CHRIST BOTH IN HIS MOTHER'S WOMB AND IN HEAVEN?

In the same manner as a man's spoken word which, even
though many hear, each hears as a whole.

43. WHY DID THE SON OF GOD APPEAR AS A MAN AND THE HOLY SPIRIT AS A DOVE?[1]

Because the Son of God came to show men a pattern for
living, whereas the Holy Spirit made his appearance to indicate the gift which virtuous living attains. Moreover, both
of these events came about in a visible manner for the sake of

---

1 Cf. Mt 3.16, Mk 1.10, Lk 3.22, and Jn 1.32.

the carnal, who must pass by degrees through the sacraments from those things which are seen with the physical eyes to those things which are understood by the mind. For words make a sound and then pass away; nevertheless, when something divine and eternal is expressed in speech, that which is signified by the words does not likewise pass away.

44. WHY DID THE LORD JESUS CHRIST COME SO LONG AFTER MAN SINNED AND NOT IN THE BEGINNING?

Because everything beautiful comes from the highest beauty which is God, and temporal beauty is achieved by the passing away and succession of things. Moreover, in each individual man each individual period of life from infancy to old age possesses its own beauty. Therefore, just as it is absurd for someone to want only youth in a man subject to time (for he would begrudge the other beauties which in the other years of a man's life have their own place and order), thus is it absurd for someone to desire one particular age for the whole of mankind, for even the race itself, in the fashion of an individual man, passes through its own sequence of ages. Nor was it necessary for a teacher to come from heaven except in the time of mankind's youth, a teacher whose example would direct man to the best morals. To this is applicable the Apostle's remark[1] that we were kept under the law like children kept under a tutor[2] until he should come whom the tutor served, he who was promised by the prophets. It is indeed one thing for Divine Providence to deal

---

1 Gal 3.23–24.
2 Cf. R 1.26 (PL 32.626): "after I mentioned that the ages of mankind were as the ages of an individual man, I said: 'Nor was it necessary for a teacher to come from heaven except in the time of mankind's youth, a teacher whose example would direct man to the best morals.' And I added: 'To this is applicable the Apostle's remark that we were kept under the Law like children kept under a tutor' (Gal 3.23–24). But one can ask why we have said elsewhere that Christ has come in the sixth age of mankind, as if in mankind's old age. [See below, Q, 58.2, and cf. DGnM 1.23.40 (PL 34.192–93).] Well then, what was said of

with individuals privately, another thing for it to be mindful of the whole of mankind publicly. For all those who have achieved true wisdom as individuals have been illumined by the same truth in accord with the opportunity of their own respective periods of life. This Truth has assumed humanity at mankind's opportune age in order that the whole of mankind might become wise.

45. AGAINST THE MATHEMATICIANS

(1) The ancients did not mean by the term *mathematician* those to whom we now give the name. Rather, they used the term for those who investigated the measure and harmony of the times by the movement of the heavens and the stars.[1] Concerning the latter the Holy Scriptures quite rightly say: "Nor, again, ought these to be excused. For if they were able to know so much that they could prize the created order,[2] how have they not more readily found its Lord?"[3] For the human mind, in passing judgement on visible things, can know that it itself is better than everything visible. Nonetheless, when the mind confesses that it too is changeable because of its failure and success in wisdom, it finds that above itself exists an unchangeable truth. Clinging to Truth itself in the manner of the psalmist: "My soul has

youth refers to the strength and fervor of faith 'which is at work through love' (Gal 5.6), but what was said of old age, to the number of years. Both, in fact, can be understood of all men taken together, but they cannot both be understood of the ages of individual men. Youth and old age cannot be the body simultaneously, but they can both be in the mind [*animo*]—youth because of its liveliness, old age because of its seriousness." Further remarks about the ages of mankind can be found below in QQ. 53.1; 58.2; and 64.2.

1 Although Augustine uses only the term *mathematicus* throughout this Q., he discusses two senses of the term, one being "mathematician" and the other being "astrologer." He is concerned to discuss both kinds of *mathematicus*, for in the first part of the Q. he deals with *mathematici* who are "mathematicians," whereas in the second he deals with *mathematici* who are "astrologers." However, it would seem that the astrologers are those whom he is most concerned to criticize.
2 *saeculum.*
3 Wis 13.8–9.

clung to you,''[4] the mind achieves happiness, even discovering within itself the Creator and Lord of all things visible.[5]
The mind accomplishes this without an external quest for
visible things, not even celestial things, which either are not
discovered or are discovered to no purpose after great effort,
unless from the beauty of these celestial things which exist
outside the mind there be discovered the artist who is within
and who causes first the superior beauties of the soul and
then the inferior beauties of physical things.

(2) However, against those who are presently called by
the name *mathematician,* who wish to subject our activities to
the heavenly bodies and to sell us to the stars and to collect
from us that price for which we are sold, there can be no
more accurate and quicker a response than the following.
They do not yield a return unless the constellations are interpreted.[6] However, in the constellations one observes parts
such as the three hundred and sixty which, so they say, the
circle of the zodiac has. Moreover, the movement of the
heavens through one hour of time traverses fifteen parts or
degrees of the zodiac, so that the movement of the heavens
through fifteen degrees of the zodiac equals one hour of
time. As for the individual degrees, they are said to have sixty minutes. However, [the mathematicians] do not ascertain
in the constellations from which they say that they predict
the future the ''minutes of the minutes,'' i.e., the seconds,

---

4 Ps 62(63).9.
5 Compare this and the preceding two sentences with Augustine's proof
   for the existence of God in DLA 2.3.7–15.39 (PL 32.1243–62).
6 *nihil uerius et breuius dici potest, quam eos non respondere, nisi acceptis constella-*
   tionibus. This sentence is difficult to interpret. For one thing, it is not
   clear how far the ''accurate and quick response'' extends. Does it
   extend to the end of the sentence or to the end of the paragraph?
   In my translation, I have understood *eos* to be the subject of *respondere*
   and Augustine's response to continue to the end of the paragraph. If
   this understanding be correct, then Augustine is claiming that the
   interpretation of the constellations as favorable or unfavorable is
   necessary to the existence of the astrologers' trade. However, he
   argues, it is impossible for the astrologers ever to produce such an
   interpretation, because they cannot take into account the seconds of
   the zodiac, which must be taken into account if there is to be any
   workable interpretation of the constellations. Therefore money spent
   on the astrologers is money wasted.

of the zodiac. However, since the conception of twins[7] is effected by the same act of intercourse, according to the testimony of medical men (whose science is much more certain and clear), this conception takes place in a point of time so small that not even two seconds elapse. What therefore is the source of so much diversity in the actions, fortunes, and choices[8] of the twins, who of necessity have the same constellation of conception, and for both of whom, as if for one man, there is one constellation given to the mathematician? Now if they should wish to restrict themselves to the constellation of birth, they are prevented from this by the twins themselves, who quite often are born one after the other in such a way that this interval of time is reduced to seconds, which they never do nor can take account of in the constellations.

Moreover, although it is said that [the mathematicians] have predicted many true things, this opinion results from men forgetting their falsehoods and errors, because they attend only to what takes place in accord with [the mathematicians'] answers and forget what is not in accord with them, and because men remember what happens not by that science (which is nothing of the kind), but by a certain unknown coincidence in things. But if men want to pay tribute to [the mathematicians'] expertise, they should also mention the fact that skilled divination belongs even to the writing on lifeless parchments, regardless of subject matter, from which parchments one's lot often times springs forth at random. But if books frequently produce lines or verses forecasting the future, and if there is no science to this, why is it surprising if the mind[9] of a man speaking produces by chance rather than by science some prediction of the future?

---

7 Compare this argument concerning twins and astrology with St. Augustine's better known discussions in C 7.6.8–10 (PL 32.737–39) and DCD 5.1–8 (PL 41.141–48). Also, see S 199 2 (PL 38.1027–28) and DDC 2.21.32–22.34 (PL 34.51–2).
8 *uoluntatum*. See above, Q. 2, n. 2.
9 *animo*.

46. ON THE IDEAS

(1) Plato is said to have been the first to use the name *ideas*. However, I do not mean to imply by this that, if there was no such name before he himself instituted it, there were accordingly no such things as those which he termed *ideas,* or that they were understood by no one. Rather, various people called them possibly by one name, possibly by another, for one is at liberty to impose any name whatever on something which is not yet defined and has no commonly accepted name. For it is not likely either that there were no wise men before Plato or that they did not understand those things which, as was said, Plato termed *ideas* (whatever they might be), since indeed so great is the importance attaching to these ideas that no one can be wise without having understood them. It is also probable that there were wise men in other countries besides Greece, to which fact even Plato himself has adequately testified, not only through travels in quest of wisdom, but also through express mention in his books. Therefore there is no need for thinking that those wise men, if they did exist, were ignorant of the ideas, although they may have possibly called them by another name. But enough of the name! Let us see the thing which above all we must contemplate and come to know, while leaving it in the power of each to call that thing which he knows by whatever name pleases him.

(2) Hence in Latin we can call the ideas either "forms" *(formae),* or "species," *(species),*[1] which are literal translations of the word.[2] But if we call them "reasons" *(rationes),*[3] we obviously depart from a literal translation of the term, for "reasons" *(rationes)* in Greek are called *logoi,* not "ideas" *(ideae).* Yet, nonetheless, if anyone wants to use "reason" *(ratio),* he will not stray from the thing in question, for in fact

1 Cf. Roche, pp. 355 ff.
2 St. Augustine is translating, of course the Greek word *idea*, which is transliterated into Latin (and English) as idea.
3 For a fuller appreciation of the word *ratio* and its uses in Augustine, one may consult Gilson, pp. 361–62.

the ideas are certain original and principal[4] forms of things, i.e., reasons, fixed and unchangeable, which are not themselves formed and, being thus eternal and existing always in the same state, are contained in the Divine Intelligence. And though they themselves neither come into being nor pass away, nevertheless, everything which can come into being and pass away and everything which does come into being and pass away is said to be formed in accord with these ideas.

However, every soul but the rational is denied the power to contemplate these ideas. This the rational soul can do by that part of itself wherein lies its excellence, i.e., by the mind and reason, as if by a certain inner and intelligible countenance,[5] indeed, an eye, of its own. And indeed, not any and every rational soul is prepared for that vision, but rather, the soul which is holy and pure. It is this soul which is claimed to be fit for that vision, i.e., which has that very eye with which the ideas are seen—an eye sound, pure, serene, and like those things which it endeavors to see.

Now what person, devout and trained in true religion, although he could not yet contemplate these [ideas], would, nonetheless, dare to deny—nay, would not even acknowledge—that all things which are, i.e., that whatever things are fixed in their own order by a certain particular nature so as to exist, are produced by God as their cause? And that by that cause all things which live do live? And that the universal soundness of things and the very order whereby those things which change do repeat with a certain regularity their journeys through time are fixed and governed by the laws of the most high God? This having been established and conceded, who would dare to say that God has created all things

---

4 The phrase *original and principal* translates the Latin adjective *principalis*. Augustine appears to have imbued the term with a twofold meaning which is reflected in the translation of the word. The *formae* or *rationes* are "original" in the sense that they are the very thoughts of God and the exemplars or plans by which he creates (see below, Q. 46.2). The *formae* or *rationes* are also "principal" in the sense that they stand at the top of a hierarchy of being in their excellence and perfection (for, of course, they are the very mind of God).

5 *facie.*

without a rational plan?[6] But if one cannot rightly say or believe this, it remains that all things are created on a rational plan,[7] and man not by the same rational plan[8] as horse, for it is absurd to think this. Therefore individual things are created in accord with reasons unique[9] to them.

As for these reasons, they must be thought to exist nowhere but in the very mind of the Creator. For it would be sacrilegious to suppose that he was looking at something placed outside himself when he created in accord with it what he did create. But if these reasons of all things to be created or [already] created are contained in the Divine Mind, and if there can be in the Divine Mind nothing except what is eternal and unchangeable, and if these original and principal reasons are what Plato terms ideas, then not only are they ideas, but they are themselves true because they are eternal and because they remain ever the same and unchangeable. It is by participation in these that whatever is exists in whatever manner it does exist.

Now among the things which have been created by God, the rational soul is the most excellent of all, and it is closest to God when it is pure. And in the measure that it has clung to him in love, in that measure, imbued in some way and illumined by him with light, intelligible light, the soul discerns—not with physical eyes, but with its own highest part in which lies its excellence, i.e., with its intelligence—those reasons whose vision brings to it full blessedness. These reasons (*rationes*), as was said, may be called ideas, or forms, or species, or reasons; and while it is the privilege of many to name them what they wish, it is the privilege of very few to see them in their reality.[10]

---

6 *irrationabiliter.*
7 *ratione.*
8 *ratione.*
9 *propriis.*
10 It is of interest to compare this entire Q. with some of Augustine's remarks concerning DO 1.11.32 in R 1.3.2 (PL 32.588-89): "However, in these books it also displeases me...that I commended the doctrine of the two worlds—one sensible, the other intelligible—not by the authority of Plato or the Platonists, but by my

47. WILL WE EVER BE ABLE TO SEE OUR OWN THOUGHTS?

It is usual to ask how, after the resurrection and transformation of the body which are promised to the saints, we
can see our thoughts. Accordingly any conjecture must start
from that part of our body which has more light, since it is
necessary to believe that the bodies of angels, such as we
hope to have, are completely full of light and are ethereal.[1] If
therefore many of the movements of our mind[2] are now
recognized in the eyes, it is probable that no movement of
the mind will be hidden, since the entire body will be an
ethereal body in comparison with which these present eyes
are flesh.

---

own authority, as if the Lord also had wanted to point this out. For he
does not say: 'My kingdom is not of the world,' but: 'My kingdom is
not of this world' (Jn 18.36). Although any number of expressions
could be devised to indicate the world in question, if another world was
meant by the Lord Christ, it could more appropriately be understood
to be that world in which will be 'the new heaven and the new earth'
(Apoc [Rev] 21.1), when there will come the fulfillment of our prayer:
'Your kingdom come' (Mt. 6.10). However, Plato has not made a
mistake in saying that there is an intelligible world, if we wish to pay
attention not to the word, which is foreign to the customary usage of
the Church in this regard, but to the thing itself. For, in fact, Plato has
termed 'the intelligible world' that very reason [*rationem*], eternal and
unchangeable, by which God has made the world. If anyone denies the
existence of such a world, it follows that he is saying that God has made
what he has made without any rational plan [*irrationabiliter*], or that
when he was making or before he made he did not know what he was
making, if he had no reason [*ratio*] for creation. But if God did have
such a reason, as he did, it appears that Plato has called it 'the
intelligible world.' Nonetheless, as for ourselves, we would not have
used this name if we had been at that time sufficiently instructed in the
language of the Church.''

---

1 Cf. R 1.26 (PL 32.626): ''I have said: 'It is necessary to believe that
the bodies of angels, such as we hope to have, are completely full of
light and ethereal.' If this body should be understood to be one without
the members which we now have and without the substance of flesh,
however much incorruptible, this is a mistake. But this issue is much
better handled in the work *On the City of God* in the place where I deal
with the question of seeing our thoughts.'' See DCD 15.23.1 and
22.29–30 (PL 41.468-69 and 796–804) for the latter reference.
2 *animi*.

48. ON WHAT CAN BE BELIEVED[1]

Three classes of things are objects of belief. First, there are those things which always are believed and never understood, e.g., history, which deals with events both temporal and human. Second, there are those things which are understood as soon as they are believed, e.g., all human reasonings either in mathematics or in any of the sciences. Third, there are those things which are first believed and afterwards understood.[2] Of such a character is that which cannot be understood of divine things except by those who are pure in heart. This understanding is achieved through observing those commandments which concern virtuous living.

---

1 Underlying this Q. is the Platonic distinction between belief (*pistis*) or opinion (*doxa*) and knowledge (*epistēmē*). According to Plato (see especially *Republic* 5–6), there are some things about which we can hold opinions but can never have knowledge (or understanding, to use Augustine's term). Any object of sensory experience is such a thing. On the other hand, there are some things about which we can have more than opinions or beliefs, for we can obtain a genuine knowledge of them. Mathematical truths are an example of such things. Plato finds the basis for this distinction primarily in the character of the objects themselves. In the first case sensible objects are contingent, transient entities which come into being and pass away. As such they are unstable foundations for knowledge, and hence they can be, at best, only objects of belief or opinion. In the second case mathematical truths are eternal and necessary and thus not subject to coming into being and passing away. As such, they can be objects of knowledge rather than simply objects of belief.

St. Augustine endorses the above distinction, and this is seen most clearly in the first of his three classes of things capable of being believed. As for the third class, this is a special class concerned with "divine things" or truths about God. Unlike the first class but like the second, these truths can be known or understood, for they are grounded in the being of the eternal and immutable God. Unlike the second class, however, knowledge of these truths is not simultaneous with believing them. Rather, this knowledge comes only to those who first believe in God so that they might afterwards attain the moral purity required for understanding these truths. (See below, Q. 81, "On Quadragesima and Quinquagesima.")

2 Cf. Is 7.9 (according to the Septuagint).

49. WHY IS IT THAT THE SONS OF ISRAEL USED TO MAKE VISIBLE SACRIFICE OF ANIMAL VICTIMS?[1]

Because there are also sacred things of a spiritual nature whose images a carnal people had to celebrate in order that the new people might be prefigured by the servitude of the old. One may also note in each one of us the same difference between these two peoples, since each person necessarily leads the life of the ''old man'' from his mother's womb until he arrives at the age of youth, where now it is not necessary to know in a carnal manner, but he can by an act of will[2] turn himself to spiritual things and be reborn within. It is a very grand thing, therefore, that what develops naturally and by training in an individual properly educated is proportionately effected and brought to completion by Divine Providence in the whole of the human race.

50. ON THE EQUALITY OF THE SON

Since God could not beget something better than himself (for nothing is better than God), then the one whom he did beget he had to beget as his equal. For if he had the desire and not the power, then he is weak; if he had the power and not the desire, then he is envious. From this it follows that God has begotten the Son as his equal.

51. ON MAN MADE IN THE IMAGE AND LIKENESS OF GOD

(1) Since the divine Scripture mentions the outer and the inner man and distinguishes them to the point that it is said

---

1 Cf. DCD 10.5 (PL 41.281–83).
2 *uoluntate*.

by the Apostle: "And if our outer man is corrupted,
nonetheless, the inner man is renewed from day to day,"[1] it
can be asked whether one of these is made in the image and
likeness of God. Now obviously it is foolish to ask, if one of
these has been so created, which one? For who hesitates to
say that it is the one who is renewed rather than the one who
is corrupted? But whether both men are so created is a big
question. For if the outer man is Adam and the inner man
Christ, both are properly understood to be so created.
However, since Adam did not remain good, as God had
made him, and since he became carnal by loving carnal
things, it does not seem an absurd possibility that Adam's
fall consisted in his losing the image and likeness of God.
And for this reason he himself is renewed, and he himself is
the inner man. How then is Adam also the outer man? Is it
in respect of the body, so that he would be the inner man in
respect to the soul, and the inner man would be resurrected
and renewed by a renewal which now comes about through
the death of the previous life, i.e., of sin, and by the rebirth
of the new life, i.e., of righteousness? Again, the outer and
the inner man are so named by the Apostle that he speaks of
one as the "old man" whom we must strip off and the other
as the "new man" who must be put on.[2] Yet again, the
Apostle terms one man the "image of the earthly man"
because he lives in accordance with the sin of the first man,
who is Adam; he terms the other the "image of the heavenly
man"[3] because he lives in accordance with the righteousness
of the second man, who is Jesus Christ. But the outer man
who is now corrupted will be renewed by the resurrection to
come, when he will have paid off that debt—death—which
he owes to nature under the terms of that law which was
given in paradise.

(2) Moreover, that there is no inconsistency in the scriptural claim that the body also was made in the likeness of
God is easily understood by the person who pays careful

1 2 Cor 4.16.
2 Col 3.9–10.
3 1 Cor 15.49.

attention to the words: "And God made all things exceedingly good."[4] For no one doubts that God himself is the
primal good. Indeed, things can be said to be similar to God
in many ways. Some, created in accordance with power and
wisdom, are similar because uncreated power and wisdom
are in him; others are similar insofar as they simply live,
because he is supremely life and the source of life; and others
are similar insofar as they have being, because he is the
highest being and the source of being. And accordingly those
things which merely exist and yet do not live or know are in
his likeness, not completely, but in a slight degree, because
even they are good in their own order, since he is that good
transcending all things from whom everything good proceeds. However, everything which lives but does not know
shares somewhat more in his likeness, for what lives also
exists, but not every existing thing also lives. Moreover, as
for those beings which know, they are so near to God's
likeness that no other created beings are closer, for what
shares in wisdom both lives and exists. However, what lives
necessarily exists, though it does not necessarily know. For
this reason, since man can participate in wisdom according
to the inner man, as such he is in the image of God in such a
way that he is formed without the interposition of any other
nature. Therefore nothing is more closely united to God, for
man knows and lives and exists and thus is unsurpassed
among created beings.

(3) If by the outer man one understands that life whereby
we sense through the body with the five celebrated senses
which we have in common with animals (for that life as well
can be corrupted by physical troubles inflicted on it by its
ordeals), this man too, and not without cause, is said to
share in the likeness of God. [This is so] not only because he
lives (a quality also apparent in animals), but more especially because he has the resources of a governing mind
which is illuminated by wisdom (an impossibility in animals
lacking reason). Moreover, the human body is unique
among the bodies of land animals in not being stretched out
prone on its stomach. However, although it could see [in

---

4 Gn 1.31.

that position], the body stands erect in order to look upon the heavens, the principle of visible things. And although it is recognized that the body has no life of its own but lives by the presence of soul, still the human body can rightly be regarded as created more in the image and likeness of God than the other bodies of animals. [Moreover, it] can be so regarded in this respect: not only because it exists and is undoubtedly good insofar as it exists, but also because it is such that it is more adapted for viewing the heavens.

Nevertheless, since a lifeless man is not rightly termed man,[5] neither the body alone nor the life alone which is present in the physical senses, but both together are perhaps more correctly understood to be the outer man.

(4) Nor is that a clumsy distinction between the image and likeness of God, which is called the Son, and that which is made in the image and likeness of God, as we understand man to have been made.[6]

There are also those who may not be mistaken in understanding the expressions *in the image* and *in the likeness* to refer to two different things, since, they claim, one expression could have sufficed if there were one thing. But also they propose that what is made "in the image" is the mind, which is formed by truth itself without the interposition of any other substance. The mind is also called spirit—not that Holy Spirit who is of the same substance as the Father and the Son, but the spirit of man. For indeed the Apostle makes this same distinction: "No one knows what goes on in a man except the man's own spirit, and no one knows what goes on

---

5 Cf. R 1.26 (PL 32.626): "what is the meaning of my statement: 'A lifeless man is not rightly termed man,' since even the corpse of a man is called man? Therefore I ought at least to have said, '...is not in the proper sense called,' where I said, '...is not rightly called.' Again, I have said: 'Nor is that a clumsy distinction between the image and likeness of God...and that which is made in the image and likeness of God, as we understand man to have been made.' This remark should not be understood as if man is not called the 'image of God,' since the Apostle says: 'A man indeed ought not cover his head, since he is the image and glory of God' (1 Cor 11.7). Still, man is also said to be 'in the image of God,' because he is not called the only begotten, who is the image alone, but not in the image."

6 See above, n. 5.

in God except the Spirit of God.''⁷ Again, concerning the
spirit of man the Apostle says: ''May he deliver your spirit
and soul and body.''⁸ For even the spirit was created by
God, as also were other created beings, for thus is it written
in Proverbs: ''Understand that the Lord knows the hearts of
men, and he who fashioned the spirit in all is the one who
knows all things.''⁹ Therefore, this spirit in which dwells the
capacity for knowing the truth is accepted without any
hesitancy as that which is made in the image of God, for it
clings to the truth without the interposition of any other
created being. They propose the suggestion that the other
parts of man are made ''in the likeness'' because every
image, of course, is a likeness, but not every likeness can
properly be called an image, although it may perhaps be
called such by an improper use of the word.

However, one must take care in such matters lest it be
thought that too much has been affirmed. It is undoubtedly
to one's advantage to keep this in mind so that one does not
believe that, because all bodies are extended in three-
dimensional space, the same holds true of the substance of
God. For the thing which is less in its part than in its totality
does not befit the dignity of the soul. How much less, then,
[does it befit] the majesty of God!

52. ON THE SCRIPTURE: ''I AM SORRY THAT I HAVE MADE MAN''¹

To raise us from the earthly and human meaning up to
the divine and heavenly, the divine Scriptures have
[themselves] come down to those words which even the most
simple customarily use among themselves. And so those
men through whom the Holy Spirit has spoken have not
hesitated to employ in those books, as the occasion best

---

7 1 Cor 2.11.
8 1 Thes 5.23.
9 Prv 16.2.

---

1 Gn 6.6.

demands, names of even those passions which our soul experiences and which the man who knows better already understands to be completely foreign to God. For example, because it is very difficult for a man to avenge something without experiencing anger, the authors of Scripture have decided to use the name *wrath* for God's vengeance, although God's vengeance is exercised with absolutely no such emotion. Again, since husbands are wont to protect the chastity of their wives through jealousy, the Scripture writers have used the expression *the jealousy of God* to indicate that providence of God whereby he admonishes the soul and seeks to prevent its corruption and, as it were, its prostitution through following after various other gods. In the same manner they also use the expression *the hand of God* for that power whereby he acts, *the feet of God* for that power whereby he perseveres in sustaining and governing all things, *the ears of God* or *the eyes of God*, for that power whereby he perceives and understands all things, *the face of God* for that power whereby he manifests himself and is known, and so on. The reason for this is that we, the people to whom this word comes, are accustomed to working with our hands, walking with our feet, going where our mind[2] directs, perceiving physical objects with our ears and eyes and other bodily senses, and being recognized by our face; and the same holds true for anything else which comes under a kind of rule like this. Therefore, in accord with this rule, since we are not easily accustomed to changing something begun and to turning to something else, except with regret, and although Divine Providence appears to observers of clear mind to administer all things by an absolutely fixed order, nonetheless, in a manner most suited to insignificant human understanding, those things which begin to be but do not continue as long as it was hoped that they would continue are said to be stopped by a kind of regret on the part of God.

---

2 *animus.*

53. *ON THE GOLD AND SILVER TAKEN BY THE ISRAELITES FROM THE EGYPTIANS*[1]

(1) Whoever considers the economies[2] of the two Testaments, which are carefully adapted in agreement with the times to the ages of the human race,[3] understands sufficiently, I think, what is appropriate to the first age of the human race and what to the later. For, subject to the harmonious governance of all things by Divine Providence, the whole series of generations from Adam to the end of the world is administered as if it were the life of a single man who from boyhood through old age marks off the progress of his life into different age-levels. Accordingly the person who devoutly attends to the divine Scriptures has to distinguish in morality levels of virtue which lead up to the highest and perfect virtue of man, lest when he discovers that at one time precepts suitable to children were imposed upon children and at another time precepts suitable to adults were imposed upon adults, he will deem those lesser commands as sin in comparison with the adult standards and think that it was not right for God to command such. But this is not the place for a lengthy discussion concerning the degrees of virtue. Still, the following is sufficient for discussing the present question.

In regard to deception, the highest and perfect virtue is to deceive no one and to display in one's conduct that saying: "Let the yes which you say be yes and the no, no."[4] But since this command was given to those to whom the kingdom of heaven was already promised, and since there is great virtue in fulfilling those adult commands for which this reward is reserved: "For the kingdom of heaven suffers violence, and the violent are those who snatch it away,"[5] there is need

---

1 Ex 3.22, 12.35.
2 *dispensationes*.
3 Further remarks about the ages of the human race can be found in QQ. 44; 58.2; and 64.2.
4 Mt 5.37.
5 Mt 11.12.

to inquire by what stages of development one attains to this height and perfection.

Undoubtedly one finds among those stages the people to whom a kingdom as yet earthly was promised, which at first they played with like children. Moreover, when from the one God, the Lord of all, they had obtained in that time the earthly joys which hitherto they only longingly gazed upon, then advancing from there and growing in spirit they dared also to hope for heavenly joys. Therefore, just as the highest and nearly divine virtue is to deceive no one, so the worst vice is to deceive everyone. For those striving toward that highest virtue from this lowest vice there is a level of virtue which involves deceiving certainly neither friend nor passer-by, though, at times, one's enemy. Hence the saying of the poet has become by now nearly an everyday proverb: "Deceit or valor? Who could care in the case of an enemy?"[6] But since even the enemy can very frequently be unjustly deceived (as when some agreement is made for a temporary peace, which they call a truce, and is not faith-fully kept, and so on), a person is much purer and much nearer that highest virtue who, though wishing to deceive the enemy, yet does not deceive him except by divine per-mission. For God alone knows, or certainly he knows far more excellently and fully than men, what punishment or reward each is worthy of.

(2) Wherefore God certainly does not deceive anyone by himself, for he is the Father of Truth, and Truth, and the Spirit of Truth. Still, in conferring rewards on the worthy (since this also is the province of justice and truth), God uses souls in accord with the merit and worth which constitute their level of attainment. Thus, if anyone merits being deceived, not only does God not deceive that person by himself, but neither does he by the man who already loves him appropriately and persists in observing the injunction, "let the yes which you say be yes and the no, no," nor does he by the angel for whom the role of deception is an un-

---

6 Virgil, *Aeneid* 2.390.

worthy one. Rather, God deceives either through the man who has not yet divested himself of such desires or through the angel who, because of his perverseness of will, has been appointed to the lowest station in nature, either in punishment for his sins or for the exercise and cleansing of those who are reborn through God's power. For we read that a king[7] was deceived by the false prediction of false prophets. The purpose of this story is to show us that the affair was not carried out apart from divine judgement, for the king was worthy of being thus deceived, nor that it was carried out by that angel for whom the office of deception was unsuited, but rather by an angel of error who on his own gladly asked that such a role be assigned to himself.[8]

Indeed in certain places in the Scripture some things are more clearly expressed which in other places the careful and devout reader would find less clearly expressed. For our God through the Holy Spirit has so directed the divine books to the salvation of souls that not only does he desire to nourish us with the plain, but also to exercise us with the obscure. Therefore, by way of this ineffable and sublime management of things which is the work of Divine Providence, natural law is transcribed, as it were, upon the rational soul so that in the conduct of this life and in their earthly ways men might preserve semblances of the workings of God. Hence it is that the judge concludes it to be unworthy of his role and execrable to slay the condemned. However, his order is carried out by the executioner, a man who, because of the character of his desire, is appointed to this office in order to slay the condemned by the directive of the law, although in his cruelty he could kill just as well even the innocent. For neither does the judge do this by himself, nor by the *princeps*,[9] the attorney, or someone upon whom, in his

---

7 I.e., Achab.

8 Cf. 3 Kgs (1 Kgs). 22.20–23.

9 I am unclear as to what Roman official St. Augustine is here referring, and so I leave the word untranslated. The word *princeps* can refer to the chief of any civil or military administrative office, hence I suspect that Augustine is referring to some sort of important police official. For a discussion of the varying official uses of the term *princeps*, see A. Berger, *Encyclopedic Dictionary of Roman Law* (Philadelphia 1953), p. 650.

official capacity, this function is inappropriately imposed. Hence it is that we also employ animals lacking reason for those things which it is outrageous for men to do. There is no doubt that a thief deserves to be chewed to pieces; still, a man does not himself do this to the thief, nor does he use his son, or a member of his household, or even his slave, but his dog whom such an activity befits due to the level of its nature. Therefore, since certain people properly suffer something which it is not proper for certain others to do to them, there are those ministers who act as instruments, upon whom appropriate duties are enjoined. The result is this: not only does justice itself use them to command someone to suffer something which it is fitting for him to suffer, but also justice inflicts the suffering through those instruments for whom it is no less appropriate to do such.

Accordingly on the one hand the Egyptians deserved being deceived, and on the other the people of Israel were then situated at such a level of morality, because of the age of the human race, that it would not be unworthy of them to deceive an enemy. It therefore came about that God commanded them (or, rather, permitted them because of their desire) to ask of the Egyptians gold and silver implements which these seekers of a kingdom as yet earthly were gazing upon longingly, even though they were not going to return them, and to take them as if they were going to return them.[10] God did not want to be unjust in the matter of the reward for such lengthy hardship and labor—a reward adapted to the level of such souls; nor did he want to be unjust in the matter of the punishment of the Egyptians, whom appropriately enough he caused to lose what they were under obligation to pay. And so God is not a deceiver. Who would not understand that it is outrageous and impious to believe that he is? Rather, he is the supremely just rewarder of merits and persons who does by his own agency some things which are worthy of him alone and befit him alone, such as illuminating souls and rendering them wise and blessed by proffering himself to them for their enjoyment.

---

10 Ex 3.22.

Other things he does by a created being subservient to
himself, ordained to this in accord with his merits by the
most impartial of laws. Through him God commands some
things and permits others, Divine Providence extending and
reaching all the while even to the aid of sparrows, as the
Lord says in the Gospel, and to the beauty of the grass, and
to the very number of our hairs.[11] Of this Providence it is
also said" "It extends powerfully from one end [of the
world] to the other, and it orders all things agreeably."[12]

(3) Moreover, that God punishes through the ministry of
souls obedient to his laws, and that he justly requites with
just penalties, though he himself abides in complete tranquillity, is quite clearly written as follows: "And as for him
who deserves not to be punished, you consider it foreign to
your power to condemn him. For your power is the source of
righteousness, and because you are the Lord of all, you act
to spare all. Indeed, you show your power when men would
not believe you to be perfect in power; but among those who
know it, you remove all grounds for presumptuousness. And
you, as the Lord of all power, judge with tranquility and
govern us with great respect."[13]

(4) Furthermore, there is proof that earthy things provide
the beginning step toward the heavenly righteousness commanded those who are already more stable. The Lord points
to this when he remarks: "If you were not faithful with that
which belongs to another, who will give you what is your
own?"[14] And that souls are taught in accord with their
degree of maturity the Lord himself also points out by saying: "I have many things to say to you, but you are not now
able to bear them."[15] The Apostle [does] likewise when he
says: "As for myself, brothers, I was not able to speak to you as
spiritual people, but as carnal. I gave you milk to drink, not
food; for you were not ready for it, neither are you now
ready, for you are still carnal."[16] We know in fact that what

11 Mt 10.29–30; Lk 12.27–28.
12 Wis 8.1.
13 Wis 12.15–18.
14 Lk 16.12.
15 Jn 16.12.
16 1 Cor 3.1–2.

happened to these people because of their level of maturity happens to the entire human race, so that, as befits the times, a carnal people were commanded one thing and a spiritual people something else. Therefore it is not surprising if the people of Israel, who yet merited deceiving an enemy, were commanded to deceive an enemy who deserved to be deceived. For they were not yet capable as are those to whom it was said: "Love your enemies."[17] Rather, they were in the condition of those to whom it was necessary to say simply: "Love your neighbor, and hate your enemy."[18] For the time was not yet at hand to teach a concept of neighbor as broadly conceived as it would have to be. Therefore a beginning was made under a tutor, while the completion was reserved for the teacher. Nonetheless, it was the same God who gave the tutor to the children, viz., the Law which was given through his servant, and the teacher to the more mature, viz., the gospel which was given through his only Son.

54. ON THE SCRIPTURE: "AS FOR MYSELF, IT IS GOOD FOR ME TO CLING TO GOD"[1]

Everything which exists is either unchangeable or not, and every soul is higher than the body. For everything which gives life is higher than that which receives life, and no one disputes that the body receives life from the soul, not the soul from the body.

Moreover, what is not a body and yet is something is either the soul or something higher than the soul. For there is nothing lower than a body, since even if someone should mention that matter from which the body comes, it is correctly termed "nothing" because it lacks all form.[2]

On the other hand, between the body and soul nothing is found which is higher than the body and lower than the soul.

17 Mt 5.44.
18 Mt. 5.43.

1 Ps 72(73).28.
2 See above, Q. 6, and n. 1.

For if there were something in between, either it would
receive life from the soul, or it would give life to the soul, or
neither; or it would give life to the body, or would receive life
from the body, or neither. But whatever receives life from
the soul is a body, and if something gives life to the soul,
then it is higher than the soul. Again, that from which a
body receives life is the soul, but there is nothing which
receives life from a body. As for that which does neither,
i.e., neither lacks life nor bestows life, either it is absolutely
nothing or something higher than both the body and soul.
However, whether there is any such thing in the universe is
another question.

Nevertheless reason has now learned that there is nothing
between the body and the soul which is higher than the body
and lower than the soul. However, that being which is
higher than the soul we call God,[3] to whom everyone who
understands him is joined. For what is understood is true,
whereas not everything which is believed is true.[4] Moreover,
whatever is true and is disjoined from the senses and the
mind can only be believed, but not sensed and understood.
Therefore that is joined to God which understands God.
Now the rational soul understands God, for it understands
that he exists ever the same and never suffers any change.
However, the body and even the rational soul itself undergo
change—the one, in time and place, the other because it is
now wise, now foolish. But what is unchangeable is obviously
higher than whatever is not so, nor is there anything higher
than the rational soul except God. When, therefore, the soul
understands something which exists ever the same, it
without doubt understands God, and he is Truth. Since in
understanding this Truth the rational soul is joined to

---

3 Cf. R 1.26 (PL 32.627): "Where I said: 'However, that being which is
  higher than the soul we call God,' I ought rather to have said
  '. . .higher than every created spirit. . .' "
4 Note carefully St. Augustine's use of the word *intelligere* ("to understand"). By definition what one understands is *true*. It would be self-
  contradictory to say that one understands something which is false. St.
  Augustine consistently and carefully adheres to this usage of *intelligere*
  in his most precise philosophic moments.

Truth, and since the soul's good lies in this, then one rightly accepts this as the meaning of the Scripture: "But as for myself, it is good for me to cling to God."[5]

55. ON THE SCRIPTURE: "THERE ARE SIXTY QUEENS, EIGHTY CONCUBINES, AND YOUNG WOMEN WITHOUT NUMBER"[1]

The number 10 can signify universal knowledge. If 10 refers to the inner and intelligible things which are signified by the number 6, this results in 10 x 6 which is 60. If 10 refers to earthly and corruptible things which are signified by the number 8, the result is 10 x 8 which is 80. Therefore the word *queens* refers to the souls which rule in the realm of the intelligible and spiritual. The word *concubines* [refers] to the souls which receive an earthly reward, concerning whom it is said: "They have received their reward."[2] The phrase

---

5 Ps. 72(73).28. This Q. contains important elements of St. Augustine's own fully developed proof for the existence of God found in DVR 29.52–31.58 (PL 34.145–48) and DLA 2.3.7–15.39 (PL 32.1243–62). The succinct remarks of G. Bardy on both this Q. and the proof of DVR and DLA are worth quoting: "This proof is grounded in the life of the mind: the possession by a contingent mind of a truth, any truth, presupposes a dependence of this mind on a perfect Truth, and this proves that Truth's existence. The heart of this proof is the principle of sufficient reason which is here applied, not to the psychological formation of the concept, but to the metaphysical import of the fact of knowledge taken in its totality, and God alone explains this fact. Illumination is the consequence of this. In this small Q. 54, St. Augustine does not develop this proof, properly speaking, but he suggests it toward the end; and one can find there a rough draft, or perhaps better yet a summary, of his full account in DLA. A little above in the same treatise, *Eighty-three Different Questions*, in Q. 45, there is also perhaps an allusion to the same thesis; and if it is purely implicit or scarcely perceived, it has, nonetheless, some value as a witness to a doctrinal tendency characterizing a frame of mind" (BA 10, p. 732, n. 56, "Amorce de la preuve de Dieu par la vie de l'esprit.")

---

1 Cant (Song) 6.7.
2 Mt 6.2.

young women without number [refers] to the souls which possess no determinate knowledge and can be imperiled by various doctrines. Hence number, as has been said, signifies the sure and certain confirmation inherent in knowledge.

56. ON THE FORTY-SIX YEARS FOR THE BUILDING OF THE TEMPLE

The numbers 6 + 9 + 12 + 10 + 8 make 45. Therefore add 1 and they make 46. This times 6 makes 276. Now it is said that human fetal development[1] reaches completion in the following way. In the first six days [the fetus] is similar to a kind of milk, in the following nine days it is changed to blood, then in the following twelve days it becomes solid, in the remaining ten and eight days the features of all its members achieve complete formation, and in the remaining time until birth it grows in size. Therefore to forty-five days add 1, which signifies the sum (because 6, 9, 12, 10, and 8 brought together into one sum make 45); add 1, as was said, and the result is 46. When this number is multiplied by 6, which stands at the head of the series, 276 results, i.e., nine months and six days. This is the time between March 25th (the day on which the Lord is believed to have been conceived, since he also suffered and died on that same day) to December 25th (the day on which he was born). Therefore it is not absurd to say that the temple, which signified his body,[2] was built in forty-six years, so that there were as many years in the construction of the temple as there were days in the completing of the Lord's body.[3]

1 *conceptio.*
2 Jn 2.20–21.
3 Cf. DT 4.5.9 (PL42.893–94) and IE 10.12 (PL 35.1473–74).

57. ON THE ONE HUNDRED
AND FIFTY-THREE FISH[1]

(1) "All things are yours, and you are Christ's, and Christ is God's."[2] If one counts from the beginning of the series, one gets 1, 2, 3, and 4.[3] Again: "The head of the woman is the man, the head of the man, Christ, and the head of Christ, God."[4] If one counts in the same way, one similarly gets 1, 2, 3, and 4. Furthermore the sum of 1 + 2 + 3 + 4 is 10. Accordingly the number 10 rightly signifies the teaching which presents God as the maker and the creature as the made. And since the perfected and indestructible body is subject to the perfected and indestructible soul, and again since the latter is subject to Christ and Christ to God (not as a dissimilar and foreign nature, but as the Son to the Father), this same 10 correctly signifies the whole of that everlasting state which, faith teaches, will follow on the resurrection of the body. And perhaps this is the reason why those who are hired for the vineyard receive a denarius as salary.[5]

Now just as the sum of 1 + 2 + 3 + 4 is 10, so (1 + 2 + 3 + 4) multiplied by 4 is 40. (2) But suppose that the body is correctly signified by the number 4 because the body consists of the celebrated four elements (the dry and the moist, the cold and the hot), and because the three-dimensional character of the body is produced by a progression, which also is contained in the number 4, from the point to the line, from the line to the plane, and from the plane to the solid. If this is so, then it is not absurd to think of the number 40 as indicating the divine plan which was carried out in the tem-

---

1 Gf. Jn 21.4–14.
2 1 Cor 3.22–23.
3 The series, from top to bottom, is: God, Christ, man, the physical universe.
4 1 Cor 11.3.
5 Mt 20.2. A denarius is a Roman coin originally containing ten Roman *asses*. Its name derives from the Latin adjective *denarius*, which means "containing ten." St. Augustine is obviously drawn to this interpretation of Mt 20.2 because the word *denarius* is also regularly used in the phrase *denarius numerus* to refer to the number 10.

poral order[6] for our salvation when the Lord assumed a body
and deigned to appear visibly to men. For the numbers 1 +
2 + 3 + 4 (which signify the creator and the creature)
multiplied by 4, i.e., represented by the body in time, make
40. For between 4 and 4x there is this difference: 4 is static,
4x is dynamic. Therefore, as 4 refers to body, thus 4x refers
to time and indicates the mystery carried out in the body and
in time for those who were entangled by a love for things
physical and were subjected to time. The number 40,
therefore, as was said, is not inappropriately thought of as
signifying that divine plan of salvation expressed in time.
Moreover, perhaps this is why the Lord fasted forty days,
showing the poverty of this present world which is driven by
the movement of bodies and time.[7] And [perhaps this is]
why he was with his disciples for forty days after the resurrection, making known to them, I think, that same temporal
program which he carried out for our salvation.[8]

Moreover, the number 40 teaches the same point when by
the addition of its factors it reaches the number 50,[9] since indeed these same factors are whole[10] numbers—whole
because physical and visible action in time, wholesomely[11]
managed, secures man's perfection. This perfection, as has
been said, is signified by the number 10. Likewise the
number 40, through the addition of its factors, generates the
number 10 because [10 is the difference when 40] reaches the
number 50 by this addition of its factors, as was said above.
For the 1 which 40 contains forty times, the 2 which it contains twenty times, the 4 which it contains ten times, the 5

---

6 *dispensatio temporalis*. *Dispensatio* has been met with earlier in Q. 53.1
  where, being in the plural, it was translated "economies." However,
  in what follows it will be translated "the divine plan (of salvation
  expressed) in the temporal order." Any serious departure from this
  will be indicated in a note.
7 Mt 4.2; Lk 4.2.
8 Acts 1.3.
9 The factors are 1, 2, 4, 5, 8, 10, and 20. These factors are enumerated
  by Augustine a few sentences below in this same paragraph. He does
  not consider 40 to be a factor, even though he considers 1 to be so.
10 *aequales*.
11 *cum aequitate*.

which it contains eight times, the 8 which it contains five
times, the 10 which it contains four times, and the 20 which
it contains two times, when added together, make 50.
Indeed, no other whole number can be a factor of the
number 40 besides these which we have enumerated and
which, added together, lead us to the number 50. Therefore,
having spent forty days after the resurrection with his
disciples committing to them what he accomplished for us in
time, the Lord ascended into heaven. After ten additional
days he sent the Holy Spirit,[12] through whom they who had
believed in visible and temporal things were brought to
spiritual perfection in order to seize hold of things invisible.
Clearly the Lord was indicating by the number 10 expressed
in these ten days preceding the sending of the Holy Spirit the
same perfection which is conferred by the Holy Spirit. And it
is this 10 which 40 produces through the addition of its whole
factors so as to make the number 50. Likewise, through the
divine plan of salvation expressed in time and wholesomely[13]
executed, one arrives at the perfection which is signified by
the number 10, which makes 50 when added to 40.

Therefore, the perfection which the Holy Spirit brings
while we yet walk in the flesh (so long as we do not walk according to the flesh, i.e., carnally)[14] is connected with this
same divine plan expressed in time. [Since this is so,] it
seems that the number 50 rightly belongs to the Church, but
now cleansed and perfected, which holds fast in love to faith
in this divine plan of salvation expressed in time and to hope
in the eternity to come, which involves, as it were, joining
the number 40 to the number 10.

Now this Church to which the number 50 belongs, either
because the Church is elected from the three kinds of men—-
Jews, Gentiles, and carnal Christians—or because it is imbued with the mystery of the Trinity, reaches the number
150 through multiplying by 3 the number by which [the
Church] is signified (for 50 x 3 = 150). If to 150 you should

---

12 Acts 1.3–9; 2.1–4.
13 *cum aequitate*.
14 See 2 Cor 10.3.

add 3 (because it must be conspicuously prominent that in the name of the Father and the Son and the Holy Spirit is the Church cleansed by the bath of regeneration[15]), the result is 153.

One hundred and fifty-three fish were found because the nets were cast to the right-hand side, and accordingly they were large,[16] i.e., perfect and fit for the kingdom of heaven. On the other hand, that parable of the net not cast on the right-hand side included both the good and the bad, who are separated on the seashore.[17] For presently among the nets of the commandments and sacraments of God the good and the evil dwell together in the Church which now exists. However, a separation takes place at the end of the present world as if at the end of the sea, i.e., on the seashore, when the righteous reign first of all in time, as it is written in the Apocalypse,[18] then forever in that city which is described there.[19] In that city where the divine plan of salvation expressed in time and signified by the number 40 has come to an end, there remains the denarius which the saints who work in the vineyard are going to receive as their reward.[20]

(3) This number can also, if carefully examined, lead us on to the holiness of the Church—a holiness realized through our Lord Jesus Christ. The reason is as follows. Since the creature corresponds to the number 7 (because 3 is assigned to the soul and 4 to the body[21]), the Lord's assumption of humanity is calculated at 3 x 7. The 3 results from the fact that the Father sent the Son, and the Father is in the Son, and by the grace of the Holy Spirit the Son was born of a virgin. And these are three: Father, Son, and Holy Spirit. But as for 7x, this is the very humanity assumed in the temporal economy[22] in order that man might become eternal.

---

15 Mt 28:19.
16 Jn 21.6, 11.
17 Mt 13.48.
18 Cf. Apoc (Rv) 22.
19 Cf. Apoc (Rv) 21.
20 See above, n. 5.
21 Recall the numbering sequence in the first paragraph of section 1 above.
22 *temporali dispensatione.*

Therefore the result is the product 21, i.e., 3 x 7. Moreover, this assumption of humanity has been efficacious for the emancipation of the Church, of which Christ is the head,[23] so that the Church itself, because it has a soul and body, is purchased under the sign of the number 7. Accordingly 21 is multiplied by 7 on account of those freed by the Lord's Man,[24] and together they become 147. To this is added the number 6, the sign of perfection, because it is equal to the sum of its factors, since nothing less than 6 nor more than 6 is found in the sum. Its factors are 1 taken six times, 2 taken three times, and 3 taken two times, which added together as 1 + 2 + 3 produce 6. Perhaps this number is also applicable to the mystery of God's having completed all his works on the sixth day.[25] Therefore, if you add 6, the sign of perfection, to 147, the result is 153. This is the number of fish discovered after the nets were cast, following the Lord's command, to the right-hand side where the sinners who belong to the left-hand side are not found.[26]

58. ON JOHN THE BAPTIST

(1) When one has carefully examined the Gospel passages concerning him, it is not absurd to think of John the Baptist as the embodiment of prophecy,[1] and this because of many cogent reasons, and especially because of what the Lord says of him: "He is more than a prophet."[2] [This is so] because, indeed, he bears the stamp[3] of all the prophecies made about

---

23 Eph 5.23.
24 See above, Q. 36, n. 6.
25 Gn 2.2.
26 St. Augustine returns to the number 153 on many occasions. Cf. IE 122.8 (PL 35.1963-64), S 248 3.3-4.4 (PL 38.1160), S 270 7 (PL 38.1244), EnP 49.9 (PL 36.571), and E 55 17.31 (PL 33.219-20). (This list of references is found in Bardy, BA 10, pp. 27-28, n. 4.) See also DDC 2.16.26 (PL 34.48). For a discussion of the authenticity of this Q., see Mutzenbecher, pp. xliii-xliv. The problem is whether section 3 is or is not a genuine part of Q. 57. Mutzenbecher argues conclusively that it is.

---

1 *prophetiae gestare personam.*
2 Mt 11.9.
3 *imaginem gestat.*

the Lord from the beginning of mankind until the Lord's
coming. However, the embodiment of the gospel foretold by
prophecy is the Lord himself, and the proclamation [of that
gospel] throughout the world from the time of the Lord's
very coming keeps on growing. But as for prophecy, it
diminishes after the coming of what it was foretelling.
Accordingly the Lord says: "The Law and the Prophets
were until John the Baptist. From now on, the kingdom of
God is proclaimed."[4] And John himself says: "That one
must increase, but I must diminish."[5] This is symbolically
represented in the days on which they were born and the
deaths which they suffered. For indeed John is born at that
time [of the year] when the days begin to diminish [in
length], while the Lord is born at that time when the days
begin to increase.[6] John is diminished by a head when he is
killed, but the Lord is raised up on a cross. Therefore, after
the prophecy represented[7] in John has pointed out as present
the one whose coming it had foretold from the beginning of
mankind, it begins to diminish, and from then on the
preaching of the kingdom of God begins to increase. Accordingly John baptized for repentance,[8] for the old life comes to
an end with repentance, and the new life begins from there.

(2) Moreover, not only among those who are called prophets, but in Old Testament history itself, one infers that
prophecy does not keep silent for those who seek devoutly
and are aided by God in investigating these things. Nevertheless, prophecy is seen chiefly in the more obvious symbols: the righteous Abel is killed by his brother,[9] and the
Lord, by the Jews; Noah's ark is guided as is the Church in
the world flood;[10] Isaac is led off to be sacrificed to God, and
a ram for Isaac's place is discovered among the thorns, as if
crucified;[11] in the two sons of Abraham—one from the

---

4 Lk 16.16.
5 Jn 3.30.
6 Augustine is referring to the summer and winter solstices.
7 *constituta.*
8 Mt 3.11.
9 Gn. 4.8.
10 Gn. 7.1 ff.
11 Gn. 22.3–13.

woman slave, the other from the free woman—the two
Testaments are understood;[12] the two peoples are presaged
in the twins Esau and Jacob;[13] Joseph, having suffered per-
secution by his brothers, is honored by strangers,[14] just as
the Lord is glorified among the gentiles while the Jews
persecute him. It is tedious to mention every single case,
since the Apostle concludes by saying: "But these things
were happening to them symbolically, and they were written
for us upon whom the end of the present world has come."[15]

Now the end of the present world, being, as it were, the
old age of an old man (if you should treat the entire human
race as an individual), is designated as the sixth age, [and it
is the age] in which the Lord has come. For there are also six
ages or periods in the life of the individual man: infancy,
boyhood, adolescence, youth, maturity, and old age.[16] Accordingly the first age of mankind is from Adam until Noah,
the second, from Noah until Abraham. These are completely obvious and well-known divisions of time. The third
is from Abraham until David, for this is the way in which
Matthew the evangelist divides it.[17] The fourth is from
David until the Babylonian exile.[18] The fifth is from the
Babylonian exile until the Lord's coming.[19] As for the sixth,
one should anticipate its [lasting] from the Lord's advent until the end of the present world. In this sixth age, the outer
man (who is called the "old man") is corrupted by old age,
as it were, and the inner man is renewed from day to day.[20]

---

12 Gal 4.22-24.
13 Gn 25.23.
14 Gn 37.41.
15 1 Cor 10.11.
16 Further remarks about the ages of mankind can be found in QQ. 44;
   53.1; and 64.2. Aside from the references in DD83, cf. DCa 17.27 and
   22.39 (PL 40.331 and 338-39), DVR 27.50 (PL 34.144), and, a most
   important reference, DGnM 1.23.39 (PL 34.190-93). For a list of
   these references, see G. Combès, J. Farges, eds., *Oeuvres de Saint
   Augustin*, BA 11: *Le Magistère Chrétien* (Paris 1949), pp. 552-54, n. 13.
17 Mt 1.17.
18 *transmigrationem.*
19 *Ibid.*
20 2 Cor 4.16.

Then comes the eternal rest which is signified by the Sabbath. In accord with this is the fact that on the sixth day man was made in the image and likeness of God.[21]

Now it is commonly known that man's present life of goal-directed activity[22] is sustained by knowledge and action. For action is thoughtless without knowledge, and without action knowledge is barren. But the early years of a man's life,[23] which no one believes, and rightly so, to be goal-directed, are given over to the five senses of the body: sight, hearing, smell, taste, and touch. Consequently the first two ages of mankind are marked off by ten generations each, as if by infancy and boyhood—the number 5[24] having been doubled because a generation is propagated by both sexes. Therefore there are ten generations from Adam until Noah, and from Noah until Abraham there are another ten. These two ages we have called the infancy and boyhood of mankind. In regard to mankind's adolescence, youth, and maturity, i.e., the periods from Abraham until David, from David until the Babylonian exile, and from the exile until the Lord's coming, they are figured at fourteen generations each—the number 7 having been doubled, because a generation is produced by both sexes.[25] As for the number 7, it results from the addition of both action and knowledge to the number 5, which is the number of the bodily senses.

---

21 Gn. 1.27.
22 *uitam...aliquid administrantem.*
23 *prima uita hominis.*
24 The number 5 is the number of the bodily senses.
25 If the first two periods of human history cover twenty generations, as Augustine has just claimed, and if the sixth period begins with the sixtieth generation, as he will shortly claim, then how does he get forty generations for the period from Abraham until the Lord's birth? For Augustine claims that that period is broken down into three subperiods of fourteen generations each, which, of course, gives us forty-two generations.

The solution to this puzzle is found in the fact that Augustine is following Matthew's genealogy (Mt 1.2–16) of the Lord. If one counts straight through the generations actually listed in those verses, one will see that forty, rather than forty-two, generations are listed. However, in v. 17 Matthew divides the ancestry of Christ from Abraham on into three periods of fourteen generations each. This means, therefore, that he has counted some generations twice for the purposes of v. 17.

Now old age usually lasts as long as all the other ages together. For since old age is said to begin with the sixtieth year, and since human life can reach one hundred and twenty years, it is clear that old age alone can be as long as all the other earlier ages. Therefore, in regard to the final age of mankind, which begins with the Lord's coming [and lasts] until the end of the present world, it is uncertain how many generations are reckoned to it. Moreover, God has willed for our benefit to hide this, as it is written in the Gospel[26] and the Apostle attests, saying that the day of the Lord will come as a thief in the night.[27]

(3) Nevertheless, the teaching of the generations detailed above establishes that in its sixth age has mankind been visited by the Lord's coming in humility. With this visit begins the clarification of prophecy whose meaning was hidden to the previous five ages. Since John personified this prophecy, as was said above, he is therefore born of aged parents, signifying that an aging world is beginning to become aware of that prophecy. For five months his mother hides herself, as it is written: "Elizabeth hid herself for five months."[28] However, in the sixth month she is visited by Mary the mother of the Lord, and the baby leaps in the womb, signifying that at the Lord's first coming, in which he has deigned to appear in humility, there would begin the clarification of prophecy. [But the prophecy is,] as it were, in the womb, i.e., not yet so evident that all may confess it to be plain as day. This we believe will happen at the Lord's second coming when he will come in glory. Elijah is looked for as the precursor of the second coming, just as John was of the first. Consequently the Lord says: "Elijah has already come, . . . and men have done many things to him; and if you wish to know, he who is going to come is really John the Baptist,"[29] because in the same spirit and in the same power, as if in the capacity of a herald who runs ahead, the

---

26 Mt 24.36.
27 1 Thes 5.2.
28 Lk 1.24.
29 Mt 17.12; 11.14.

latter has already come and the former is going to come. On
that account is it said that this John, with the prophetic spirit
which filled his father, will be the precursor of the Lord in
the spirit and power of Elijah.

Now when Mary had spent three months with Elizabeth,
she left.[30] The number 3 seems to me to signify the
Trinitarian creed and baptism in the name of the Father and
the Son and the Holy Spirit, by which mankind is initiated
[into the faith], thanks to the Lord's coming in humility, and
is lifted up at his future coming in glory.

59. ON THE TEN VIRGINS

(1) Among the parables spoken by the Lord, what is said
concerning the ten virgins habitually occupies serious investigators. Indeed many investigators have observed here
many things which are not contrary to faith; but what needs
to be worked out is an explanation of the parable which will
fit together all of its parts. I have also read in a certain
apocryphal text something which is not contrary to Catholic
faith, but it seemed to me to be an interpretation poorly
matched to this passage, if one considers all the pieces of the
parable. Nevertheless, I dare make no rash judgements
about this explanation lest perhaps my difficulty be caused,
not by its disagreement [with the passage], but by my
slowness to find in the explanation its agreement. However,
what seems to me, and not absurdly, to be taught by this
passage I shall set forth briefly and carefully to the best of my
ability.

(2) Therefore, when our Lord was questioned privately
by the disciples about the end of the present world, among
many other things which he said he also said this: ''Then the
kingdom of heaven will be likened to ten virgins who took
their lamps and went to meet the bridegroom. Now five of
them were foolish, and five were wise. But the five foolish
virgins, when they had gotten their lamps, did not take any

---

30 Lk 1.56.

oil with them. However, the prudent ones took oil with them in their containers along with the lamps. Now when the bridegroom was late, they all became drowsy and slept. But in the middle of the night a cry arose: 'Look! The bride-groom comes! Arise to meet him!' Then the virgins got up and prepared their lamps, and the foolish ones said to the wise: 'Give us some of your oil because our lamps are going out.' The wise virgins answered, however, and said: 'Lest there not be enough for us and for you, go rather to the ven-dors and buy for yourselves.' While the foolish virgins were gone to buy, the bridegroom came, and those who were ready went inside with him to the wedding, and the door was closed. And last of all the remaining virgins came saying: 'Master, Master, open up for us!' But he said in response: 'I speak the truth to you—I do not know you.' Be watchful, therefore, because you know neither the day nor the hour.''[1]

Obviously, that five of the ten virgins are admitted and five excluded signifies the separation of the good and the evil. Accordingly, if the name *virginity* is an honorable one, why is it common to those welcomed and those shut out? Again, what does the number 5 mean, the number for both groups? Moreover the significance of the oil appears a source of puzzlement. Again, it is puzzling that the wise virgins do not share with those asking, since it is not right for those to begrudge [their oil] who are so perfect that they are received by the bridegroom (a name which undoubtedly signifies our Lord Jesus Christ), and since it is necessary for them to be merciful and give of that which they have in ac-cord with their knowledge of the injunction of the Lord who says: ''Give to everyone who asks of you.''[2] And what is it that cannot in the giving suffice for both? These questions greatly increase the difficulty of the present issue, the fact notwithstanding that other things as well [do so] when carefully considered. [Therefore] great caution must be employed in order that everything come together in one in-

---

1 Mt 25.1–13.
2 Lk 6.30.

telligible explanation, and nothing be said in one part that
obstructs another.

(3) Consequently the five virgins seem to me to signify a
five-part self-restraint from the attractions of the flesh. For
the desire of the soul must be restrained from the delight of
the eyes, the delight of the ears, the delight of smelling,
tasting, and touching. But since this self-restraint is exercised sometimes before God in order to please him in the inner joy of conscience and sometimes before men alone in
order to capture human glory, there are said to be five wise
virgins and five foolish. Nonetheless, both groups are virgins
because both practice self-restraint, although the joy of this
self-restraint has different sources. Moreover, the lamps,
because they are carried in the hand, are the works which
are done in accord with this self-restraint, and it is said:
"Let your works shine before men."[3]

Now indeed all "took their lamps and went to meet the
bridegroom." Therefore one must understand those in
question to be known by the name of Christ, for they who
are not Christians cannot go to meet the bridegroom, Christ.
"But the five foolish virgins, when they had gotten their
lamps, did not take any oil with them." Indeed, although
many hope greatly in Christ's goodness, nevertheless, they
have no joy while living continently except in the praises of
men. Therefore they have no oil with them, for oil, I think,
signifies joy. "For that reason," says [the Psalmist], "has
God, your God, anointed you with the oil of exultation."[4]
But he who receives no joy from pleasing God within does
not have any oil with him. "However, the prudent ones took
oil with them in their containers along with the lamps," i.e.,
they effected in heart and conscience the joy of good works in
accord with the Apostle's warning: "But let a man prove
himself, and then he will have cause for praise in himself and
not in [the opinion of] someone else."[5]

"Now when the bridegroom was late, they all became
drowsy," because those who are of the two classes of self-

---

3 Mt 5.16.
4 Ps 44(45).8.
5 Gal 6.4.

restrained men (those who exult before God and those who
find pleasure in the praises of men) experience death in this
interval of time extending until the resurrection of the dead
at the Lord's coming. [The passage continues:] "But in the
middle of the night," i.e., no one knowing or expecting,
since in fact the Lord himself says: "However, concerning
that day and hour no one knows."[6] Moreover the Apostle
says: "The day of the Lord will come as a thief in the
night,"[7] which means that his coming will be completely
secret. "A cry arose: 'Look! The bridegroom comes! Arise
to meet him!' " In the twinkling of an eye and at the last
trumpet we shall all rise from the grave.[8] Therefore, "all the
virgins got up and prepared their lamps," i.e., prepared to
give an account of their works. For it is necessary that we be
brought before the judgment seat of Christ so that each one
may receive in recompense there what he did in the body,
whether good or evil.[9]

"And the foolish ones said to the wise: 'Give us some of
your oil because our lamps are going out,' " for those whose
deeds are sustained by the praise of another are left wanting
when that praise is withdrawn, and from habit the soul
always seeks that from which it customarily derives its joy.
Accordingly they wish to have before God, who is the
examiner of the heart, the witness of men who do not see the
heart.

But what did the wise virgins answer? "Lest there not be
enough for us and for you," for each and every one will give
an accounting of himself, nor before God, to whom the
secrets of the heart are manifest, is anyone helped by the
testimony of another. Each person is hardly sufficient in
himself so that his own conscience might bear witness for
him. In fact, who will boast that he has a pure heart?[10]
Hence the Apostle says: "But as for me, it matters very little
that I am judged by you or by human judgment. Rather,

---

6 Mt 24.36.
7 1 Thes 5.2.
8 1 Cor 15.52.
9 2 Cor 5.10.
10 Prv 20.9.

neither do I judge even myself.''[11] Wherefore, since each
either cannot at all or can scarcely have a true opinion about
himself, how can he judge another person when no one
knows what goes on in a man except the man's own spirit?[12]

"Go rather to the vendors and buy for yourselves." The
wise virgins must be thought of not as having given advice,
but as having brought up obliquely the fault of the foolish
virgins. For the sellers of oil are the flatterers who send souls
into error with false and uninformed praise, and who, by
providing empty delights for them as if for the foolish,
receive some kind of recompense from them, whether it be
food or money or honor or some temporal advantage,
because these foolish ones do not understand the saying:
"Those who call you happy send you into error."[13] Rather
is it better to be rebuked by a righteous man than to be
praised by a sinner. "The righteous man," it is said, "will
correct me in mercy and will reprove me, but the oil of the
sinner will not fatten my head."[14] "Now then go rather to
the vendors and buy for yourselves," i.e., let us now see
what help you get from those who are accustomed to selling
you praises and to leading you into error so that you seek
praise, not before God, but from men.

"While the foolish virgins were gone to buy, the
bridegroom came," i.e., while they were inclining
themselves to external things and were seeking pleasure in
the usual things, because they did not know the inner joys,
the one who judges came. "And those who were ready,"
i.e., those whose conscience was bearing good witness for
them before God, "went inside with him to the wedding,"
i.e., to the place where the upright soul is joined to the pure,
perfect, and eternal Word of God in order to be made fruit-
ful. "And the door was closed," i.e., after those were received who have been transformed into the angelic life.
"For," it is said, "we shall all rise from the grave, but we
shall not all be transformed."[15] Access to the kingdom of

11 1 Cor 4.3.
12 1 Cor 2.11.
13 Is 3.12.
14 Ps 140(141).5.
15 1 Cor 15.51.

heaven has been closed, for after the judgment no opportunity for prayers and merits remains open. ''And last of all
the remaining virgins came saying: 'Master, Master, open
up for us!' '' It is not said that they bought oil, and therefore
they must be understood to have reached the point of im-
ploring God in their distress and great affliction, since the
delight in the praises of others no longer remains. But great
is God's severity after the judgment when his ineffable
mercy was granted in advance before the judgment. And so
answering, the bridegroom says: ''I speak the truth to
you—I do not know you.'' The bridegroom does this in virtue of that rule whereby the Art of God,[16] i.e., the Wisdom
of God, is not required to let those enter his joy who
appeared to act before him in accord with his commandments, though they intended to please men. And thus the
conclusion: ''Be watchful, therefore, because you know
neither the day nor the hour.'' Not only does no one know
the day or hour of that last moment in time when the
bridegroom will come, but no one knows the day or hour of
his own death. However, whoever is prepared even for
sleep, i.e., for even the death which is a debt all must pay,
will also be found prepared when in the middle of the night
that voice will sound which will awaken all.

(4) Now as for the remark that the virgins went to meet
the bridegroom, I think that it should be understood in this
way: the virgins stand for the one called the bride.
(Analogously, all Christians gathering together into the
Church, the sons are said to be gathered to the mother,
although what is called the mother consists of these same
sons united together.) For at present the Church is betrothed
and is a virgin to be led to the wedding, i.e., the Church is
preserving itself from the corruption of the world; but she
will be wed in that time when, with the passing away of

16 The interesting expression *ars Dei* (''the Art of God'') is used as a
synonym for *sapientia Dei* ('the Wisdom of God''), the second person of
the Trinity, in several other places. See below, Q. 78, and cf. DCD
11.7 and 29 (PL 41.322 and 343), and DT 6.10.11 (PL 42.931). Also,
cf. DVR 31.57 (PL 34.147), DCD 11.21 (PL 41.334), and DT 6.10.12
(PL 42.932).

everything mortal in her, she enjoys an immortal union. "I
have betrothed you," it is said, "to one husband in order to
present you to Christ as a chaste virgin."[17] In saying "you"
and "virgin," the Scripture moves from the plural to the
singular. Therefore the words *virgins* and *virgin* can be used
interchangeably. Moreover, it has been explained, I believe,
why there are said to be five virgins.

However, now we see obscurely, but then face to face;
now we see partially, but then completely.[18] But the present
ability to see in the Scriptures obscurely and partially
something which, nonetheless, is in accord with Catholic
faith is the work of the pledge which was received at her
bridegroom's lowly coming by the virgin Church, who will
be wed at his final coming when he will come in glory, and
when she will then behold face to face; for he has given to us
a pledge which is the Holy Spirit, as the Apostle says.[19] And
therefore this explanation views nothing as certain except
that it is in accord with faith, nor does it pass judgment on
other explanations which are possibly no less in accord with
faith.[20]

60. "CONCERNING THAT DAY AND HOUR NO ONE KNOWS, NEITHER THE ANGELS IN HEAVEN NOR THE SON OF MAN—NO ONE EXCEPT THE FATHER"[1]

God is said to know even when he causes someone to
know, as it has been written: "The Lord your God puts you
to the test that he might know if you love him."[2] Now this
manner of speaking does not mean that God does not know;

17 2 Cor 11.2.
18 1 Cor 13.12.
19 2 Cor 5.5.
20 Cf. E 140 31.74-37.84 (PL 33.571-77) and S 93 (PL 38.573-80) for
other studies of the parable of the ten virgins.

1 Mt 24.36.
2 Dt 13.3.

rather, [it was said] in order that men might know how far they have progressed in the love of God—a thing which is not fully recognized by them except by way of the testings which come about. As for the expression *he puts to the test*, it means that God permits testing. Therefore, when it is also said that God does not know, this means either that he does not approve, i.e., does not recognize [as conformable to] his discipline and teaching, as it has been said: "I do not know you,"[3] or that he causes men not to know for their own good, because it serves no useful purpose for them to know. Accordingly the text "the Father alone knows" is correctly grasped if understood to say that he causes the Son to know, and the text "the Son does not know," if understood to say that the Son causes men not to know, i.e., does not disclose to them what would serve no useful purpose for them to know.

61. ON THE GOSPEL STORY THAT THE LORD FED THE MULTITUDE ON THE MOUNTAIN WITH FIVE LOAVES OF BREAD

(1) The five barley loaves with which the Lord fed the multitude on the mountain signify the Old Law, either because that Law was given to those not yet spiritual but still carnal, i.e., to those given over to the five bodily senses, for the multitude itself numbered five thousand men,[1] or because the Old Law was given through Moses, for Moses wrote five books.[2] The fact that the loaves were of barley aptly signifies either: (1) the Law itself, which was so given that its life-sustaining nourishment of the soul was covered over by mysteries of a physical character, for the barley

---

3 Mt 25.12.

1 For the story of the feeding of the five thousand, see Mt. 14.13-21, Mk 6.30-44, Lk 9.10-17, and Jn 6.1-14.
2 Cf. IE 24.5-6 and 25.6 (PL 35.1594-95 and 1599) for other explanations of the five loaves.

kernel is enveloped by a very tightly gripping hull; or (2) the people themselves when not yet deprived of the carnal desire which was sticking to their hearts like a barley hull, i.e., when not yet circumcised in heart so that not even with the threshing of the tribulations[3] during their forty-year wanderings in the desert did they lay aside the carnal coverings from an intellect having been laid bare, just as barley itself is not stripped of that enveloping hull by being threshed on the threshing floor. Accordingly it was fitting to give a law of this sort to that people.

(2) The two fish, however, which gave a good taste to the bread, seem to signify the two persons, namely, the kingly and the priestly, to whom also belonged the holy anointing.[4] By them the people were being ruled so that they might receive the direction of their counsels. It was their duty never to be broken and misled by the storms and floods [of protest] on the part of the people, frequently to break up like opposing waves the violent objections of the multitudes, occasionally to yield to them with their integrity as a safeguard

---

3 See above, Q. 27, for Augustine's remarks on the etymology of the word *tribulation*.

4 In R 1.26 (PL 32.627) St. Augustine says: "Where I said: 'the two fish...signify the two persons, namely, the kingly and the priestly, to whom also belonged the holy anointing,' I ought rather to have said, 'especially belonged,' since we read that at times the prophets were also anointed. Again I said: 'Luke, having presented Christ the priest as if ascending after the destroying of sins, ascends through Nathan to David, because there had been sent Nathan the prophet by whose reproof the penitent David obtained the annulling of his sin.' This should not be understood as if the prophet Nathan was David's son, because not even here [in the disputed passage] is it said: 'because he [the son] was sent as a prophet'; rather, it is said: 'because there had been sent Nathan the prophet,' so that the mystery should be understood not in the same man, but in the same name."

St. Augustine later on makes a revision similar to the latter when commenting on a passage from his DCns 2.4.12 (PL 34.1076–77). In R 2.16 (PL 32.637) he states: "Again, where I have said: 'However, Luke ascends to the same David through Nathan, the prophet by whom God has made satisfaction for David's sin,' I ought rather to have said: 'the prophet of the same name [as David's son],' lest it be thought that the prophet was [David's son], when actually he was a different person, but just called by the same name." See below, n. 15.

—in a word, to conduct themselves in the troubled governance of the people in the manner of fish in a stormy sea.

These two roles,[5] however, prefigured our Lord, for he alone maintained both roles, and not in a figurative sense, because he alone was the genuine fulfillment of them. For the Lord Jesus Christ is our king who has shown us an example of fighting and conquering by taking our sins upon his mortal flesh, by not yielding to the seductive and dreadful temptations of the enemy, by afterwards divesting himself of flesh, by resolutely despoiling empires and powers, and by triumphing over them in himself.[6] Consequently under his leadership we are freed, as if from Egypt, from the burdens and labors of this our sojourning, and our sins, in pursuit of us, are engulfed by the sacrament of baptism while we escape. As long as we have hope in his promise which we do not yet see, we are led, as it were, through the desert, our source of comfort being the word of God in the Holy Scriptures, just as manna from heaven was for the Hebrew people. Under his same leadership we are confident that we can be brought into the heavenly Jerusalem, as if into the land of promise, and can there be kept safe forever under his reign and protection. This is the evidence that our Lord Jesus Christ is our king. Also, our priest forever according to the order of Melchizedek,[7] he offered himself a holocaust[8] for our sins, and recommended the reenactment[9] of that sacrifice to be celebrated in memory of his suffering and death, so that what Melchizedek offered to God[10] now we see offered in the Church of Christ throughout the whole world.

Therefore, since our king has assumed our sins that he might also show us an example of fighting and conquering, the evangelist Matthew, by way of indicating the assumption of the same sins and of the kingly role, undertakes his

---

5 *duae personae.* See above, Q. 58, n. 1.
6 Col 2.15.
7 Ps. 109(110).4 = Heb 5.6.
8 The Latin *holocaustum* is from the Greek, meaning a whole burnt-offering.
9 *similitudinem.*
10 Gn 14.18.

human lineage from Abraham who is the father of the people
of faith and, counting down through the succession of off-
spring, comes to David in whom the steadfastness of royal
authority is most clearly apparent; and from there having
continued the royal line through Solomon, born of the
woman with whom his father had sinned, Matthew arrives
at the birth of the Lord.[11] However, Luke, the other
evangelist, since he also undertakes to display the Lord's
human ancestry, but in the priestly role to which belong the
cleansing and destroying of sins, does not begin to follow up
the lineage of the Lord's ancestors at the beginning of his
Gospel, as does Matthew. Rather, Luke begins to follow up
step by step the lineage at that place where Jesus was baptized, and where he prefigured purification from our sins. Nor
does he move down the list from the earlier to the later, as
did Matthew, who was showing him as if descending for the
assumption of sins. Rather, he moves up from the later to
the earlier as if he were presenting the Lord ascending, as it
were, after the destroying of sins. Nor does he name the
same ancestors as does Matthew.[12] For there was another
and priestly line which [was continued] on through one of
David's sons, who selected a wife, according to custom,
from the priestly tribe. The result was that Mary descended
from each of the two tribes, i.e., from the royal and the
priestly, for when Joseph and Mary registered for taxing, it
was written that they were of the house, i.e., of the stock, of
David,[13] and Elizabeth, who is described as no less a relative
of Mary, was of the priestly tribe.[14] But just as Matthew,
presenting Christ the king as if descending for the assumption of our sins, thus descends from David through
Solomon, because Solomon was born of her with whom
David had sinned, so Luke, presenting Christ the priest as if
ascending after the destroying of sins, ascends through

11 Cf. Mt 1.1-17.
12 Cf. Lk 3.23-28.
13 Lk 2.4.
14 Lk 1.35-36.

Nathan to David, because Nathan the prophet had been sent, and by his reproof the penitent David obtained the annulling of his sin.[15]

Accordingly, after Luke gets past David, he does not disagree with Matthew about the names in the genealogy, for he gives the same names ascending from David to Abraham as does Matthew in descending from Abraham to David. It is after David that the line has been divided into two families, the kingly and the priestly, and, as was said, Matthew, going down [the list], has followed the kingly family, while Luke, going up, has followed the priestly. As a result, our Lord Jesus Christ, our king and priest, would come from a priestly line, and, nonetheless, would not be from a priestly tribe, i.e., the tribe of Levi; rather, he would be from the tribe of Judah, i.e., from the tribe of David whose members do not serve the altar. Therefore he also is especially called the son of David according the flesh, because both Luke and Matthew, ascending and descending respectively, met together in David. In fact, it was necessary that he who was going to nullify the sacrifices being made by the Levitical priesthood according to the order of Aaron not be from the tribe of Levi. Otherwise to the same tribe and to the same priesthood, which was a foreshadow in time of the one to come, would appear to belong the purifying of sins which the Lord executed by the offering of his own holocaust, which was figuratively represented in the old priesthood; and the likeness of his holocaust he has given to be celebrated in the Church in memory of his suffering and death so that he might be a priest forever, not according to the order of Aaron, but according to the order of Melchizedek.[16] It is possible to consider yet more closely the mystery in all these things, but let it suffice that we have treated to this extent the two fish in which we said were represented two kinds of person, the kingly and the priestly.

---

15 Cf. 2 Kgs (2 Sm) 12.1–13. See above, n. 4
16 Heb 6.20.

(3) Now as for the multitude's having reclined upon the
grass, this signifies that those who had accepted the Old
Covenant,[17] because a temporal kingdom and a temporal
Jerusalem were promised them, were established in a carnal
or fleshly hope (for "all flesh is grass and the glory of man is
like the flower of grass"[18]). However, the filling of the twelve
baskets with morsels from the leftovers signified that the
Lord's disciples, among whom the number 12 had a special
place, were filled from an opening up and discussion of the
very Law which the Jews had left and abandoned. Indeed,
the New Testament writings did not yet exist when the
Lord, as if by breaking and opening what was hard and en-
cased in the Law, filled the disciples during that period after
the resurrection when he opened to them the Old Testament.[19] He began from Moses and all the prophets and interpreted to them everything in the Scriptures which was
about him, for indeed then was it that two of them recognized the Lord in the breaking of bread.[20]

(4) Accordingly the second feeding of the people,[21] which
involved seven loaves of bread, is correctly understood to
refer to the preaching of the New Testament, for it was not
said by any of the gospel writers that these loaves were of
barley, as John said of the previous five. This feeding
therefore refers to the grace of the Church which is nourished and recognized through the well-known sevenfold working of the Holy Spirit.[22] Consequently it is not written here
that there were two fish, as in the Old Law where only two—
the king and the priest—were habitually anointed; rather,
there were a few fish, i.e., those who first believed in the
Lord Jesus Christ, and were anointed in his name, and were
sent to preach the gospel and to withstand the stormy sea of

17 *Testamentum.*
18 Is 40.6.
19 *scripturas ueteres.*
20 Lk 24.27-31.
21 Mt 15.32-38.
22 Cf. Is 11.2-3 in the Latin Vulgate. St. Augustine is referring to the
    seven gifts of the Spirit catalogued in those verses: wisdom,
    understanding, counsel, courage, knowledge, piety, and fear of the
    Lord. Also cf. DDC 2.7.9-11 (PL 34.39-40).

this world so that they might serve as ambassadors,[23] as the apostle Paul says, for that one great fish, i.e., for Christ. Nor in that throng were there five thousand men as in the other, where the fleshly recipients of the Law, i.e., those devoted to the five senses of the flesh, are signified. Rather, there were four thousand, which signifies the spiritual, because of the four virtues of the soul[24] by which one lives spiritually in this life, viz., prudence, moderation, courage, and justice. The first of these is the knowledge of things to be sought after and things to be avoided; the second, the bridling of desire for temporal pleasures; the third, strength of mind[25] in the face of temporal setbacks; and the fourth, the love of God and neighbor, which is diffused through all the others.[26]

(5) As we know, the gospel writers recount that there were five thousand men in one case and four thousand in the other, not counting women and children.[27] In my opinion, the point of this is that we understand that among the Old Testament people were some who were weak in fulfilling the righteousness which is according to the Law (a righteousness in which Paul says that he lived without reproach[28]), and again that there were others who were led astray into idol worship. These two kinds [of difficulty], i.e., weakness and error, are indicated by the words *women* and *children,* for the female sex is weak in acting, while childhood is given to playing. And what is as similar to the play of children as the worshipping of idols, inasmuch as even the Apostle has compared this kind of superstition to play when he says: "And do not worship idols as some of them did. As it is written: 'The people sat to eat and to drink, and they got up to play'''?[29] Therefore there was a similarity to women in those

23 2 Cor 5.20.
24 *animi.*
25 *animi.*
26 See above, Q. 31.1, for Cicero's treatment of the four cardinal virtues. Cf. in St. Augustine the following places: DME 1.15 (PL 32.1322), DLA 2.19.52 (PL 32.1268), CI 4.3.17 (PL 44.745–46), S 341 6.7–7.9 (PL 39.1497–98), and DCD 19.4.3–4 (PL 41.728–29). (These references are found in BA 10, p. 737, n. 67.)
27 Mt 15.38.
28 Phil 3.6.
29 1 Cor 10.7. The apostle Paul is himself quoting Ex 32.6.

who, amid the hardships of waiting until they had achieved
the things promised of God, had not manfully persevered
and thus had tempted God, and to children in those who sat
to eat and to drink and got up to play. However, not only are
the Old Testament people to be compared to women and
children, but also the New Testament people who do not endure to the attaining of perfect manhood[30] due to either lack
of strength or fickleness of mind. For it is said to the one
group: "if, nonetheless, we should hold fast to the elements
of his being"[31] and to the other: "Do not become children in
your thinking, but be infants in relation to malice that you
might be fully mature in your thinking."[32] And for that
reason neither in the Old Testament nor in the New are such
people numbered. Rather, in one case there are said to be
five thousand [33] and in the other, four thousand, the women
and children having been excluded from the count.[34]

(6) However, although in both the former and the latter
case it is because of Christ himself, who is constantly called a
mountain in the Scripture, that both groups of people were
fed, appropriately enough, on a mountain, nonetheless, in
the latter case the people do not recline "on the grass"[35] but
"on the ground."[36] The reason is that in the former cir-
cumstance the eminence of Christ is covered over by a carnal
hope and desire because of carnal men and an earthly
Jerusalem, whereas in the latter, all carnal or fleshly
coveting having been removed, the foundation of a permanent hope, like the solid and grassless mass of the mountain
itself, was directly supporting the New Testament dinner
companions.[37]

(7) Seeing that the apostle Paul quite rightly says:
"Before faith came, we were being kept in custody under the

---

30 Eph 4.13.
31 Heb 3.14.
32 1 Cor 14.20.
33 Mt 14.21.
34 Mt 15.38.
35 Mt 14.19.
36 Mt 15.35.
37 *conuiuias Noui Testamenti*.

Law,"[38] the Lord also seems to mean this when he says of those whom he was going to feed with the five loaves: "They do not need to go—you feed them."[39] With these words they are figuratively detained, like those to be kept in custody, although the disciples had advised him to send them away. However, as for the multitude associated with the seven loaves, he felt a spontaneous pity for them, because it was already the third day since they had joined themselves to him in fasting, for, given the entire life span of the human race, this period in which the grace of Christian faith is given is the third period. The first is before the Law, the second, under the Law, and the third, under grace.[40] Since there yet remains a fourth period in which we shall achieve the abundant peace of the heavenly Jerusalem for which all strive who correctly believe in Christ, the Lord therefore says that he will refresh that multitude in order that they might not expire along the way. For this period in God's plan,[41] in which the Lord has deigned to appear in time and visibly as a man and has given to us as a pledge the Holy Spirit,[42] by whose sevenfold working we are given life (apostolic authority having been added like the seasoning of a few fish), what else therefore does this period in God's plan effect but the possibility of attaining the prize of the heavenly calling without [our] powers failing us? "For we walk by faith and not by sight."[43] Even the apostle Paul says that he has not yet seized hold of the kingdom of God. He says: "But, having forgotten those things which are behind, stretched out toward those things which are in front, I pursue in accord with my design the prize of the heavenly calling. . . . Nonetheless, what we have attained, let us walk in that."[44] [The Apostle makes the latter remark] because, in cleaving to the Lord during the third day and in being fed by him, we shall not expire along the way.

---

38 Gal 3.23.
39 Mt 14.16.
40 See below, Q. 66.3–7.
41 *dispensatio*.
42 2 Cor 5.5.
43 2 Cor 5.7.
44 Phil 3.13, 16.

(8) Here as well, of course, the multitude could not finish
eating everything, and there was food left over. For not in
vain was it said of the future: "Do you think that the Son of
Man will find faith upon the earth at his coming?"[45] I
believe that this will be so because of the women and
children. But, nonetheless, the leftovers filled seven baskets,
and these refer to the sevenfold Church, which is also
described in the Apocalypse,[46] i.e., it refers to everyone who
will have persevered to the end. For that one who said: "Do
you think that the Son of Man will find faith upon the earth
at his coming?" indeed meant that it is possible for his food
to be left and forsaken at the end of the meal. However,
since he himself has also said: "He who perseveres to the
end will be saved,"[47] he has signified the unfailing Church
which would receive these same seven loaves with an abundance greater than the number seven and would keep [them]
by the expanse of love[48] which [their] very continuance[49] in
the baskets seems to signify.[50]

62. ON THE GOSPEL PASSAGE: "THAT JESUS WAS BAPTIZING MORE THAN JOHN, ALTHOUGH HE HIMSELF BAPTIZED NO ONE. RATHER, HIS DISCIPLES [WERE BAPTIZING]"[1]

The question is whether they received the Holy Spirit who
were baptized at the time when, according to the gospel, the
Lord through his disciples had baptized more than John, for
in another place in the gospel it says: "For the Spirit had not
yet been given, because Jesus had not yet been glorified."[2]

---

45 Lk 18.8.
46 Cf. Apoc (Rv) 1.4; 2.1–3.19.
47 Mt 24.13.
48 *latitudine cordis.*
49 *perseuerantiam.*
50 The Latin text printed in BA 10 reads: "which seems to signify [their]
very continuance in the baskets." However, there is a variant reading
found in at least two manuscripts which seems to make better sense,
and therefore I have translated in accord with that variant reading.

---

1 Jn 4.1–2.
2 Jn 7.39.

The easiest answer to the question is this: they did receive the Holy Spirit, because the Lord Jesus, who was raising even the dead, could have prevented any of them from dying until after his glorification, i.e., his resurrection from the dead and ascension into heaven.

However, there comes to mind that famous thief to whom it was said: "Truly I say to you, today you will be with me in paradise,"[3] and who had not even received baptism.[4] Although Cornelius and those gentiles with him who had believed had likewise received the Holy Spirit before their baptism,[5] nonetheless, I do not see how even that thief could have said without the Holy Spirit: "Remember me, Lord, when you come into your kingdom."[6] For as the Apostle says: "No one says 'Lord Jesus' unless in the Holy Spirit."[7] The Lord himself has indicated the outcome of the thief's faith by saying: "Truly I say to you, today will you be with me in paradise."

Therefore, just as by the inexpressible power and righteousness of the ruler God even baptism was imputed to the believing thief and considered as received in his free mind,[8] because he could not have received it in a body hung upon a cross, so also was the Holy Spirit habitually given in secret before the Lord's glorification; but after the manifestation of his divinity the Holy Spirit was given more openly. And this

---

3 Lk 23.43.
4 Cf. R 1.26 (PL 32.627): "I have said: '. . .that famous thief to whom it was said: "Truly I say to you, today you will be with me in paradise" (Lk 23.43), and who had not even received baptism.' We have found that other leaders of the holy Church before us have as well set forth this view in their writings; but with what proofs it could be satisfactorily shown that that thief was not baptized, I do not know. We have discussed this matter more carefully in certain of our later works, especially in that one, *On the Origin of the Soul*, which we wrote to Vincentius Victor." For the latter reference, cf. DAO 3.9.12 (PL 44.516–17). As for the "other leaders of the holy Church," see BA 10, p. 738, n.68. Bardy refers us to, among others, St. Cyprian, *Epistula* 73.22 (PL 3.1170), and St. Hilary of Poitiers, *Tractatus super Psalmos* 1.9 and 65(66).26 (PL 9.255 and 435), and *De Trinitate* 10.34 (PL 10.370–71.)
5 Acts 10.44–47.
6 Lk 23.42.
7 1 Cor 12.3.
8 *animo.*

the Scripture has said: "But the Spirit had not yet been given,"[9] i.e., had not yet so appeared that all might acknowledge that he had been given. Likewise even the Lord had not yet been glorified among men, but still his eternal glorification never ceased to be. Likewise as well his very manifestation in mortal flesh is called his coming, for he came to that place where he already was, because "he came to his own possession,"[10] and because "he was in this world, and the world was made by him."[11] Therefore, just as one understands the Lord's coming to be his physical manifestation, yet before this manifestation he himself spoke through all the holy prophets as the Word of God and the Wisdom of God, so also the coming of the Holy Spirit is likewise the Holy Spirit's manifestations even to bodily vision, when fire was seen distributed upon [the apostles], and they began to speak in [different] languages.[12]

Obviously, if there was in fact no Holy Spirit in men before the visible glorification of the Lord, how could David have said: "And take not your Holy Spirit from me"?[13] Or how were Elizabeth and her husband Zacharias filled so that they might prophesy, and Anna and Simeon, about all of whom it is written that, filled with the Holy Spirit, they have said those things which we read in the gospel?[14] But it is part and parcel of God's providential government to do some things in secret, but others out in the open through a visible created thing. By this providence all the divine actions are executed by an exceedingly beautiful succession[15] and distinction of times and places, although divinity itself neither is bound by space nor moves about in it, nor is it either extended or changed in time. And just as the Lord himself was undoubtedly in possession of the Holy Spirit in that humanity which he was bearing when he went to John to be baptized, and yet, after he was baptized, the Holy

---

9 Jn 7.39.
10 Jn 1.11.
11 Jn 1.10.
12 Acts 2.3–4.
13 Ps 50(51).13.
14 Lk 1.41–45, 60–79; 2.25–38.
15 *ordine.*

Spirit was seen to descend upon him with the appearance of a dove,[16] so it should be understood that, even before the open and visible coming of the Holy Spirit, it was possible for all saintly men to possess him without visible show.

We have, of course, said all this so that we might by all means understand that by this visible manifestation of the Holy Spirit (which is called his coming), his fulness, in an ineffable and even yet inconceivable way, has been poured out more bountifully into the hearts of men.

63. ON THE WORD

"In the beginning was the Word."[1] The Greek word *logos* signifies in Latin both "reason"[2] and "word."[3] However, in this verse the better translation is "word," so that not only the relation to the Father is indicated, but also the efficacious power with respect to those things which are made by the Word. Reason, however, is correctly called reason even if nothing is made by it.

64. ON THE SAMARITAN WOMAN[1]

(1) The gospel mysteries signified by the words and deeds of our Lord Jesus Christ are not open to all, and some, through interpreting them less attentively and less circumspectly, very often occasion destruction in place of salvation and error in place of knowledge of the truth. Among these mysteries is the Scripture passage that the Lord at the sixth hour of the day had come to Jacob's well, sat wearied from the journey, requested a drink from a Samaritan

---

16 Mt 3.13-16.

---

1 Jn 1.1.
2 *ratio.*
3 *uerbum.*

---

1 Jn 4.5-43. Cf. IE 15.5-33 (PL 35.1512-22).

woman, and the other things requiring discussion and investigation which are mentioned in the same Scripture passage. In regard to such an enterprise, this above all must be kept in mind, that in all Scripture it is necessary for one to maintain the highest vigilance so that the expositon of the divine mystery be according to the faith.

(2) Accordingly, at the sixth hour of the day, our Lord came to the well. I see in the well a gloomy depth. I am therefore led[2] to understand [by this] the lowest parts of the universe, i.e., the earth, to which our Lord Jesus came at the sixth hour, i.e., at the sixth age of mankind as if in the old age of the "old man," whom we are commanded to strip off in order that we might put on the new who is created after the likeness of God.[3] For the sixth age is old age, since the first is infancy; the second, boyhood; the third, adolescence; the fourth, youth; the fifth, maturity.[4] Consequently the life of the old man, which is lived out in a carnal way under the condition of time, is concluded in the sixth period by old age. In mankind's old age, as I have said, our Lord came as both our Creator and Restorer so that (with the death of the old man, of course) he might constitute in himself a new man whom he might convey, divested of earthly stain, into the heavenly kingdom. Therefore now the well, as was said, signifies by its gloomy depth the earthly toil and error of this [lowest part of the] universe.

Moreover the old man is the outer man, and the new the inner, for it is said by the Apostle: "And if our outer man is corrupted, nonetheless, the inner man is renewed from day to day."[5] Therefore, since all visible things pertain to the outer man and [thus] are renounced by the Christian code of conduct,[6] it is altogether fitting that the Lord came to the well at the sixth hour, i.e., at midday when already this world's visible sun begins to set in the west. [For] the delight in things visible is diminished for us who have been called by Christ, so that the inner man, recreated by the love of things

---

2 *admoneor.*
3 *secundum Deum.* Cf. Eph 4.22–24.
4 See above, QQ. 44; 53.1; and 58.2.
5 2 Cor 4.16.
6 *christiana disciplina.*

invisible, is turned to the inner light which never sets, and it seeks, in accord with the Apostle's teaching, not "those things which are seen, but those things which are not seen, for the things seen are temporal, but the things not seen are eternal."[7]

(3) Moreover, that the Lord was tired when he came to the well signifies the infirmity of the flesh, [and] that he sat, humility, because he assumed on our behalf even the weakness of flesh and deigned to appear in so humble a manner as a man among [other] men. About this infirmity of the flesh the prophet says: "He was a man situated in affliction, knowing how to bear weakness."[8] As for the humility, the Apostle speaks with these words: "He has humbled himself, having become obedient even to the point of death."[9] However, the fact that he sat, since it is customary for teachers to sit, could indicate on another interpretation not the unassuming character of humility, but the role of a teacher.

(4) Nonetheless, one can ask: Why did the Lord request a drink of the Samaritan woman who had come to fill her jar with water, when afterwards he himself was going to say that he could give the gushing of a spiritual fountain to those asking? Well, obviously, the Lord was thirsty for the trust of that woman, because she was a Samaritan, and Samaria usually represents idolatry. For, separated from the Jewish people, they had delivered the dignity of their souls over to the images of dumb animals, i.e., to golden cows. However, our Lord Jesus had come that he might lead the multitude of nations who were serving idols to the protection of Christian faith and uncorrupted religion. "For," he says, "the healthy have no need of a physician—only the ill."[10] Therefore he is thirsty for the trust of those for whom he shed his blood. Consequently Jesus said to the woman: "Woman, give me a drink."[11]

---

7 2 Cor 4.18.
8 Is 53.3.
9 Phil 2.8.
10 Mt 9.12.
11 Jn 4.7.

Moreover, to see [12] what our Lord was thirsty for, [note that] after a little while come his disciples, who had gone into the city to buy food, and they say to him: " 'Rabbi, eat.' But he said to them: 'I have food to eat of which you have no knowledge.' Therefore his disciples say to one another: 'Has anyone brought him [anything] to eat?' Jesus said to them: 'My food is to do the will of him who has sent me and to complete his work.' "[13] There is here no doubt, is there, that these two things—the will of the Father who has sent him and the work of the Father which Jesus answers that he wants to complete—are nothing other than our conversion from the ruinous error of the world to faith in him? Therefore Jesus's drink is the same as his food. Accordingly he was thirsty for this in the woman, that he might do in her the Father's will and complete his work.

However, understanding in a carnal manner, she answers: "Since you yourself are a Jew, how do you ask of me a drink, since I am a Samaritan woman? For the Jews have no dealings with the Samaritans."[14] Our Lord said to her: "If you knew the gift of God and who it is who says to you: 'Give me a drink,' you rather would have asked of him, and he would have given you living water."[15] [He said this] to show her that he had not asked for the kind of water that she herself had understood, but that he himself was thirsty for her trust and was desirous of giving the Holy Spirit to her in her own thirst, for we correctly understand this living water to be the gift of God, as the Lord himself says: "If you knew the gift of God." Likewise the same evangelist John testifies in another place with these words: "that Jesus was standing and crying out: 'If anyone is thirsty, let him come and drink. He who believes in me, as the Scripture says, out of his belly will flow rivers of living water.' "[16] Jesus speaks altogether consistently when he says: "He who believes in me, out of his belly will flow rivers of living water," because we first

---

12 *ut noueris*.
13 Jn 4.31-34.
14 Jn 4.9.
15 Jn 4.10.
16 Jn 7.38-39.

believe in order to merit these gifts. Therefore these rivers of living water, which the Lord wanted to give to that woman, are the reward of the trust which he was first thirsting for in her. The evangelist provides the interpretation of this living water when he says: "But he was saying this about the Holy Spirit whom those who would believe in him were going to receive. However, the Spirit had not yet been given, because Jesus had not yet been glorified."[17] Consequently this gift is the Holy Spirit, a gift which he gave to the Church after his glorification, as the Scripture elsewhere says: "Ascending to the heights, he has taken captive capivity, he has given gifts to men."[18]

(5) Still, however, the woman understands in a carnal manner, for she answers thus: "Lord, you have no bucket, and the well is deep. How are you going to give me living water? Are you greater than our father Jacob who gave us this well, and he himself drank from it, as well as his sons and his livestock?"[19] But now the Lord explains his words: "Everyone who drinks of that water will thirst again; but he who drinks of the water which I give will never thirst, but the water which I give will become in him a fountain of water springing up into eternal life."[20] Still, nonetheless, the woman continues to embrace a carnal interpretation, for she responds: " 'Lord, give me this water so that I may not be thirsty nor come here to draw.' Jesus says to her: 'Go, call your husband, and come here.' "[21] Since he knew that she had no husband, why did he say this? For when the woman had said: "I do not have a husband," Jesus says to her: "You have well said that you have no husband, for you have had five husbands, and the one whom you now have is not your husband. You have spoken the truth in this matter."[22] However, these things are not to be understood in a carnal way, lest we ourselves just now seem like the Samaritan

---

17 Jn 7.39.
18 Ps 67(68).19 = Eph 4.8.
19 Jn 4.11–12.
20 Jn 4.13–14.
21 Jn 4.15–16.
22 Jn 4.17–18.

woman. But if we have already tasted something of that gift
of God, let us treat these matters spiritually.

(6) The five husbands some understand to be the five
books given through Moses. And as for the words: "and the
one whom you now have is not your husband," they understand the Lord to have spoken them concerning himself. The
passage would thus mean: You have served the five books of
Moses in the manner of five husbands, but now the one
whom you have, i.e., whom you hear, who speaks with you,
is not your husband, because you have not yet believed in
him. However, since she was, of course, still bound to those
five husbands, i.e., the five books, because she did not yet
believe in Christ, there arises the question how it is possible
to say: "You have had five husbands," as if now she no
longer had them, although as yet she would surely be living
subject to them. Moreover, since the five books of Moses
proclaim nothing other than Christ, as he himself says: "If
you believed in Moses, you would perhaps[23] have also
believed in me, for he wrote about me,"[24] how can a man be
thought to abandon those five books to go over to Christ,
when he who believes in Christ embraces those five books all
the more avidly in order to understand them spiritually
rather than to leave them behind?

(7) There is therefore another interpretation: the five
husbands are understood to be the five senses of the body.
The first belongs to the eyes, and by it we see this [world's]
visible light and all colors and bodily forms. The second is
that of the ears, and by it we sense the vibrations[25]
[emanating from] voices and all sounds. The third is that of
the nose, and by it we delight in various pleasant odors. The
fourth, being in the mouth, is taste, which senses things
sweet and bitter, and which is the tester of all savors. The
fifth covers the whole body, and, by touching, it distinguishes things cold and hot, soft and hard, smooth and
rough, and whatever else we sense by touching. Consequently the first age of man is steeped in these five senses of

---

23 *forsitan* = *an* in the Greek text.
24 Jn 5.46.
25 *momenta*.

flesh by the necessity of a mortal nature whereby we are begotten in such a state after the sin of the first man that, the
light of the mind not yet restored, we are subject to senses of
flesh, and we spend life engrossed in the flesh[26] without any
understanding of the truth. Such is necessarily the condition
of infants and small children, who are not yet capable of
reason. And because these senses which govern the first age
are natural and have been granted by God the creator, they
are appropriately called husbands, i.e., spouses, as if legitimate, since it is not error through its own depravation, but
nature through the creative activity of God that has imparted
them.

However, when each one reaches that age at which he is
capable of reason, then, if he can immediately comprehend
the truth, he will no longer use those senses as guides.
Rather, he will possess a husband, the rational spirit, to
which he renders those senses subject, bringing his body into
subjection, because the soul is no longer subject to the five
husbands, i.e., the five senses of the body, but has the divine
Word as its lawful husband. Clinging in union to this Word
(since man's spirit itself will cling to Christ, because Christ
is the head of the husband[27]), the soul enjoys through a
spiritual embrace eternal life without any fear of separation.
For who will be able to separate us from the love of Christ?[28]

However, because that woman was in the grip of an error
which signified the mass of people in a world subjugated by
empty superstitions[29] following the era of the five senses of
flesh which ruled the first age, as we have said, [therefore]
the Word of God had not taken her in marriage, but the
devil was holding her fast in an adulterous embrace. And so
the Lord, recognizing that she is carnal, i.e., that she
understands in a carnal manner, says to her: "Go, call your
husband, and come here," i.e., withdraw yourself from the
carnal state of mind in which you are now fixed so that you
are incapable of understanding what I say, "and call your

---

26 *carnalem uitam...transeamus.*
27 1 Cor 11.3.
28 Cf. Rom 8.35.
29 The error in question is idolatry or paganism. See below, Q. 83.

husband," i.e., be present with the spirit of understanding,
for the spirit of man is in some way a kind of husband of the
soul, and the spirit, like a spouse, rules the soul's dispositions. [The spirit in question is] not that Holy Spirit who,
unchangeable, abides with the Father and the Son and is
immutably given to worthy souls, but the spirit of man of
which the Apostle says: "No one knows what goes on in a
man except the man's own spirit." Indeed that Holy Spirit
is the Spirit of God, about whom [the Apostle] speaks again
and in this manner: "and no one knows what goes on in
God except the Spirit of God."[30] Therefore, when this spirit
of man is present, i.e., attentive, and when it submits itself
in piety to God, then man understands spiritual words.
When, however, the error of the devil rules the soul, just as
if the intellect were absent, then man is adulterous.
Therefore he says: "Call your husband," i.e., the spirit that
is within you, whereby a man can understand spiritual
things if the light of truth illumines him, [and] let this spirit
be present when I speak with you, so that you can receive
spiritual water. And when she said: "I do not have a husband," he says: "You have spoken well, for you have had
five husbands," i.e., the five senses of the flesh which ruled
you in the first age, "and the one whom you now have is not
your husband," because there is not in you the spirit which
understands God and with which you could have a lawful
union, but rather, the error of the devil dominates, the error
which corrupts you with the defilement of an adulteress.

(8) Furthermore, perhaps to indicate to those of
understanding that the five bodily senses mentioned above
are signified by the expression *five husbands*, after five
responses of a carnal nature, the woman in her sixth
response names Christ. For her first response is "Since you
yourself are a Jew, how do you ask of me a drink?"[31] the
second: "Lord, you have no bucket, and the well is deep";[32]
the third: "Lord, give me this water so that I may not be

---

30 1 Cor 2.11.
31 Jn 4.9.
32 Jn 4.11.

thirsty nor come here to draw'';[33] the fourth: ''I do not
have a husband'';[34] and the fifth: ''I see that you are a
prophet. Our fathers have worshipped on this mountain.''[35]
Certainly even this response is carnal, for an earthly place
had been given to the carnal where they might pray; but the
Lord has said that the spiritual are going to pray in spirit and
in truth. But, after he spoke, the woman in her sixth
response confesses the Christ to be the teacher of all such
people, for she says: ''I know that the Messiah will come,
who is called the Christ. When he comes, he himself will
make known to us all things.''[36] Nevertheless, she still errs,
because she does not see that he whom she hopes will come
has already come. Still, this adulterous error, as it were, is
now expelled through the Lord's mercy, for Jesus says to
her: ''I who speak with you am he.''[37] Upon hearing this,
the woman does not answer, but, leaving her water jar
behind, she immediately departs and hastens to the city, so
that she might not only believe, but also proclaim the gospel
and the Lord's advent. Nor should one carelessly pass over
the fact that she departed leaving the water jar behind. For
perhaps the jar signifies the love of this world, i.e.,
covetousness, by which men draw for themselves from the
gloomy depth which the well symbolizes (i.e., from their
earthly manner of life) a pleasure which, once experienced,
inflames men again with a longing for it, as Jesus says: ''He
who drinks of that water will thirst again.'' However, it was
necessary for the woman, believing in Christ, to renounce
the world and to demonstrate her relinquishing of worldly
coveting by the abandoned jar. She not only believes in her
heart ''unto righteousness,'' but also she will confess with
her mouth ''unto salvation'' and will proclaim what she has
believed.[38]

---

33 Jn 4.15.
34 Jn 4.17.
35 Jn 4.19-20.
36 Jn 4.25.
37 Jn 4.26.
38 Rom 10.10.

65. ON THE RESURRECTION OF LAZARUS[1]

Although we have complete confidence in the gospel history of the resurrection of Lazarus, nonetheless, I have no doubt that the event also has an allegorical significance. However, when events are interpreted allegorcially, they do not lose their historical value. For example, Paul explains the allegory of the two sons of Abraham, that they are the two Covenants.[2] But then did Abraham not exist, and did he not have those two sons? Therefore let us understand Lazarus in the tomb as an allegory for the soul buried by earthly sins, i.e., all mankind. In another place the Lord represents the soul by the one lost sheep for whose deliverance he says that he has descended, the ninety-nine other sheep having been left in the mountains.[3]

Jesus's question, "Where have you laid him?"[4] signifies, I think, our calling which comes about in secret, for the predestination of our calling is secret. The sign of this secret event is the Lord's question, as if he does not know (although we are the ones in ignorance, as the Apostle says: "that I may know even as I am known"[5]), or the Lord's claim elsewhere that he does not know sinners, expressed in the words: "I do not know you,"[6] which the burial of Lazarus signified because in his teaching and commandments there is no sin. To this question corresponds that one in Genesis: "Adam, where are you?"[7] because Adam had sinned and had hidden himself from the face of God. The burial of Lazarus signifies this hiding, so that the dead man corresponds to the one who sins, and the buried man, to the one who hid from God's face.

"Take away the stone,"[8] he says. This signifies, I think,

1 Jn 11.1–45. Cf. IE 49.1–24 (PL 35.1746–57).
2 Gal 4.22–24.
3 Lk 15.4.
4 Jn 11.34.
5 1 Cor 13.12.
6 Mt. 7.23.
7 Gn 3.9.
8 Jn 11.39.

those who wanted to impose the burden of circumcision on the gentiles coming to the Church, against whom the Apostle writes in various ways,[9] or [it signifies] the ones who live corruptly in the Church and are a cause of stumbling to those wishing to believe. Martha says to Jesus: "Lord, it is already the fourth day, and he stinks."[10] The last of the four elements is earth, therefore this word signifies the stench of earthly sins, i.e., of carnal desires. "You are earth," the Lord says to Adam when he had sinned, "and to earth you will return."[11]

Once the stone was removed, Lazarus went out of the tomb with his hands and feet wrapped, and his face was covered with a handkerchief. That he went out of the tomb signifies the soul withdrawing from carnal vices. That he was wrapped in bandages, however, signifies this: although we withdraw from carnal things and with the mind serve the Law of God, nonetheless, while situated in the body, we cannot be free from the vexations of the flesh as the Apostle says: "with the mind I serve the Law of God, but with the flesh, the law of sin."[12] And that his face was covered with a handkerchief signifies that we cannot have full knowledge in this life, as the Apostle says: "Now we see by way of an indistinct mirror reflection, but later, face to face."[13] And Jesus said: "Loose him, and allow him to go,"[14] which means that after this life all coverings will be removed so that we may see face to face.

Moreover, [the passage in question] provides an understanding of how great a difference there is between the man whom the Wisdom of God assumed, through whom we have been set free, and other men, because Lazarus is not loosed except by going out of the tomb. This means that, although the soul is reborn, as long as it sees the Lord by way of an indistinct mirror reflection, it cannot be free from all sin and ignorance except by a loosening from the body.

9 Cf. Gal 2.
10 Jn 4.39.
11 Gn 3.19.
12 Rom 7.25.
13 1 Cor 13.12.
14 Jn 11.44.

However, the linen sheets and handkerchief of Jesus, who did not sin and was not in ignorance, were found in the tomb,[15] for he alone of all flesh was not only not overcome by the tomb so that some sin should be found in him,[16] but neither was he enveloped by the winding linen sheets so that something should hide him or hinder him from going.

66. ON THE TEXT: "OR DO YOU KNOW, BROTHERS (FOR I SPEAK TO THOSE WHO KNOW THE LAW), THAT THE LAW IS THE MASTER OF A MAN AS LONG AS HE LIVES?" TO THE TEXT: "HE WILL BRING EVEN YOUR MORTAL BODIES TO LIFE THROUGH HIS SPIRIT LIVING IN YOU"[1]

(1) The Apostle in this analogy, in which he says of a husband and a wife that the wife is bound by law to the husband, commends three things for consideration: the wife, the husband, and the law, i.e., the wife subject to the husband through the bond of law, from which bond she is freed by the death of the husband to marry whom she wants. For he says the following: "For the woman subject to a husband is joined by law to the husband while he is alive; but if her husband should die, then she is released from the law of the husband. Therefore, while the husband is alive, she is called an adulteress if she is with another man; but if her husband has died, then she is freed from the law so that she is not an adulteress if she is with another man."[2] The analogy ends here. Then the Apostle begins to speak of the substantive issue for whose explanation and proof he brought forward the analogy.

In this issue too three things are likewise to be considered: man, sin, and the Law, for the Apostle says that as long as man lives in sin he lives under the Law, just as the woman,

---

15 Jn 20.7.
16 Is 53.9.

---

1 Rom 7.1–8.11.
2 Rom 7.2–3.

as long as the husband lives, lives under the law of the husband. Now the sin in question must here be understood as that sin which has come about through the Law; and this sin, the Apostle says, is beyond measure because, although it already appears as sin, it nonetheless is augmented in its commission by the addition of transgression. "For where there is no law, there is no transgression."[3] What he means is this: "in order that, owing to the commandment, sinner or sin be beyond measure."[4] Wherefore, he says, although the Law forbids sin, nonetheless, it has not been so given that it frees from sin. Rather, the Law points out the sin from which the soul in its subservience must turn itself to the grace of the Deliverer so that it might be set free from sin. "For through the Law is the knowledge of sin."[5] Again, the Apostle says in another place: "But sin, that it might be seen as sin, has effected my death through that which is good."[6] Therefore, where the grace of the Deliverer is not present, the forbidding of sins increases the desire for sinning. However, this serves the purpose of making the soul aware that it is not sufficient in itself to extricate itself from enslavement to sin, so that in this way, with the subsiding and extinction of all pride, it might become subject to its Deliverer, and so that a man might say with sincerity: "My soul has clung to you."[7] In this state one is no longer under the law of sin, but in the law of righteousness.

The Apostle speaks of "the law of sin," not because the Law itself is sin, but because it is imposed on sinners. Likewise also [he speaks] of the "law of death," because "sin's wage is death,"[8] [and] "the sting of death is sin, but

---

3 Rom 4.15.
4 Rom 7.13. Augustine's Latin translation of the Greek text is faulty here, for the Greek should be translated: "in order that, owing to the commandment, sin become sinful beyond measure." In reading the Greek text, somebody (Augustine himself?) had read *he* ("the") as *e* ("or") and translated into Latin accordingly. Once this happened, the Greek word *hamartolos* was then understood as a noun, *sinner*, rather than as an adjective, *sinful*.
5 Rom 3.21.
6 Rom 7.13.
7 Ps 62(63).9.
8 Rom 6.23.

the power of sin, the Law."[9] Indeed, by sinning we slip
down into death, for, where the Law forbids, we sin more
seriously than if we were not forbidden by the Law.
However, when grace is added, we then fulfill without difficulty and most willingly that very thing which the Law had
oppressively commanded. Accordingly the law of sin and
death, i.e., the Law imposed upon sinning and dying men,
merely commands that we not covet, and, nonetheless, we
do covet.

However, the Law of the spirit of life—a law which
belongs to grace and sets free from the law of sin and
death—causes us not to covet, and causes us to fulfill the
commands of the Law, no longer slaves of the Law through
fear, but friends through love and slaves of the righteousness
which was the very source of the Law's promulgation.
Moreover, righteousness must be served, not in the manner
of a slave, but in the manner of a free man, i.e., out of love
rather than out of fear. Consequently it is quite rightly said:
"Do we therefore make the Law null and void through
faith? Not at all! Rather, we confirm the Law,"[10] for faith
brings about what the Law commands. Therefore the Law is
confirmed through faith. Apart from faith the Law merely
commands, and it holds guilty those who do not fulfill its
commands so that it might thereafter turn to the grace of the
Deliverer those groaning in their inability to do what is
commanded.

(2) Therefore, although we see three things in the
analogy: the wife, the husband, and the law, and three again
in the question for which the analogy was employed: the
soul, sin, and the law of sin, there is here only the following
difference. In the analogy the husband dies with the result
that the wife marries whom she wants, and she is released
from the law of the husband; but in the question at issue the
soul itself dies to sin that it should marry Christ, and when it
dies to sin, it also dies to the law of sin. "And so, my
brothers," the Apostle says, "you yourselves have died to
the Law through Christ's body so that you might belong to

9 1 Cor 15.56.
10 Rom 3.31.

another who raised you from the dead, so that we might bear
fruit for God. For when we were in the flesh,'' i.e., held fast
by fleshly desires, ''the sinful passions brought about by the
Law were working in our members so that they bore the fruit
of death.''[11] Along with the evil desire forbidden by the
Law, a desire which grew in the absence of faith, there was
also added to the accumulated mass of sins that of transgression, because ''where there is no law, there is no transgression.''[12] These, he says, are ''the passions brought about by
the Law,'' passions which ''worked in our members so that
they bore the fruit of death.'' Before the coming of the grace
brought about by faith, the soul was living subject to these
passions, as if subject to the domination of a husband.
Therefore he who now serves with the mind the Law of God
dies to these passions, although the passions themselves are
not yet dead as long as he serves with the flesh the law of sin.
Consequently there still remains in the one under grace
something which, [although] incapable of overcoming him
or taking him captive, [will persist, nonetheless,] until the
mortification of all that which draws its strength from the
habits of sin and which is the reason why the body even now
is said to be dead as long as it does not give perfect obedience
to spirit. But there will come a time when it will give perfect
obedience, and this when even the mortal body itself has
been infused with life.

(3) From this we grasp that there are four different phases
even in [the life of] one man, and after the progressive completion of these he will abide in eternal life. Indeed, because
it was necessary and just that we be born in an animal, carnal state after our nature had sinned and lost the spiritual
blessedness which is signified by the name *paradise*, the first
phase is [our] activity prior to the Law; the second, under
the Law; the third, under grace; and the fourth, in peace.
Prior to the Law we live in ignorance of sin and as followers
of carnal desires. Under the Law we now live forbidden to
sin, and yet, overcome by sin's habits, we sin because faith

11 Rom 7.4–5.
12 Rom 4.15.

does not yet assist us. The third phase of life is when now we trust fully in our Deliverer and do not attribute anything to our own merits, but, by loving his mercy, we are no longer overcome by the pleasure of evil habit when it strives to draw us into sin. But, nonetheless, we still suffer from its attempted seductions, although we are not betrayed to it. The fourth phase of activity is when there is absolutely nothing in man which resists the spirit, but all things, joined and connected harmoniously to one another, maintain unity by a steadfast peace. This will happen when the mortal body has been infused with life, when this which is corruptible has put on incorruptibility, and when this which is mortal has put on immortality.[13]

(4) In order to show the first phase of activity there come to mind for the present the following proof texts: "Through one man sin has entered the world, and through sin, death; and thus [death] has extended to all men in that all men have sinned. For until the Law, sin was in the world, but sin was not imputed in the absence of the Law."[14] And again: "For without the Law sin is dead, and there once was a time when I myself was living without the Law."[15] For this expression *is dead* means the same as the previous expression *was not imputed*, i.e., was concealed. This is expressly said in the following passage: "But sin, that it might be seen as sin, has effected by death through that which is good,"[16] i.e., through the Law, because the Law is good if someone uses it lawfully.[17] Therefore, if the Apostle here says, "that it might be seen as sin," it is clear that, in the above passage, he was saying "dead" and "is not imputed" because sin was not seen as such before the prohibitions of the Law had disclosed it.

(5) For the second phase of activity, the following proof texts are suitable: "But the Law entered by stealth in order that it might increase the offence,"[18] for there was added

---

13 1 Cor 15.53–54.
14 Rom 5.12–13.
15 Rom 7.8–9.
16 Rom 7.13.
17 1 Tm 1.8.
18 Rom 5.20.

transgression where there was none. And [there is] that passage already cited: "For when we were in the flesh, the sinful passions brought about by the Law were working in our members so that they bore the fruit of death."[19] Again: "What then shall we say? Is the Law sin? Not at all! Nonetheless, I did not know sin except through the Law, for I would not have been aware of evil desire if the Law had not said: 'Shun evil desire!' But, once the opportunity was there, sin through the commandment produced in me every kind of evil desire."[20] And a little later the Apostle says: "With the coming of the commandment, sin came back to life, but I died, and the commandment, whose purpose was life, proved to be the cause of my death. For, once the opportunity was made available through the commandment, sin deceived me and struck me down."[21] By the expression *I died* the Apostle means: "I knew that I was dead," because now he also sins with transgression who sees by way of the Law what he ought not to do and yet does it. As for the claim: "Once the opportunity was made available through the commandment, sin deceived me,"[22] he means either that pleasure's persuasion to sin is more powerful where something is forbidden, or that, even if a man did do something in accord with the Law's requirements, if there is yet no faith resting in grace, then he endeavors to attribute this to himself rather than to God, and he sins the more because of pride. Therefore the Apostle continues by saying: "And so the Law is indeed holy, and the commandment holy and just and good. Therefore has what is good become my death? Not at all! But sin, that it might be seen as sin, has effected my death through that which is good, in order that sinner or sin, transgressing because of the commandment, might be beyond measure. And we know that the Law is spiritual, but as for myself, I am carnal,"[23] i.e., I consent

---

19 Rom 7.5.
20 Rom 7.7–8.
21 Rom 7.9–11.
22 Rom 7.11.
23 Rom 7.12–14.

to the flesh, not yet set free by spiritual grace,[24] "sold under sin,"[25] i.e., sinning for the price of temporal pleasures. "For I do not know what I am doing," i.e., I am not aware of being in the commandments of truth wherein is true knowledge.[26] In accord with this manner of speaking, the Lord says to sinners: "I do not know you."[27] Indeed nothing is hidden from him, but rather, because sins are not found among the prescriptions of the commandments belonging to truth, therefore Truth itself says to sinners: "I do not know you," for just as darkness is sensed by the eyes because they do not see, thus the mind is aware of sins because it does not know.[28] I think that this is the meaning of a remark in the

---

24 Cf. R 1.26 (PL 32.627-28): "Wishing to explain the Apostle's words: 'And we know that the Law is spiritual, but as for myself, I am carnal' (Rom 7.14), I said: ' . . . i.e., I consent to the flesh, not yet set free by spiritual grace.' This should not be understood thus, as if the spiritual man established under grace could not also say this of himself; and the same applies to everything up to the point where the Apostle says: 'Wretched man that I am! Who will set me free from the body of this death?' (Rom. 7.24). I taught this later on, as I have already acknowledged earlier (cf. R 1.23.1 [PL 32.620-21]). Again, explaining the Apostle's words: ' . . . then indeed the body is dead by reason of sin' (Rom. 8.10), I say: ' . . . the body is dead as long as it is in such a state that it disturbs the soul with the need for physical things.' But later on (cf. DPB 1.7.7 [PL 44.113]), it seemed to me much better to say that the body is dead by reason of the fact that at present the body necessarily dies, which was not the case before sin."
25 Rom 7.14.
26 Rom 7.15. This perplexing comment seems to mean the following. "Only truth can be known. Therefore my sinful life lived contrary to the commandments is not something which I can properly be said to know, for sin does not partake of truth." See below, n. 28.
27 Mt 25.12. See above, Q. 60 and Q. 65.
28 For St. Augustine, darkness is the absence of light, and sin is the absence of good, i.e., the failure of a moral agent to be all that God intends it to be. (Cf. DLA 2.20.54 [PL 32.1269-70].) Hence we do not, properly speaking, *see* darkness. Rather, we are aware of darkness precisely because of the fact that we do *not* see anything. Likewise, we do not, properly speaking, *know* sins. Rather, we are aware of sins precisely because of the fact that we do *not know* anything. In both cases, there is nothing positive to grasp; rather, there is only the felt *absence* of a positive reality.
  Cf. DDS 1, Q. 1.8 (PL 40.105-6) for a considerably less metaphysical interpretation of Rom 7.15. There Augustine argues that the expression *I do not know* means "I do not approve." Moreover, he applies the same analysis to Christ's remark in Mt 25.12. (However, it should be noted that in Q. 60 above, Augustine has already presented this interpretation of Christ's words.)

Psalms: "Who understands sins?"[29] "For I do not what I want; rather, I do what I hate. And if I do what I do not want, I am in agreement with the Law that it is good. Moreover, now I no longer am the one doing that, but that sin living in me; for I know that there lives in me, i.e., in my flesh, nothing good. Indeed the desire for good lies in me, but I do not find [the wherewithal] to accomplish it, for I do not do the good that I want, but I do the evil that I do not want. Moreover, if I do what I do not want, then I myself am not doing that, but the sin which lives within me. Therefore, I find it to be a law that, when I wish to do good, evil lies close at hand to me. For I am delighted with the Law of God in the inner man, but I see another law in my members, one fighting against the law of my mind and taking me captive by the law of sin which is in my members."[30]

Up to this point we have the words of a man situated under Law and not yet under grace, a man who, though he does not want to sin, is overcome by sin. For the habits of the flesh have prevailed, as well as the natural fetter of mortality, a fetter with which we have been begotten since the time of Adam. Therefore let him who is in this situation appeal for help, and let him know that his fall was of his own doing, while his rising up is not. In fact, once he has been set free and recognizes the grace of his Deliverer, he says: "Wretched man that I am! Who will set me free from the body of this death? The grace of God through Jesus Christ our Lord!"[31]

(6) And now begin the words spoken by a man situated under grace in the activity which we have described as the third phase. In this phase the mortal flesh indeed continues its resistance, though not overpowering a man and taking him captive to win agreement to sin. For he speaks in this way: "Therefore, as for myself, with the mind I serve the Law of God, but with the flesh, the law of sin. Therefore there is now no condemnation for those who are in Christ Jesus, for the law of the spirit of life in Christ Jesus has set

---

29 Ps 18(19).13.
30 Rom 7.15–23.
31 Rom 7.24–25.

me free from the law of sin and death. Indeed this was
impossible for the Law, because it was continually enfeebled
through the flesh,"[32] i.e., through fleshly or carnal desires.
For the Law was not being fulfilled because there was not yet
any love for righteousness itself—a love which would possess
the mind by an inward delight, lest the mind be drawn to sin
by the delight of temporal things. Therefore the Law was
continually enfeebled through the flesh, i.e., it did not make
righteous those given to the flesh. But, "God sent his Son in
the likeness of sinful flesh."[33] Indeed [his flesh], which was
not begotten of carnal pleasure, was not sinful flesh; but,
nonetheless, there was in him a likeness to sinful flesh in that
his flesh was subject to death. However, Adam did not merit
death except by sinning. But what did the Lord accomplish?
"With respect to sin, he condemned sin in the flesh,"[34] i.e.,
by assuming the flesh of sinful man, and by teaching how we
should live, he has condemned sin in the flesh itself, in order
that the spirit, burning with a love for eternal things, might
not be taken captive to consent to pleasure. "So that the
righteousness of the Law," he says, "might be fulfilled in us
who walk, not according to the flesh, but according to the
spirit."[35] Consequently the commandments of the Law,
which could not have been carried out through fear, are
fulfilled through love. "For those who live after the flesh
have a taste for the things of the flesh,"[36] i.e., they hunger
after fleshy or carnal goods as the highest goods. "But those
who are spiritual are influenced by the things of spirit. For
the flesh's way of thinking is death, whereas the spirit's way
of thinking is life and peace, because the flesh's way of thinking is inimical to God."[37] In case someone should think that
another and opposing principle has been introduced, the
Apostle himself explains the meaning of *inimical,* for he sub-
joins the following remark: "for it is not subject to the Law

---

32 Rom 7.25–8.3.
33 Rom 8.3.
34 *Ibid.*
35 Rom 8.4.
36 Rom 8.5.
37 Rom 8.5–7.

of God, nor in fact can it be.''[38] Therefore to act contrary to the Law is to be inimical to God. [It is] not that anything can harm God; rather, whoever resists the will of God harms himself, for he kicks against the goad, as the voice from heaven said to the apostle Paul while he was still presecuting the Church.[39] Moreover, to say: "for it is not subject to the Law of God, nor in fact can it be,''[40] is analogous to saying: "Snow does not produce heat, nor in fact can it." For as long as it is snow, it does not produce heat; but it can be dissolved and brought to a boil so that it does produce heat. However, when it does this, it is no longer snow. The same is said of the flesh's way of thinking when the soul hungers after temporal goods as the highest goods, for as long as such an appetite is in the soul, the soul cannot be subject to the Law of God, i.e., it cannot fulfill the Law's demands. However, when the soul begins to desire spiritual goods and to despise temporal, then the flesh's way of thinking ceases, and there is no resistance to spirit. For indeed the same soul is said to possess the flesh's way of thinking when it longs for lower things, and the spirit's way of thinking when it longs for higher things. [It is] not that the flesh's way of thinking is a substance which the soul puts on or takes off; rather, it is a disposition of the soul itself, and it completely disappears when the soul turns itself entirely to things on high. "But those who are in the flesh," the Apostle says "cannot please God,''[41] i.e., those who are satisfied with the pleasures of the flesh; for lest someone think that this is said of those who have not yet departed from this life, he adds at the first opportunity: "However, as for yourselves, you are not in the flesh but in the spirit.''[42] Obviously he is still speaking to those who are in this life, who, certainly, were in the spirit because they were finding their satisfaction in faith and hope and the love of things spiritual. "If, nonetheless," he says,

---

38 Rom 8.7.
39 Acts 26.14.
40 Rom 8.7.
41 Rom 8.8.
42 Rom 8.9. It is unclear whether Augustine understands the word *spirit* in this verse to mean the spirit of man or the Spirit of God.

"the Spirit of God lives in you. But if anyone does not have
the Spirit of Christ, he does not belong to him. If, however,
Christ is in you, then indeed the body is dead by reason of
sin, but the spirit is life by reason of righteousness."[43] The
Apostle says that the body is dead as long as it is in such a
state that it disturbs the soul with the need for physical
things[44] and induces it to desire earthly things through certain agitations arising from that need. Nonetheless, be there
ever so many agitations, the mind which now serves the Law
of God and is established under grace does not consent to doing that which is forbidden, for this is the point of what was
said above: "with the mind I serve the Law of God, but with
the flesh, the law of sin."[45] Furthermore, that man is now
described as being under grace who does not yet have the
perfect peace which will come about through the resurrection and transformation of the body.

(7) It remains therefore to speak of this same peace of the
resurrection of the body, a peace which is the fourth phase of
activity, if, nonetheless, it is appropriate to use *activity* for
that which is rest in the highest degree. For the Apostle continues by saying: "If therefore the Spirit of him who raised
Jesus from the dead lives in you, then he who raised Jesus
from the dead will bring even your mortal bodies to life
through his Spirit living in you."[46] Here also is a very
explicit witness to the resurrection of the body, and it is sufficiently clear that, as long as we are in this life, there will be
no lack of both the annoyances occasioned by the mortal
flesh and some excitations arising from carnal pleasures. For
although he does not yield who, established under grace,
serves with the mind the Law of God, nonetheless, he serves
with the flesh the law of sin.

When a man has been perfected in these degrees, no
existing thing[47] is found to be evil; nor is the Law evil which
shows to a man the fetters of sin in which he lies so that

43 Rom 8.9–10.
44 See above, n. 24.
45 Rom 7.25.
46 Rom 8.11.
47 *substantia.*

through faith, the deliverer's help having been implored, he might merit being released and raised up and firmly established. Therefore, in the first [phase of] activity, which is prior to the Law, there is no struggle with the pleasures of this world; in the second, which is under the Law, we struggle but are overcome; in the third, we struggle and overcome; in the fourth, we do not struggle, but we rest in perfect and eternal peace. For our lower nature is subject to us, which previously was not subject because we had forsaken the God who is higher than we.

67. ON THE TEXT: "FOR I DO NOT CONSIDER THE SUFFERINGS OF THIS WORLD TO BE WORTH MUCH IN COMPARISON WITH THE FUTURE GLORY WHICH WILL BE REVEALED IN US," TO THE TEXT: "FOR WE HAVE BEEN SAVED BY HOPE"[1]

(1) This section is obscure because it is not sufficiently clear here what the word creature[2] refers to under these circumstances. Now, according to Catholic teaching, creature

---

1 Rom 8.18–24.

2 *creatura.* The word *creation* is another appropriate translation of the term. However, throughout Q. 67 I use the word *creature.* The reasons for this are the following. (1) The basic meaning of *creature* is wholly consistent with the material being discussed by Autustine, for, according to the OED, the first meaning of the term is, "anything created; a created being, animate or inanimate; a product of creative action; a creation." (2) Moreover the connotations of *creature* allow more flexibility than do those of *creation,* for Augustine concentrates most of his discussion on that portion of the created order which is made up of living beings or "creatures," as we commonly say.

However, regardless of the translation finally adopted, St. Augustine's problem in this Q. requires one to use that translation *consistently* rather than to switch back and forth between them for the sake of clarity. For Augustine's problem is to interpret a Pauline text whose difficulty is caused in part by the fact that St. Paul himself uses *creatura* (*ktisis*) consistently but ambiguously throughout. Thus, by using only one English term to translate *creatura,* the translator allows Augustine rather than himself the task of interpreting Paul's meaning for the reader.

refers to whatever has been made and created by God the Father through the only begotten Son in the unity of the Holy Spirit. Therefore, not only the body, but even our souls and spirits are included in the term *creature*. However, the text says the following: "the creature itself will be delivered from the bondage of destruction to the freedom of the glory of the sons of God,"[3] as if we are not creatures, but the sons of God to whose glorious freedom the creature will be delivered from bondage. Again it is said: "For we know that every creature groans and suffers pain up to the present time; and not only they, but also we ourselves,"[4] as if we are one thing [and] every creature something else. Therefore the entire section needs to be examined in detail.

(2) "For I do not consider," the Apostle says, "the sufferings of this world to be worth much in comparison with the future glory which will be revealed in us."[5] This is clear, for he had said earlier: "but if you by the spirit put to death the deeds of the flesh, you will live."[6] This is not possible without suffering, for which patience is necessary. A slightly earlier statement also applies to the above: "if, nonetheless, we suffer together that we might be glorified together."[7] Consequently the Apostle's statement: "For the creature in its expectancy awaits the revelation of the sons of God,"[8] means the following, in my opinion. This in us which suffers pain when we put to death the deeds of the flesh, i.e., when we hunger and thirst through abstinence, when we curb sexual pleasure through chastity, when we endure the lacerations of injustice and the stings of reproach through patience, when we toil for the benefit of Mother Church, our own pleasures having been neglected and despised, whatever in us, I say, suffers pain in this and similar abrasive experiences is creature. For the body together with the soul, which undoubtedly is a creature, are in pain, and

---

3 Rom 8.21.
4 Rom 8.22–23.
5 Rom 8.18.
6 Rom 8.13.
7 Rom 8.17.
8 Rom 8.19.

they await the revelation of the sons of God, i.e., they await
the time when that which has been called will make its
appearance in that glory to which it has been called. Indeed,
since the only begotten Son of God cannot be given the name
creature (since indeed through him has been made all that
God has made), then it is we who, prior to that manifestation of glory, are distinctly called by the name *creature*, and it
is we who are distinctly called by the name *the sons of God*,
although we merit this by adoption, for the only begotten is
the Son by nature. Therefore "the creature in its expectancy," i.e., we in our expectancy, "awaits the revelation of
the sons of God,"[9] i.e., awaits the time of the appearance of
what has been promised, the time of the manifestation of the
reality which we now are by hope. For, "we are the sons of
God, and it has not yet appeared what we will be. However,
we know that when it appears, we will be like him, because
we will see him as he is."[10] It is the very revelation of the
sons of God which now the creature awaits in expectancy. [It
is] not that the creature awaits the revelation of another
nature which may not be a creature, but that in its present
condition it awaits the time of its future condition.[11] This is
analogous to one saying that, a painter having supplied
himself with paints and prepared them for his work, the
paints in their expectancy await the appearance of the picture. [It is] not that then they are one thing and will be
another, or will not be paints, but only that they will have
another dignity.

---

9 *Ibid.*
10 1 Jn 3.2.
11 Note that 1 Jn 3.2 speaks of two revelations—the revelation of God
("we will see him as he is") and the revelation of the sons of God in
their eternal and heavenly form ("we know that when it appears").
The latter, of course, is contingent upon the former, because without
God's disclosure of himself there can be no disclosure of what the sons
of God will be. For the sons of God will be (as much as creatures can
be) what God is, "because we will see him as he is." Consequently,
when St. Augustine claims that the creature does *not* await "the revelation of another nature which is not a creature," he is speaking of the
second disclosure rather than the first.

(3) "For the creature," says the Apostle, "has been subjected to vanity."[12] That is: "The vanity of the foolish! All is vanity! What advantage is there for man in all the toil at which he toils under the sun?"[13] To man it was said: "You will eat your bread through toil."[14] Therefore, "the creature has been subjected to vanity though not of its own will."[15] It was appropriately added, "though not of its own will," inasmuch as man has sinned of his own will, but has not been condemned of his own will. Thus his willful sin was to act contrary to the commandment of truth; but the punishment for his sin, to be subject to deception. Therefore the creature has not been subjected to vanity of its own will, "but on account of him who has subjected it in hope,"[16] i.e., on account of the righteousness and mercy of him who has neither left sin unpunished nor wished the sinner to be without remedy.

(4) "Because even the creature itself. . ." This means man himself, since he has remained only a creature, the mark of the image having already been lost on account of sin.[17] And so, "even the creature itself," i.e., even that which is not yet called a son in the fullest sense,[18] but is only

---

12 Rom 8.20.

13 Eccl 1.2–3.

14 Gn 3.19.

15 Rom 8.20.

16 *Ibid.*

17 Cf. R 1.26 (PL 32.628): "While explaining the verse: ' . . . even the creature itself will be delivered from the bondage of destruction' (Rom 8.21), I said: ' " . . . even the creature itself . . . . " This means man himself, since he has remained only a creature, the mark of the image having already been lost on account of sin.' This must not be understood as if man has completely lost what he was having of the image of God. For if he had not lost the image at all, there would have been no reason for saying: 'Be transformed in the newness of your mind; (Rom 12.2), and: 'We are being transformed into the same image' (2 Cor 3.18). But again, if man had completely lost the image, there would have remained no reason for saying: 'Although man walks in the image, nonetheless, he is agitated in vain; (Ps 38 [39].7). Again, as for my remark: ' . . . the highest angels live by the spirit and the lowest, by the soul,' I spoke more boldly about the lowest angels than is warranted from the holy Scriptures or the facts themselves. Even if, peradventure, this can be shown, it can be done only with the greatest difficulty."

18 *quae nondum uocatur filiorum forma perfecta.*

called a creature, "will be delivered from the bondage of destruction."[19] Consequently the Apostle's words, "even it will be delivered," mean, "even it, just as we ourselves." That is, there need be no despair for those who are not yet called the sons of God because they have not yet believed, but are only called creatures; for they also are going to believe and will be delivered from the bondage of destruction, just as we who already are the sons of God, although it has not yet appeared what we will be. Therefore they will be delivered "from the bondage of destruction to the freedom of the glory of the sons of God,"[20] i.e., in the perfect life which they will have as sons of God they will be freed from bondage and brought to glory from the dead.

(5) "For we know that every creature groans and suffers pain up to the present time."[21] Every creature is considered to be in man, not because in him are all the angels and the powers and authorities above, or heaven and earth and sea and all the things which are in them, but because the whole creature is partly spirit, partly soul, partly body. But let us examine these, starting from the lower. The creature which is body is extended in space; the creature which is soul, however, gives life to body; the creature which is spirit governs the soul, and it governs well when it in turn subjects itself to the governance of God. However, when the spirit transgresses his commandments, it is enveloped in toils and hardships through the very same things which it was capable of governing. Therefore he who lives according to the body is called a carnal or animal[22] man. [He is called] carnal or fleshly because he follows after the things of the flesh, but animal, because he is carried along by the dissolute las-

19 Rom 8.21.
20 *Ibid.*
21 Rom 8.22.
22 The Latin here is *animalis* ("of or pertaining to life, soul"). It is the adjectival form of *anima* ("soul"). For St. Augustine, any creature which is *animalis* is energized by a life-principle, i.e., by a soul. Hence the English adjective *animal* does not carry the important nuance of the Latin adjective, because the English term ordinarily refers to living creatures other than human beings, and it is supposed that these creatures do *not* have souls. For Augustine's understanding of *anima*, see above, Q. 27, n. 2.

civiousness of his own soul, which the spirit neither governs nor restrains within the limits of the natural order, for even the spirit itself does not submit itself to the rule of God. But he who rules the soul by the spirit and the body by the soul (which cannot be done unless he also has God as his ruler, because just as the head of the wife is the husband, so the head of the husband is Christ)[23] is called spiritual. The life of the spiritual man is, at present, subject to some annoyance, but later on it will suffer none of this. Now, since the highest angels live by the spirit and the lowest, by the soul,[24] but the beasts and all animals, by the flesh (though the body does not live, but is made to live), every creature is in man, because he understands by the spirit and senses by the soul and is moved in space by the body. Consequently every creature in man groans and suffers pain. For the Apostle did not say "the entire creature,"[25] but "every creature,"[26] just as if someone should say that every healthy man sees the sun, but not that the entire man sees it, because he sees only with the eyes. Thus every creature is in man, because he understands and lives and has a body; but the entire creature is not in him, because besides him there are angels who understand and live and exist, and animals which live and exist, and bodies which simply exist, since to live is better than not to live, and to understand is itself better than to live without understanding.[27] Therefore, when wretched man groans and suffers pain, every creature groans and suffers pain up to the present time. Moreover, the Apostle was correct in saying, "up to the present time," because even if already there are some in Abraham's bosom,[28] and even if the famous thief established with the Lord in paradise did cease from pain the day on which he believed,[29] nevertheless, up to the present time every creature groans and suffers pain, because every creature, by way of spirit and soul and body, is in those who have not yet been delivered.

---

23 I Cor 11.3.
24 See above, n. 17.
25 *totam creaturam.*
26 *omnem creaturam.*
27 Cf. DLA 2.3.7 (PL 32.1243–44).
28 Lk 16.23.
29 Cf. Lk 23.43.

(6) "And not only" every creature groans and suffers pain, he says, "but also we ourselves," i.e., not only the body and soul and spirit in man together suffer pain from the troubles of the body, but also we ourselves, apart from our bodies, "groan within ourselves, having [our] spirits as firstfruits."[30] The Apostle has fittingly said, "having [our] spirits as firstfruits," referring to those whose spirits have already been offered to God as if in sacrifice and have been encompassed[31] by the divine fire of love. Man's firstfruits are these, because the truth first takes hold of our spirit in order that through our spirit the rest may be encompassed.[32]

---

30 Rom 8.23. St. Augustine presents here an interpretation of v. 23 which is based, apparently, upon reading *spiritus* as accusative plural ("spirits"), to which *primitias* is apposed, rather than as a genitive singular ("of the spirit"), which is the more usual way of reading the word in this verse. (The Greek text is unequivocal, since it has *tou pneumatos* ["of the spirit."]) However, this translation of Augustine's words is warranted by his own subsequent commentary on v. 23, for he explicitly says: our "spirits have already been offered to God as if in sacrifice" and: "we souls who have already offered our minds to God as firstfruits".

This exegesis differs from the usual contemporary understanding of v. 23, which interprets the verse as referring to the Holy Spirit of God rather than to created spirits. Thus, translating the very same Latin text used by Augustine, the verse is read: "we groan within ourselves, having the first fruits of the Spirit." This means: "we groan within ourselves, possessing as much of the Spirit as has been poured out so far." (For this latter interpretation, cf. W. Arndt and F. Gingrich, *A Greek-English Lexicon of the New Testament* (Chicago 1967), *s.v.* "*aparkhē,*" 2b.

On this whole question of the *primitiae spiritus* in St. Augustine, see M. Skutella, ed., *Oeuvres de Saint Augustin,* BA 14: *Les Confessions* 8-13 (Paris 1962), pp. 552-55, n. 11. Here, A. Solignac lists the various places in other works of Augustine where this verse is cited or alluded to, gives a nice resume of recent scholarly debate on the topic, and sets out his own opinion. While agreeing with my view that Augustine does not refer the term *spiritus* in Rm 8.23 to the Holy Spirit, as most modern commentators have done, Solignac does not agree that *spiritus* should be read as an accusative plural to which *primitias* is apposed. Hence he does not agree that Augustine, in Q. 67.6, is speaking of the spirit itself as a firstfruit offering to God. Rather, he understands St. Augustine to be speaking of "an *attitude of the spirit in relation to God,* . . . an attitude of sacrifice . . . and love . . . , an attitude which opens up the soul to the truth and thus grants to it a right judgment concerning all things" (BA 14, p. 554, author's emphasis).

31 *comprehensi sunt.*

32 *comprehendantur.*

Therefore he already has the firstfruits offered to God who
says: "with the mind I serve the Law of God, but with the
flesh, the law of sin."[33] The same is true of him who says:
"God, whom I serve in my spirit."[34] Of this man it is said:
"Indeed the spirit is ready, but the flesh is weak."[35] But
since he still says: "Wretched man that I am! Who will set
me free from the body of this death?",[36] and since it is still
said to such: "He will bring even your mortal bodies to life
by means of the Spirit who abides in you,"[37] he is not yet a
holocaust;[38] but he will be when death is swallowed up into
victory,[39] when it is said to death: "Where, O death, is your
contending? Where, O death, is your sting?"[40]

Therefore, the Apostle says, at the present time not only
every creature, the body included, "but even we ourselves
having [our] spirits as firstfruits," i.e., we souls who have
already offered our minds to God as firstfruits, "groan
within ourselves," i.e., apart from the body. [We do so]
"awaiting adoption, the redemption of our body,"[41] whose
purpose is that even the body itself, privileged to receive the
adoption of sons for which we have been called, might clearly
show that we, having been completely set free by way of the
cessation of all troubles, are the sons of God in every respect.
"For we have been saved by hope; but hope which is seen is
not hope."[42] Therefore the reality which is now hope will
come at that time, "when it will appear what we will be,"
i.e., "like him, because we will see him as he is."[43]

(7) If this section is explained in the manner in which it
has been handled, then we do not fall into those difficulties

---

33 Rom 7.25.
34 Rom 1.9.
35 Mt 26.41.
36 Rom 7.24.
37 Rom 8.11. The word *spirit* in this verse refers to the Holy Spirit.
Augustine has already quoted this verse in Q. 66 above, and there the
text clearly reads "his Spirit" *(spiritum eius)*.
38 See above, Q. 61, n. 8.
39 1 Cor 15.54.
40 1 Cor 15.55.
41 Rom 8.23.
42 Rom 8.24.
43 1 Jn 3.2.

whereby most men are compelled to say that all the angels and the heavenly powers are in pain and groanings before we ourselves are fully delivered, since it is said: "every creature groans and suffers pain."[44] For although they aid us by virtue of their nobility while obedient to God, who has deigned to send even his only Son for our sakes, nonetheless, we must believe that they do this without groaning and pain, lest they be thought to be miserable, and lest that Lazarus, a mortal like ourselves who now rests in Abraham's bosom,[45] be happier. [We must believe this,] particularly since the Apostle has said that the same creature which groans and suffers pain has been subjected to vanity, which is a monstrous thing to believe about those supreme creatures who are possessed of surpassing power and authority. The Apostle then went on to say that the creature is to be delivered from the bondage of destruction, a destruction into which we cannot believe those creatures to have fallen who live in complete bliss in heaven.

Nevertheless, nothing ought to be affirmed rashly, but the divine words must be treated again and again with devout care, lest perhaps the creature which groans and suffers pain and is subjected to vanity can be understood in some other way, so that one can without impiety think this of the highest angels insofar as they, at our Lord's command, aid us in our weakness. But whether that exposition which we have pursued or some other exposition of this section be proferred, one must take care for this one thing: that he not violate or rend Catholic faith. For I know that deceptive heretics[46] have boasted of many impious and absurd things concerning this section.[47]

---

44 Rom 8.22.
45 Lk 16.24.
46 The heretics in question are the Manichaeans, as St. Augustine indicates in ExR 53 (PL 35.2074).
47 St. Augustine's explanation of the term *creature* in the puzzling verses from St. Paul is not without its own difficulties. A quick reading of Q. 67 will disclose that Augustine assigns the word more than one meaning. He does this deliberately, as can be seen from ExR 53 (PL 35.2074-76), which is a discussion contemporaneous with Q. 67. The treatment of Rom 8.19-23 in ExR is much more concise and ordered

68. ON THE SCRIPTURE: "O MAN, WHO ARE YOU TO ANSWER BACK TO GOD?"[1]

(1) Although the Apostle seems to have reproached the prying by saying: "O man, who are you to answer back to God?" they raise a question about this very matter and do not cease to pry about that judgment by which prying itself was rebuked. And indeed the impious do this in an abusive way, saying that the Apostle failed to solve the question and rebuked inquirers because he could not explain what was under investigation. Moreover, some heretics,[2] because they do not deceive except when they promise a knowledge which they do not produce, and who are enemies of the Law and the prophets, charge that whatever the Apostle has injected about them into his discussion is false and has been introduced by corrupters. These heretics have preferred to number even this passage among those which they say are interpolated and to deny that Paul said: "O man, who are

---

than that of Q. 67, and hence it can help in illuminating St. Augustine's explanation of *creature* in that Q. In ExR Augustine explains that the word takes on two different meanings in the development of St. Paul's argument. It refers, on the one hand, to mankind as a whole (creature$_1$) and, on the other hand, only to Christian believers. The second group breaks down in turn into two subgroups: those who have not yet believed but will (creature$_{2a}$) and those who are now believers (creature$_{2b}$). Applying Augustine's analysis in schematic fashion to the verses from Romans 8, we have:

vv. 19–20	creature$_1$
vv. 21–22	creature$_{2a}$
v. 23	creature$_{2b}$

This schematic arrangement differs somewhat from that which can be abstracted from Q. 67. There we have the following suggested arrangement:

v. 19	creature$_{2b}$
v. 20	creature$_1$
v. 21	creature$_{2a}$
v. 22	creature$_1$
v. 23	creature$_{2b}$

However, regardless of the exactness of the two schemata, it is clear that St. Augustine means to distinguish the two fundamental senses of *creature* that we have discussed.

1 Rom 9.20.
2 Probably the Manichaeans.

you to answer back to God?'' For if the passage speaks to the very ones who practice calumny in order to deceive men, then without doubt they will be silent, nor will they dare to promise to the ignorant whom they wish to deceive any knowledge of the will of the omnipotent God.

Now certain people who read the Scriptures with a good and devout intention[3] inquire what answer they can give in this case to the authors of abuse and calumny. But as for us who to our advantage cling to the apostolic authority, and who think that the books preserved in Catholic teaching have been in no way falsified, let us perceive the truth: those to whom the divine secrets are closed are unworthy of and incapable of understanding them. When those who murmur and are indignant that they do not learn the counsels of God begin to say: ''Therefore he has mercy on whom he wants, and he hardens whom he wants. What then does he still complain about? For who resists his will?''[4] and when with these words they begin either to misrepresent the Scriptures or to seek a pretext for their sins so that they might defy the commandments which lead to the moral life, to them, I say, let us boldly respond: ''O man, who are you to answer back to God?'' Nor let us, out of regard for them, give what is holy to dogs or cast our pearls before swine[5] (if, nonetheless, we ourselves are no longer dogs and swine), and, subject to the Holy Spirit's revelation concerning the merit of souls, let us raise our thoughts up to something lofty and far removed from commonplace conjecture, even if partially and dimly grasped.

(2) Now the Apostle in this passage has not prohibited the saints, but those who have not yet been rooted and grounded in love, from inquiry, so that they might be able to comprehend with all saints the breadth, length, height, and depth, and the other things which he describes in the same passage.[6] Therefore he has not prohibited inquiry who says: ''However, the spiritual man judges all things, but he

---

3 *mente.*
4 Rom 9.18–19.
5 Mt 6.6.
6 Eph 3.18–19.

himself is judged by no one,". and especially this:
"However, as for us, we have not received the spirit of this
world, but the Spirit who is of God, so that we might know
what has been bestowed upon us by God."[7] Therefore,
whom has he forbidden except those of clay and earth who,
not yet reborn and nourished within, bear the image of that
man who first was made of the earth from the ground?[8] And
since he did not want to obey him by whom he was made, he
fell back into that from which he was made, and, after sin,
he deserved to hear: "You are earth, and to earth you will
return."[9] Accordingly to such men the Apostle says: "O
man, who are you to answer back to God? Does the thing
molded say to him who has molded it: 'Why have you made
me this way?' " Therefore, insofar as you are a thing
molded [and] not yet a finished son, because you have not
yet exhausted the full abundance of grace whereby is given
to us the power to become the sons of God[10] that you might
be able to hear [the words]: "No longer will I call you servants,...but friends,"[11] then "who are you to answer back
to God" and to want to know God's intention? If you had
wanted to know the intentions of a man [who is] your equal,
you would have acted impudently unless first you had
become friends with him. Therefore, as we have borne the
image of the earthly man, let us bear the image of the
heavenly,[12]   taking off our old man and putting on the
new,[13] so that no one can say to us as to something molded of
clay: "Does the thing molded say to him who has molded it:
'Why have you made me this way?' "

(3) In order that it might be clear that these things are
said to the earthly clay rather than to the sanctified spirit,
note what follows: "Or has not the potter of the clay the
authority to make from the same lump one vessel for honor

7 1 Cor 2.15, 12.
8 1 Cor 15.47–49.
9 Gn 3.19.
10 Jn 1.12.
11 Jn 15.15.
12 1 Cor 15.49.
13 Col 3.9–10.

and another for shame?''[14] Therefore, given that our nature sinned in paradise, we are [now] formed through a mortal begetting by the same Divine Providence, not according to heaven, but according to earth, i.e., not according to the spirit, but according to the flesh, and we have all become one mass of clay, i.e., a mass of sin. Since therefore we have forfeited our reward through sinning, and since, in the absence of God's mercy, we as sinners deserve nothing other than eternal damnation, who then does the man from this mass think he is that he can answer God and say: "Why have you made me this way?" If you want to know these things, do not be clay, but become a son of God through the mercy of him who has given to those believing in his name the power to become the sons of God, although he has not so given, as you want, to those desiring to know divine things before they believe. For the reward of knowledge is paid to the deserving, and such merit is obtained by believing. However, the very grace which is given through faith is given prior to any merit that we might have. What then is the merit of the sinner and the ungodly man? Christ has died for the ungodly and for sinners[15] in order that we might be called to faith, not by merit, but by grace, and that by believing we might also establish merit. Therefore sinners are commanded to believe in order that they might be purged of sins through believing, for sinners do not have a knowledge of what they will see by living rightly. For this reason, since they cannot see except they live rightly, nor are they capable of living rightly except they believe, it is clear that they must start from faith, so that the commandments by which believers are turned from this world might produce a pure heart capable of seeing God. For, "Blessed are the pure in heart, because they will see God."[16] Moreover, it is said by way of prophecy: "Seek him in simplicity of heart."[17]

---

14 Rom 9.21.
15 Rom 5.6.
16 Mt 5.8.
17 Wis 1.1.

Consequently, to men who dwell in the old age of life and on that account have obscured vision of soul, one is right in saying: "O man, who are you to answer back to God? Does the thing molded say to him who has molded it: 'Why have you made me this way?' Or has not the potter of the clay the authority to make from the same lump one vessel for honor and another for shame?"[18] Clean out the old yeast that you might be a new lump,[19] and in that lump itself be no longer a child in Christ who needs to drink milk,[20] but attain to perfect manhood that you might be among those of whom it is said: "We speak wisdom among the perfect."[21] Then at last will you hear correctly and without distortion whether there are any secrets of the almighty God concerning the deeply hidden merits of souls and concerning grace or righteousness.

(4) Now, in Pharaoh's case, there is a simple response. His prior mistreatment of the foreigners in his kingdom merited for him as a fitting consequence hardness of heart so that he could not believe even the most obvious signs decreed by God. Therefore, from the same mass (of sins, that is), he brought forth both vessels of mercy to succor when the sons of Israel prayed to him, and vessels of wrath, i.e., Pharaoh and his people, to instruct Israel by their punishment, because, although both peoples were sinners and on that account belonged to one mass, still it was necessary to treat differently those who had made their lament to the one God. Therefore, "He endured with much patience the vessels of wrath which were made for destruction."[22] By the expression *with much patience*, the Apostle has adequately indicated the previous sins for which God endured Pharaoh and his people so that he could opportunely exact vengeance at a time when vengeance on them was necessary to help those being liberated, "and that he might

---

18 Rom 9.20-21.
19 1 Cor 5.7.
20 1 Cor 3.2.
21 1 Cor 2.6.
22 Rom 9.22.

make known the riches of his glory in the vessels of mercy which he has prepared for glory.''[23]

Here, perhaps troubled, you return to that question: ''he has mercy on whom he wants, and he hardens whom he wants. What then does he still complain about? For who resists his will?''[24] By all means he has mercy on whom he wants, and he hardens whom he wants, but this will of God cannot be unjust. For it springs from deeply hidden merits, because, even though sinners themselves have constituted a single mass on account of the sin of all,[25] still it is not the case that there is no difference among them. Therefore, although they have not yet been made righteous, there is some preceding thing in sinners whereby they are rendered worthy of righteousness, and again, there is some preceding thing in other sinners whereby they are deserving of obtuseness. You have the same Apostle saying elsewhere: ''Because they did not see fit to have a knowledge of God, God gave them up to an unsound mind.''[26] God gave them up to an unsound mind—this is how he hardened Pharaoh's heart,[27] and they did not see fit to have a knowledge of God—this is how they showed themselves worthy of being given up to an unsound mind.

(5) Nonetheless, it is true that ''it is not of him who wills nor of him who runs, but of God who shows mercy.''[28] For even if each person with petty sins or genuinely grave and numerous sins, however many, is yet worthy of God's mercy by virtue of a great lament and the anguish of repentance, this does not depend on himself, who would perish if abandoned, but on God who shows mercy and who comes in response to his prayers and anguish. For it is not enough to will except God show mercy; but God, who calls to peace,

---

23 Rom 9.23.
24 Rom 9.18–19.
25 The Latin for ''the sin of all' is *generale peccatum.* St. Augustine is referring to the original sin of Adam with which all mankind became infected.
26 Rom 1.28.
27 Ex 4.21.
28 Rom 9.16.

does not show mercy except the will have preceded,[29] because on earth peace is to men of good will.[30] And since no one can will unless urged on and called, whether inside where no man sees, or outside through the sound of the spoken word or through some visible signs, it follows that God produces in us even the willing itself.[31] In fact, to that prepared feast of which the Lord speaks in the Gospel, not all who were called wanted to come, nor could those come who did come except they were called.[32] Accordingly neither should those who came give themselves the credit, for they came by invitation, nor should those who did not want to come blame it on another, but only on themselves, for they had been invited to come of their free will. Therefore, before merit, the calling determines the will. For this reason, even

---

29 Cf. R 1.26 (PL 32.628): "I have said: 'For even if each person with petty sins or genuinely grave and numerous sins, however many, is yet worthy of God's mercy by virtue of a great lament and the anguish of repentance, this does not depend on himself, who would perish if abandoned, but on God who shows mercy and who comes in response to his prayers and anguish. For it is not enough to will except God show mercy; but God, who calls to peace, does not show mercy except the will for peace have preceded.' This is said of the time after repentance. For God's mercy precedes even the will itself, and in the absence of this mercy, 'the will would not be prepared by the Lord' (Prv 8.35). To that mercy belongs also the very calling, which precedes faith as well. When I considered the calling a little later, I said: 'Moreover, this calling which works through the opportune circumstances of history, whether this calling be in individual men or in peoples or in mankind itself, springs from a decree both lofty and profound. To this pertains the following passage: "In the womb have I sanctified you" (Jer 1.5); and: "When you were in your father's loins I saw you"; and: "Jacob have I loved, but Esau have I hated" (Rom 9.13; Mal 1.2–3),' and so on. As for the testimony: 'When you were in your father's loins I saw you,' I do not know how it occurred to me that it was from the Scriptures." The source for this latter quotation in Q. 68 still remains unidentified. [For an analogous wording. cf. Heb 7.10. Editor's note.]
    These same Scriptural themes, subject to practically the same exegesis, are treated with a great deal more order and clarity in a work of the same period as these QQ. on Romans. Cf. ExR 60–64 (PL 35.2078–81) and St. Augustine's very useful reconsiderations in R 1.23.2–4 (PL 32.621–22).
30 Lk 2.14.
31 Phil 2.13.
32 Lk 14.16–24.

if someone called takes the credit for coming, he cannot take
the credit for being called. And as for him who is called and
does not come, just as his calling was not a deserved reward,
so his neglecting to come when called lays the foundation for
a deserved punishment. There will thus be the following two
things: "Of your mercy and judgement will I sing, O
Lord."[33] To mercy belongs the calling; to judgement
belongs the blessedness of those who have come when called
and the punishment of those who did not want to come.
Therefore, was Pharoah ignorant of how much good came
upon the land through Joseph's coming?[34] The knowledge of
that fact, therefore, was Pharaoh's invitation to a gratitude
expressed through merciful treatment of the people of Israel.
However, because he did not want to obey this invitation,
but exercised cruelty on those to whom he owed humanity
and mercy, he deserved punishment. As a consequence, his
heart was hardened, and he suffered such a blindness of the
mind that he did not believe God's signs, though so many
and so great and so manifest. [All this was] to the end that
his punishment, whether the hardening or the ultimate, visible drowning, might serve as a lesson for the people by
whose affliction Pharaoh merited for himself both his hidden
obtuseness and his drowning in the sight of all.[35]

(6) Moreover, this calling, which works through the
opportune circumstances of history,[36] whether this calling be
in individual men or in peoples or in mankind itself, springs
from a decree both lofty and profound. To this pertains the
following passage: "In the womb have I sanctified you";[37]
and: "When you were in your father's loins I saw you";
and: "Jacob have I loved, but Esau have I hated,"[38]
although this was said before they were born. Nor can this
calling be comprehended, except perhaps by those who love
God with all their heart and with all their soul and with all

33 Ps 100(101).1.
34 Cf. Gn 41.
35 Cf. Ex 5–14.
36 *quae . . . per temporum opportunitates operatur.*
37 Jer 1.5.
38 Rom 9.13; Mal 1.2–3; cf. above, n. 29.

their mind, and who love their neighbors as themselves.[39] For, established in so great a love, they can perhaps already comprehend with the saints the length, breadth, height, and depth.[40] Nevertheless, one must hold to the following with an absolutely steadfast faith: God does not do anything unjustly, nor is there any nature which does not owe to God what it is. For to God is owed all splendor and beauty and the congruence of parts which, if pursued into the inmost recessess and removed from things right to the very last part, leaves nothing remaining.

69. ON THE SCRIPTURE: "THEN EVEN THE SON HIMSELF WILL BE SUBJECT TO HIM WHO HAS SUBORDINATED ALL THINGS TO HIM"[1]

(1) Those who contend that the Son of God is not equal to the Father[2] customarily and habitually make use of the Apostle's claim in which he says: "But when all things have been subordinated to him, then even the Son himself will be subject to him who has subordinated all things to him, in order that God may be all in all."[3] Their error, to be sure, could not spring up clothed with the name *Christian* except from a failure to understand the Scriptures. For they say: "If the Son is equal, how will he be subject to the Father?" This, of course, is similar to a question in one of the gospels: If the Son is equal, how is the Father greater? For the Lord himself says: "because the Father is greater than I."[4]

However, the rule of Catholic faith is this: when the Scriptures say of the Son that he is less than the Father, the Scriptures mean in respect to the assumption of humanity; but when the Scriptures point out that he is equal, they are

39 Mt 22.37–39.
40 Cf. Eph 3.18.

1 1 Cor 15.28.
2 The Arians were the most noteworthy proponents of this view.
3 1 Cor 15.28.
4 Jn 14.28.

understood in respect to his deity. Therefore the meaning of the following passages is clear: "the Father is greater than I," and, "I and the Father are one",[5] and, "the Word was God," and, "The Word became flesh",[6] and, "He did not deem equality with God a prize to be snatched up, but he emptied himself by assuming the form of a slave."[7]

Nonetheless, since many things also are said of the Son which concern the constitutive character of the [divine] person apart from what belongs to the assumption of humanity, so that it is necessary for the Father to be understood as nothing other than the Father and the Son as nothing other than the Son, the heretics think that equality is impossible in those passages which are so expressed and understood. For it is written: "Everything has been made *through him*,"[8] the Son undoubtedly, i.e., the Word of God. By whom[9] has it been made except by the Father? But nowhere is it written that the Son has produced any created thing through the Father.[10] Again, it is written that the Son is the image of the Father,[11] but nowhere is it written that the Father is the image of the Son. Again, [it is written] that the one begets while the other is begotten, and other such things which do not concern equality of substance, but properties peculiar to the persons. When those heretics, because they employ minds too dense to fathom these things, say that equality among the persons is impossible, one must come down hard on them with the weight of authority. For if in these passages one could not perceive the equality of him through whom[12] everything has been made and him by whom[13] it has been made, of the image and that whose image he is, of the begotten and the begetter, the Apostle would under no circumstances employ even the very word to stop the mouths of

---

5 Jn 10.30.
6 Jn 1.1, 14.
7 Phil 2.6–7.
8 Jn 1.3 (emphasis mine). In Latin: *"Omnia per ipsum facta sunt."*
9 *a quo.*
10 *per Patrem.*
11 Col 1.15.
12 *per quem.*
13 *a quo.*

contentious men by saying: "He did not deem equality with God a prize to be snatched up."[14]

(2) Therefore, since those things which are written for the distinguishing of the Father and the Son have been thus written partly on account of the constitutive features of the [divine] persons, partly on account of the assumption of humanity, while the deity and unity and equality of the Father and the Son nonetheless remain intact, it is appropriate to inquire at this point whether it is in respect to the constitutive features of the persons or in respect to the assumption of humanity that the Apostle has said: "Then even the Son himself will be subject to him who has subordinated all things to him." The Scriptural context usually sets the meaning in a clear light when the surrounding verses which bear on the question at hand are treated to careful examination. Accordingly we find that this passage comes after an earlier statement: "Now, however, Christ has arisen from the dead, the firstfruits of those who sleep."[15] For he was concerned with the resurrection of the dead, a thing which, in the Lord's case, was realized insofar as he had become a man, even though this would follow quite plainly when he would say: "Indeed, since death came through a man, the resurrection of the dead also comes through a man. For just as in Adam all die, so also in Christ all will be made alive, but each one in his turn: Christ the firstfruits; then those who are Christ's, at his coming; then the end, when he will hand the kingdom over to God and the Father, when he will destroy every dominion, and every authority and power. For it is necessary for him to reign until he places all his enemies under his feet. Death, the very last enemy, will be destroyed, for he has placed all things under his feet. However, when [the Scripture] says that all things have been placed under, it is clear that it makes an exception of him who has placed all things under him. But when all things have been subordinated to him, then even the Son himself will be subject to him who has subordinated all

---

14 Phil 2.6.
15 1 Cor 15.20.

things to him, in order that God may be all in all.''[16] Therefore it is clear that the passage speaks with the assumption of
humanity in mind.

(3) However, the heretics usually raise questions in
regard to other places in this section which I have cited in its
entirety. In the first place, there is the statement: ''when he
will hand the kingdom over to God and the Father,'' as if the
Father does not presently possess the kingdom. Then it is
said: ''For it is necessary for him to reign until 'he place all
enemies under his feet,' '' as if afterwards he is not going to
reign. This is also supported by the earlier statement, ''then
the end.'' Though a sacrilegious opinion, they understand
the verse thus, as if it meant by *end* the consummation of his
kingdom, although it is written in the gospel: ''And of his
kingdom there will be no end.''[17] Finally, it is said: ''But
when all things have been subordinated to him, then even
the Son himself will be subject to him who has subordinated
all things to him.'' They wish to understand this in the
following way, as if now either something is not subject to
the Son, or he himself is not subject to the Father.

(4) In these circumstances, the character of the language
provides the solution to the problem. For very often the
Scripture speaks in such a way that what is always the case is
said to become the case in something at the moment when it
ought to be acknowledged in it. For this we say in the
[Lord's] Prayer: ''May your name be hallowed,''[18] as if
there is a time when it is not holy. Therefore, just as the
expression ''may it be hallowed'' means ''may it be
recognized as holy,'' so also the passage ''when he will hand
the kingdom over to God and the Father'' means ''when he
will show that the Father reigns,'' so that what is now taken

---

16 1 Cor 15.21–28. St. Paul himself is quoting Ps 109(110).1 and Ps 8.8.
    No doubt, on the first reading of this passage as translated, one will be
    quite perplexed about whom Paul is speaking in any given verse in the
    passage quoted. Does he mean God the Father, or is he speaking of the
    Son? However, the ambiguity of reference in my translation reflects
    the same ambiguity in the Latin text of Augustine, which in turn
    reflects the same ambiguity in the Greek text.
17 Lk 1.33.
18 Mt 6.9.

on faith by believers and is not accepted by unbelievers will become evident through [its] appearance and manifestation. Moreover, he will destroy every dominion and authority through the express manifestation of the kingdom of the Father so that all may know that no ruler and no authority, be they heavenly or earthly, have possessed any dominion and authority of themselves, but by him from whom are all things, not only in respect of their existing, but also in respect of their ordering. For in that appearing there will remain no hope for anyone in any ruler or in any man. This is said even now by way of prophecy: "It is good to hope in the Lord rather than to hope in man; it is good to hope in the Lord rather than to hope in princes."[19] Thus, with this meditation, the soul rises up even now to the kingdom of the Father, neither placing much value in the power of anyone besides him, nor, to its own destruction, flattering itself about its own.

Therefore Christ will hand the kingdom over to God and the Father when through him the Father will be known by sight, for his kingdom consists of those in whom he now reigns through faith. In fact, in one sense Christ's kingdom means his divine power according to which every created thing is subject to him; and in another sense his kingdom means the Church in respect to the faith which it has in him. In accord with this meaning is the prayer of him who says: "Possess us,"[20] for it is not the case that [Christ] himself does not possess all things. This is also the meaning of the following statement: "When you were the slaves of sin, you were free from righteousness."[21] Therefore he will destroy every dominion and every authority and power, so that he

19 Ps 117(118).8–9.
20 Is 26.13 (according to the Septuagint).
21 Rom 6.20. Beckaert, the French translator of DD83 in BA 10, notes: "The meaning appealed to is this: one belongs to either one or the other. The one who is yet the slave of sin is not free in regard to righteousness in the sense that he is legitimately exempt from it, but in the sense that he considers himself to be exempt from it. St. Paul's thought is as follows: Well, what advantage have you derived from this license? (ironical). St. Augustine's application is that by destroying the tyranny of sin, Jesus Christ will take possession again of those whom sin took away from righteousness; (BA 10, pp. 290–91, n. 2).

who sees the Father through the Son will neither require nor be pleased with repose in his own or the power of any created thing.

(5) "For it is necessary for him to reign until 'he place all his enemies under his feet,' "[22] i.e., it is necessary for Christ's kingdom to be manifested to such a degree until all his enemies confess that he does reign, for this is what is meant by the claim that his enemies are going to be under his feet. Now if we understand this of the righteous, then the word *enemies* is used because the righteous are justified from among the unrighteous, and they become subject to him by faith. However, in regard to the unrighteous who do not have a share in the future blessedness of the righteous, the passage must be understood in this sense, that even they, confounded at the very manifestation of his kingdom, will confess that he reigns. Therefore, given the text: "It is necessary for him to reign until 'he place all enemies under his feet,' " this does not mean that when he has placed his enemies under his feet he will then no longer reign. Rather, "It is necessary for him to reign until 'he place all his enemies under his feet.' " That is, the Apostle says, it is necessary for him to make his reign so clearly evident until his enemies dare not at all deny that Christ reigns. For it is written: "Thus are our eyes toward our Lord God until he show us mercy";[23] but nonetheless, when he has shown us mercy, we should not turn our eyes from him. For our blessedness is in direct proportion to our enjoyment of God in contemplation. Therefore the text signifies this: our eyes do not seek after and reach out for the Lord except for the obtaining of his mercy, not that afterwards they may then turn away, but that from then on they may require nothing more.[24] The word *until*, therefore, is to be understood as equivalent to *nothing more*. What more, i.e., what greater manifestation, will the appearance of Christ's kingdom require, save only that sufficient to make all his enemies confess that he does reign? Therefore it is one thing not to be

---

22 1 Cor 15.25.
23 Ps122(123).2.
24 *nihil amplius.*

any more manifest; it is another not to continue anymore. *Not to be any more manifest*[25] means "not to become more evident"; *not to continue anymore*[26] means "not to keep on any longer." But when will Christ's kingdom be more evident than when it has become visible to all his enemies?[27]

(6) "Death, the very last enemy, will be destroyed."[28] For there will be nothing else to destroy after this which is mortal has put on immortality. "For 'he has placed all things under his feet,' " and this for the purpose of destroying death. "However, when [the Scripture] says that 'all things have been placed under,' " as, of course, the prophet says in the Psalms,[29] "it is clear that it makes an exception of him who has placed all things under him."[30] The intent is that the Father be understood as having placed all things under the Son (as the same Lord in many places in the gospel teaches and proclaims), not only by reason of [the Son's] form [as a] slave, but also by reason of the principle from which he is and by which he is equal to him from whom

---

25 *non amplius manifestari.*

26 *non amplius permanere.*

27 This whole paragraph is better grasped if one remembers Augustine's earlier remark that "very often the Scripture speaks in such a way that what is always the case is said to become the case in something at the moment when it ought to be acknowledged in it" (Q.69.4). He then argues that this interpretative principle is the key which unlocks an otherwise problematic 1 Cor 15.25. First, it notifies us that Christ's kingdom is an abiding reality. Second, it notifies us that the word *until* is not a temporally limiting term signifying an end to Christ's reign at the subordination of all enemies to himself. Rather, the word focuses our attention on a critical moment in the history of the permanent and continuing kingdom of Christ—the moment when the realization that Christ's is an everlasting kingdom breaks in upon those who previously did not acknowledge this. Hence Augustine thinks that his interpretative principle makes it clear that here the word *until* really means "nothing more." Thus, with these two results of his principle in mind, he in effect restates 1 Cor 15.25 as follows: Nothing more is required for the subjection of Christ's enemies than the clear manifestation of the abiding reality which is Christ's kingdom. This is a paraphrase of Augustine's response to a question which he himself asks in these words: "What more, i.e., what greater manifestation, will the appearance of Christ's kingdom require, save only that sufficient to make all his enemies confess that he does reign?" (Q.69.5).

28 1 Cor 15.26.

29 Ps 8.8.

30 1 Cor 15.27.

he is. For he is wont to refer everything to one principle whose image, as it were, he is, although in [the image] dwells all the fulness of divinity.[31]

(7) "But when all things have been subordinated to him, then even the Son himself will be subject to him who has subordinated all things to him."[32] Not that this is not the case now, but rather, then will it be manifest (in accord with the mode of expression discussed above). "In order that God may be all in all."[33] He himself is the end which was mentioned above, when the Apostle wanted first to compress the whole into a few words in order then to explain and set it forth piece by piece, as it were. For he was speaking of the resurrection where he says: "Christ the firstfruits; then those who are Christ's, at his coming; then the end."[34] Clearly this is the end in question, "that God may be all in all." For there is one meaning of *end* which refers to consummation, another, to consumption. For, on the one hand, a tunic is ended by [the completion of] the weaving; on the other, a meal is ended through eating. God, however, is said to be all in all, with the result that no one of those who cling to him loves his own will in opposition to loving him, and with the result that it is manifest to all what the same Apostle says in another place: "But what do you have that you have not received?"[35]

(8) Again, as for the following passage: "It is necessary for him to reign until 'he place all his enemies under his feet,' "[36] there are some[37] who understand it in such a way that they say that here *to reign* has a meaning different from that of *the reign*, of which the Apostle says, "when he will

---

31 Cf. Col 1.15 and 2.9.
32 1 Cor 15.28.
33 *Ibid.*
34 1 Cor 15.23–24.
35 1 Cor 4.7.
36 1 Cor 15.25.
37 It is not known whom St. Augustine has in mind here. Their exegesis of 1 Cor 15.25 continues to the end of section 8 of Q. 69.

hand the reign over to God and the Father.''[38] Hence the
phrase *the reign* would refer to God's rule over the entire
created order, whereas *to reign* would be understood in terms
of leading an army against an enemy or defending a city, so
that he would therefore say: ''It is necessary for him to reign
until 'he place all his enemies under his feet,' '' because
there will be no reason for the sort of reign military leaders
have, once the enemy has been so subjected that he cannot
offer resistance. For it is clearly stated in the gospel: ''And of
his reign there will be no end,''[39] and this because he reigns
forever. However, in respect to the war waged under him
against the devil, this conflict will obviously continue ''until
he place all his enemies under his feet''; but afterwards there
will be no conflict, since we shall enjoy an everlasting peace.

(9) Now there is value in these remarks if they cause us to
recognize the need for considering more carefully this next
question: In what respect does the Lord presently reign during this special period characterized by the mystery which is
his incarnation and passion?[40] For, insofar as he is the Word
of God, his kingdom is both without end and without beginning, as well as without interruption. But insofar as the
Word was made flesh,[41] he began to reign in those who
believe by faith in his incarnation. This is the reason for the
following verse: ''The Lord has reigned from the tree.''[42]
Moreover from here has he destroyed every dominion and
every authority and power, while those believing in him are

---

38 1 Cor 15.24. I have here translated *regnum* by *reign* rather than by the
   word *kingdom* used elsewhere in this Q. in the translation of this particular word. I do so here and in Lk 1.33 below in order to bring out
   the proposed contrast in meaning between *regnare* (''to reign'') in v. 25
   and *regnum* (''the reign'') in v. 24.
39 Lk 1.33.
40 *dispensatione sacramenti sui per incarnationem atque passionem.*
41 Jn 1.14.
42 Ps 95(96).10. The word *lignum* (''tree'' or ''wood'') is an ancient
   Christian term for the cross of Christ. While Augustine's Latin Old
   Testament apparently had the words *from the wood,* they are lacking in
   both the Hebrew and the best Septuagint manuscript traditions. [For a
   brief discussion on this text, see H. Swete, *An Introduction to the Old
   Testament in Greek* 2d ed. (Cambridge 1914, reprinted 1968), p. 424, n.
   1 and p. 467. Editor's note.]

saved, not through his glory, but through his humility. This is hidden from the wise and the clever and revealed to little ones,[43] since it pleased God through the foolishness of preaching to save those who believe.[44] Nor does the Apostle say that he, numbered among the little ones, knows anything except Jesus Christ and him crucified.[45] This preaching is necessary for so long a time until all enemies are placed under his feet, i.e., until all worldly pride yields and is subject to his humility (which is signified, I think by the word *feet*); and this has already happened for the most part, and we see it happening daily.

However, for what end do these things transpire [but] that he hand over the kingdom to God and the Father, i.e., that he lead those nourished by faith in his incarnation to the actual seeing of his equality with the Father? For already he was speaking to those who had believed when he said: "If you abide in my word, truly you are my disciples, and you will know the truth, and the truth will make you free."[46] For he will hand over the kingdom to the Father when he will reign in those contemplating the truth through that whereby he is equal to the Father, and when through himself, the only begotten, he will cause the Father to be seen by sight. For now he reigns in believers by his self-emptying and the acceptance of the form of a servant,[47] but then he will hand over the kingdom to God and the Father when he will have destroyed every dominion and authority and power. With what will he destroy except with humility and forbearance and weakness? For what dominion will not be destroyed when the Son of God reigns in believers by reason of the fact that the princes of the world have judged him? What authority will not be destroyed when the very one through whom all things were made reigns in believers by reason of the fact that he was so subject to the authorities that he could say to a man: "You would have no authority over me except it had been granted you from above"?[48] What power will

---

43 Mt 11.25.
44 1 Cor 1.21.
45 1 Cor 2.2.
46 Jn 8.31–32.
47 Phil 2.7.
48 Jn 19.11.

not be destroyed when the very one through whom the
heavens were established reigns in believers by reason of the
fact that he became weak to the point of the cross and death?
Moreover, it is proper for the Son to reign in this manner in
the faith of believers, for one cannot say that the Father
either became flesh or was judged or crucified. But through
the actual seeing of his equality with the Father, he reigns
with the Father in those who contemplate the truth.
However, in that [the Son] will hand the kingdom over to
God and the Father by leading those who now believe in him
from faith in his incarnation to the vision of divinity, he
himself loses nothing, but both offer themselves, to those
contemplating, as a single entity to be enjoyed. However, it
is necessary among men not yet capable of beholding the
equality of the Father and the Son by the clear light of the
mind that Christ reign for so long a time through that which
such men can grasp and which he himself has assumed as his
own, i.e., the humility of the incarnation, until he place all
enemies under his feet, i.e., until all worldly pride be subjected to the humility of his incarnation.

(10) "Then even the Son himself will be subject to him
who has subordinated all things to him." Certainly, in
regard to this text, although it speaks of the assumption of
humanity, because this question was occasioned by an
investigation of the resurrection of the dead, it nonetheless is
proper to ask whether the text speaks of Christ only insofar
as he is the head of the Church,[49] or insofar as he is the
universal Christ who encompasses the body and its
members. For the Apostle says to the Galatians: "[The
Scripture] does not say 'and to descendants,' as if referring
to many, but, as if referring to one, 'and to your
descendant,' who is Christ."[50] However, lest we should
understand in this place only the Christ himself who was
born of the Virgin Mary, he afterwards says: "For you are
all one in Christ Jesus. But if you are Christ's, you are
therefore a descendant of Abraham."[51] And when he was

---

49 Eph 5.23.
50 Gal 3.16.
51 Gal 3.28–29.

speaking to the Corinthians of love, he draws a comparison with the members of the body by saying: "For just as the body is one and has many members, and all the members of the body, though many, are one body, so also Christ."[52] He did not say, "so also Christ's," but "so also Christ,"[53] showing that Christ is also properly spoken of as universal, that is, as the head with his body which is the Church. Moreover, we find that Christ is also referred to in this way in many places in the Scripture, so that he is understood with all his members to whom it was said: "You yourselves are Christ's body and members."[54] Therefore, as for the verse: "Then also the Son himself will be subject to him who has subordinated all things to him," we do not absurdly understand it if we understand *the Son* to mean not only the head of the Church, but also all the saints with him. They are one in Christ, the one descendant of Abraham, and [their] subjection is in respect to the contemplation of eternal truth for the obtaining of blessedness, there being no opposing motion of the soul or opposing part of the body, "in order that," no one loving his own authority in that life, "God may be all in all."

---

52 1 Cor 12.12.
53 The difference cited here is, in the Latin text, the difference between *ita et Christi* ("so also Christ's") and *ita et Christus* ("so also Christ").
54 1 Cor 12.27. [For a succinct discussion of this wording, see T. O'Malley, *Tertullian and the Bible* (Nijmegen 1967), pp. 58–59, 175–76. Editor's note.]

*70. ON THE APOSTLE'S CLAIM: "DEATH HAS BEEN
SWALLOWED UP INTO VICTORY. WHERE,
O DEATH, IS YOUR CONTENDING? WHERE.
O DEATH, IS YOUR STING? NOW THE STING
OF DEATH IS SIN; BUT THE POWER
OF SIN, THE LAW"*[1]

I think that *death* in this passage signifies a carnal habit[2]
which resists the good will through a delighting in temporal
pleasures. For the passage would not say, "Where, O death,
is your contending?" if there had not been resistance and
struggle. The "contending" of [the carnal habit] is also
described in the following passage: "The flesh has longings
contrary to the spirit's, and the spirit, contrary to the flesh's;
for these resist and are opposed to one another, so that you
do those things you do not want to do."[3] Therefore perfect
sanctification achieves this: every carnal desire is made subject to our spirit [now] illumined and made alive, i.e., to the
good will. And, just as now we see that we are free of
boyhood delights which, if denied, used to grieve us keenly
as boys, so should we believe that this will happen to every
carnal delight when perfect holiness restores wholeness to
man. At present, however, as long as there is something in
us which resists the good will, we need God's help through
good men and good angels so that, until our wound is
healed, it may not so torment us that it destroy even the
good will.

This death, moreover, we have merited by sin, because in
the beginning sin was the result of a totally free choice [exer-
cised] at a time when in paradise no pain from a forbidden

---

1 1 Cor 15.54–56.
2 *Consuetudo,* here translated "habit," can also mean "a love affair"
   and "illicit intercourse." Augustine could possibly be employing that
   sense of the word for this particular passage.
3 Gal 5.17. The word *spirit* is ambiguous in its reference. Does it refer to
   the spirit in man, to the Holy Spirit, or to both? Many recent English
   translations of the New Testament take Paul to be referring to the
   Holy Spirit, but Augustine seems to view the passage otherwise. His
   use of the Scripture passage in Q. 70 would indicate that he
   understands the word *spirit* to be referring to the spirit of man.

delight opposed the good will, as is true now. For example, if there is someone who has never taken pleasure in hunting, he is completely free as to whether he wants to hunt or does not want to, nor does the one who forbids him cause him pain. But if, abusing this freedom, he hunts contrary to the order of him who forbids, then pleasure, stealing unawares upon the soul little by little, inflicts death upon it so that if the soul wants to restrain itself, it cannot do so without vexation and anguish, since previously it did not act with full equanimity. Therefore "the sting of death is sin," because through sin there has come about a delight which can now resist the good will and be kept back [only] with pain. This delighting we rightly call death, because it is the failing of a soul become degenerate.

"But the power of sin is the Law," because what is forbidden by law is done with much more viciousness and shamefulness than if forbidden by no law. Hence death will be swallowed up into victory at that time when carnal delight will be eclipsed through the sanctification of the whole man by a perfect delight in things spiritual.

71. ON THE SCRIPTURE: "BEAR ONE ANOTHER'S BURDENS, AND IN THIS WAY WILL YOU FULFILL THE LAW OF CHRIST"[1]

(1) Because obedience in the Old Testament was characterized by fear, there could be no clearer an indication that the gift of the New Testament is love than in this passage where the Apostle says: "Bear one another's burdens, and in this way will you fulfill the law of Christ." For one understands *the law of Christ* to refer to the fact that the Lord himself commanded us to love one another, placing so much weight on the significance of the maxim that he said: "In this will one know that you are my disciples, if you love one another."[2] Moreover, the responsibility of this love is that we bear one another's burdens. But this responsibility,

---

1 Gal 6.2.
2 Jn 13.34–35.

which is not an eternal one, leads doubtless to an eternal blessedness in which there will be no burdens for us which we shall be required to bear for one another. Now, however, while we are in this life, i.e., on this journey, let us bear one another's burdens so that we can achieve that life which is free of every burden. Indeed, take the example of deer, whom some people learned in such areas of knowledge have written about. When deer swim across a channel to an island in search of pasture they line themselves up in such a way that the weight of their heads carried in the antlers is borne by one another thus: the one behind, by extending its neck, places its head on the one in front. Moreover, because there must be one deer which is at the head of the others and thus has no one in front of itself to lay its head on, they are said to take the lead by turns, so that the one in front, wearied by the weight of its head, retires to the end of the line, and the one whose head it was supporting while travelling in the lead takes its place. In this way, bearing one another's burdens, they traverse a channel until they come to solid ground.[3] Perhaps Solomon had this characteristic of the deer in mind when he said: "Let the deer of friendship and the foal of your affections converse with you."[4] For nothing so proves friendship as the bearing of a friend's burden.

(2) Nonetheless, we would not bear one another's burdens if the two parties who bear their burdens did so at the same time or had the same kind of weakness. However, different times and different sorts of weakness enable us to bear one another's burdens. For example, you will bear the anger of your brother at a time when you yourself are not angry at him, so that he in turn may support you by his own gentleness and calm at a time when anger will have seized hold of you. This example refers to a case in which both parties bear their burdens at different times, although the weakness itself is not different, for they bear one another's anger.

---

3 Cf. H. Rackham, trans., *Pliny, Natural History,* Book 8 (Cambridge, Mass. 1956), p. 83.
4 Prv 5.19.

For a case in which the sort of weakness is different, one has to look at another example. Take the case of someone who has overcome talkativeness in himself and has not yet overcome obstinacy, while the other person is talkative but no longer obstinate. The former ought to bear in love the talkativeness of the latter and the latter, the stubborness of the former, until they each be cured of their respective ills.

Of course, if the same infirmity afflicts both parties at the same time, then they cannot give support to one another while each party is at odds with himself. Now obviously against some third party two angered people are in accord with one another and support one another, although one ought not to say that they support one another, but rather, encourage one another. Take also those who are sad about a particular matter: they support one another and, as it were, lean upon one another, which they would not do if one were sad and the other happy. But if they were sorrowing about one another, obviously they cannot give support to one another. And therefore, in respect to such states of mind, you must take on somewhat the very affliction from which you want the other person to be freed through your efforts, and you must take it on in this way for the purpose of being able to give help, not to achieve the same degree of misery. Analogously, a man bends over and extends his hand to someone lying down, for he does not cast himself down so that they are both lying, but he only bends down to raise up the one lying down.

(3) Furthermore, there is not anything which causes us to expend our energy willingly in bearing the burdens of others (a thing which we are obliged to do) except for the thought of how much the Lord has endured for us. For on this account the Apostle says in an admonitory fashion: "Have the same thoughts in yourselves as were in Christ Jesus, who, though being in the form of God, did not deem equality with God a prize to be snatched up, but, assuming the form of a slave, emptied himself, having been made into the likeness of men. And having been found with the appearance of a man, he abased himself by becoming obedient even to the point of death—the death of the cross." For he had said previously:

"each one looking not to his own interest, but to that of others."[5] To this thought he joined the passage cited, for that passage ensues in the following way: "Have the same thoughts in yourselves as were in Christ Jesus." The precise point is this: just as that one did not look after his own interest but ours, in that as the Word he became flesh and lived among us,[6] and he assumed our sins, although he was without sin, so also should we, in imitation of him, willingly bear one another's burdens.

(4) To this consideration the Apostle adds the other, viz., that he became a man. Now we ourselves are men, and we ought to consider that we too could have had or can have the sickness of soul or body which we see in another man. Therefore let us proffer to the one whose weakness we wish to bear what we would want him to proffer to us, if perchance we ourselves were subject to that weakness, and he himself was not. To this pertains the remark of the Apostle himself: "I have become all things to all in order that I might win all,"[7] [and this,] you see, by reflecting upon the fact that even he himself could have been caught in that vice from which he was desiring to free another. For he was trying to do that more by having compassion, not by lying, as some surmise, and especially those who seek the protection of some illustrious example for the needed defense of their own undeniable lies.

(5) Next, one must reflect on this: there is no man who could not have some good quality, albeit hidden, which you do not yet have [and] by which he could doubtlessly be superior to you. This consideration is of importance in crushing and subduing pride, lest you think, because certain of your own good qualities stand out and are conspicuous, that no one else therefore has any good qualities, even hidden and perhaps of greater significance, by which he excells you without your knowing it. For the Apostle enjoins us not to deceive, or rather, not to employ flattery, when he says:

5 Phil 2.4–8.
6 Jn 1.14.
7 1 Cor 9.22.

"not by strife nor by empty conceit, but in lowliness of mind, the one valuing the other as superior to himself."[8] We ought not to value the other in such a way that we do not value him but instead pretend to value him. Rather, let us genuinely consider the possibility of there being something hidden in the other by which he may be superior to us, even though our moral fitness, by which we seem to be superior to the other, is not hidden. These reflections, which crush pride and kindle charity, result in brothers carrying one another's burden, not only with equanimity, but also with the greatest willingness. Moreover, in the case of some man whom one does not know, one must not pass any judgment at all; and no one is known except through friendship. And for this reason do we bear more steadfastly the bad points of our friends, because their good points delight and captivate us.

(6) Accordingly one must not reject the friendship of anyone who offers himself for the association of friendship. [It is] not that he should be received immediately, but he should be desired as one worthy of being received, and he should be so treated that he can be received. For we can say that a person has been received into friendship to whom we dare pour out all our plans. And if there is someone who lacks the courage to offer himself [to us] in the making of friendship, because restrained by some temporal honor or rank of ours, we must come down to him and must offer to him with a certain gentleness and humility of soul what he himself does not of himself dare ask. Although somewhat rarely, of course, nonetheless it does happen from time to time in regard to someone whom we want to receive into friendship that we learn of his bad qualities before we learn of his good, and offended and, as it were, driven back by them, we give up on him and do not pursue an investigation of his good qualities, which are perhaps somewhat hidden. For this reason the Lord Jesus Christ, who desires that we become followers of his example, admonishes us to bear that person's weaknesses so that through the steadfast endurance of love we may be led to certain wholesome qualities which

8 Phil 2.3.

bring us joy—a joy which satisfies. For he says: "The whole have no need of a physician—only the ill."[9] Therefore, we ought not, for the sake of Christ's love, to reject from our lives[10] a person who is ill in possibly every respect, since he can be made whole by the Word of God. [If this is so,] how much less [ought we to reject] him who can appear to us to be totally ill for the reason that we could not endure certain ills of his in the very beginnings of friendship, and, what is more serious, for the reason that we dared, in our displeasure, to pass a rash and prejudiced judgment on the whole man, not fearing the words: "Judge not, that you be not judged," and: "The measure with which you measure, the same will be used in turn to measure you."[11]

Often, however, the good qualities appear first. In regard to these you must also beware of a rash judgment which springs from goodwill, lest, when you think the person completely good, his bad qualities afterwards come to light and find you free of doubt and unprepared, and they shock you all the more, so that the one whom you had thoughtlessly loved you will hate more intensely, which is absolutely wrong. For even if none of his good qualities preceded, and [even if] the first qualities to stand out were the ones [mentioned above] which afterwards appeared bad, still they ought to have been endured until you had done everything with him which ordinarily brings healing to such ills. [This being so], how much more [is it necessary] when those good qualities preceded which ought, like pledges, to constrain us to put up with what comes afterwards!

(7) Therefore it is the very law of Christ that we bear one another's burdens. Moreover, by loving Christ we easily bear the weakness of another, even him whom we do not yet love for the sake of his own good qualities, for we realize that the one whom we love is someone for whom the Lord has died. This is the love which the apostle Paul pressed upon us when he said: "And the weak one will perish because of your knowledge, the brother for whom Christ has died."[12]

---

9 Mt 9.12.
10 *ab animo.*
11 Mt 7.1–2.
12 1 Cor 8.11.

Paul's intent was that if, because of the moral failing whereby he is weak, we love that weak person less, we should then consider the person in relation to him who died on his behalf. For this reason, with great care and the mercy of God having been implored, we must purpose not to neglect Christ because of the weak person, since we ought to love him because of Christ.

72. ON THE ETERNAL TIMES

One can inquire into the meaning of the apostle Paul's expression, *before the eternal times*.[1] For if times, how are they eternal? However, perhaps he wanted us to understand "before all times," because if he had said, "before the times," and not added the adjective *eternal*, we could understand, "before certain times which were preceded by other times." But he preferred to use the word *eternal* rather than *all* for possibly this reason, that time does not begin from time.[2] Or did *the eternal times* signify the *aeuum*,[3] the difference

---

1 Ti 1.2. In the Greek New Testament, the phrase is *pro khronōn aiōniōn* which is rendered by the New American Bible as "in endless ages past."

2 In order to understand Augustine's discussion, we must keep in mind one thing: Augustine apparently thinks what whatever else the apostle Paul may be saying in Ti 1.2, he is saying that God's promise mentioned there is before time. Augustine then tries to give an interpretation of the perplexing Latin reading of the text, *ante tempora aeterna*, which will square with his understanding of the general intent of the whole verse, with a meaningful use of language, and with the requirement of Christian faith that time be a "creature," i.e., created.

3 This is the only place in DD83 that St. Augustine uses this word. It is possible to be translated "eternity," a meaning which it sometimes has in other classical authors, e.g., Cicero. Used in this way, *aeuum* would here replace *aeternitas*, which is Augustine's usual term for eternity. If this is what he means by *aeuum*, then his proposal in the last sentence of Q. 72 would seem to suggest that he had in mind the following exegesis of Ti 1.2. God's promise made "before the eternal times" is a promise made in eterniy, i.e., made by the eternal God, and it is as unchangeable as eternity itself.

   Some later medieval thinkers distinguished *aeuum* from *aeternitas* in rather subtle and interesting ways. Cf. St. Thomas Aquinas, *Quaestiones Quodlibetales* 5.4.7c.

between the latter and time being this: the *aeuum* is
unchangeable, whereas time is subject to change?[4]

73. ON THE SCRIPTURE: "AND HAVING BEEN FOUND IN THE [BODILY] HABIT (HABITUS) OF A MAN"[1]

(1) We use the word *habit* (*habitus*) in many ways. We use
it to refer to a "habit" (*habitus*) of the mind, e.g., the comprehension, strengthened and established by usage, of any
body of knowledge, or to the "habit" (*habitus*) of the body in
respect to which we say that one is more vigorous and robust
than another (the more appropriate and usual word here is
condition [*habitudo*]), or to the "habit" (*habitus*) which is fitted
onto us externally, in respect to which we say that one is
clothed, shod, armored, and other such things. In all these
cases, since indeed this noun is derived from the verb *to have*
(*habere*), it is clear that *habit* (*habitus*) refers to that thing
which is added[2] to someone in such a way that he could just
as well not have it. For knowledge is added to the mind, and
vigor and strength, to the body; and clothing and armor,
there is no doubt but that they are added to our bodily
members. [However, they are added] in such a way that the
mind could be ignorant if no knowledge were added to it,
and the body could be weak and languid without its internal
fluids[3] and strength, and a man could be naked without

---

4 Compare Q. 72 with DCD 12.16 (PL 41.365-66) where Augustine
   discusses the same problem of the *tempora aeterna*. It is interesting to
   note, among other things, that he does not speak of *aeuum* there.

---

1 Phil 2.7. St. Augustine's Latin text reads: "Et *habitu* inuentus ut
   homo" (my emphasis). The meaning of *habitus* is the topic for discussion in this Q. The word *habit* has for the sake of clarity been used
   throughout to translate *habitus*.
2 *accidit.*
3 *sine succo uiscerum.* Another possible translation is "without digestive
   juices." In the two other places in this paragraph in which Augustine
   speaks of the condition of the body, he uses the words *succulentior* and
   succus, which have been translated as "vigorous" and "vigor" respectively.

clothing, and defenseless without armor, and barefoot without shoes. Therefore *habit* (*habitus*) refers to that thing which we have once it is added to us.

Nonetheless, there are differences here, because certain things added to us to produce a habit (*habitus*) are not changed by us, but they themselves change us, while in themselves they remain whole and undisturbed. For example, wisdom, when added to a man, does not itself change, but it does change the man, making a wise man out of a fool. However, certain things are so added that they both change and are changed. For example, food, while itself losing its own character, is turned into our body, and we, refreshed by the food, are changed completely from a state of weakness and languor to one of strength and vigor. But there is a third classification: the very things added are changed in order to produce a habit (*habitus*) and are in some way shaped by the things for which they produce the habit (*habitus*). For example, take clothing: certainly when it has been laid or cast aside, it does not have that shape which it assumes when it is put on and drawn over one's members. Therefore, when put on, it receives a shape which it did not have while off, although the members themselves, with the clothes on or off, remain in the same state. There can also be a fourth classification: those things which are added to produce a habit (*habitus*) neither change the things to which they are added nor are themselves changed by those things. An example is the ring in relation to the finger, if one does not give too much attention to detail here. Nonetheless, this kind [of habit] either comes to nothing, if you should examine it very carefully, or is very, very rare.

(2) Therefore, when the Apostle was speaking of the only begotten Son of God, relative to his divinity and insofar as he is most truly God he said that he is "equal to the Father." This was not for him some kind of "prize to be snatched up,"[4] i.e., another's property, as it were, to be grasped after

---

4 *rapinam* (Phil 2.6). This usually means "robbery" or "plunder." According to G. Richards, the term translates the Greek word which means "prize to be snatched." However, Richards continues, "whether the translator meant that by *rapina* is uncertain, but possible,

if, ever continuing in that equality, he did not wish to be
clothed with humanity[5] and appear to men as a man. Rather,
"he emptied himself," not by changing his own form, but by
"assuming the form of a slave." Nor was he changed or
transmuted into a man at the cost of his enduring
immutability. But yet, by assuming a genuine humanity, he
who assumed it, "having been made into the likeness of
men," not for himself, but for them to whom he had
appeared in his humanity, "was found with the [bodily]
habit (*habitus*), of a man,"[6] i.e., by having humanity (*haben-
do hominem*), he was found as a man. For it was impossible
for him to be found as God by those who had unclean hearts,
and was impossible for them to see the Word with the Father
except by his assuming something which they could see, and
something by which they might be led to that inner light.

However, this [bodily] habit (*habitus*) is not of the first
kind, for human nature, in its own abiding character, has
not changed the nature of God. Nor is it of the second kind,
for it is not the case that man has both changed God and
been changed by him. Nor [is it] of the fourth kind, for he
did not assume humanity in such a way that this humanity
neither changed God nor was changed by him. But rather, it
is of the third kind, for he took up humanity in such a way
that it was transformed for the better, and it was filled out[7]
by him in a manner more inexpressibly excellent and
intimate than is a garment when put on by a man.
Therefore, by this name *habit* (*habitus*), the Apostle has adequately indicated what he meant by saying, "having been
made into the likeness of men," because he became a man
not by way of a transformation, but by way of a habit (*habitus*)
when he was clothed with a humanity which he, in some way
uniting and adapting to himself, joined to [his] immortality
and eternity.

as the word is found meaning 'booty.' " See G. Richards, *A Concise
Dictionary to the Vulgate New Testament* (London 1934), *s.v.* *"rapina."*
These remarks would seem to apply even if Augustine was using the
Old Latin Bible instead of the later Vulgate of St. Jerome.
5 *nollet homine indui.*
6 Phil 2.6–7.
7 *formaretur.*

But, in fact, that habit (*habitus*) which consists in the comprehension of wisdom and knowledge is called *hexis* by the Greeks, but the one whereby we speak of being clothed or armored they prefer to call *skhēma*. For this reason we understand the Apostle to have spoken of the latter kind of habit (*habitus*) since indeed in the Greek texts there is written *skhēmati*,[8] which we have as habit (*habitus*) in our Latin texts. In regard to this term, it is necessary for one to understand that the Word was not changed by the assumption of humanity, just as the members clothed by a garment remain unchanged, although that assumption has joined in an inexpressible manner the thing assumed to the one assuming it. But, insofar as human words can be fitted to the ineffable, in order to prevent one from thinking that God was changed by the assumption of human frailty, it was decided to express that assumption by *skhēma* in Greek and habit (*habitus*) in Latin.[9]

74. ON THE TEXT IN PAUL'S LETTER TO THE COLOSSIANS: "IN WHOM WE HAVE REDEMPTION AND REMISSION OF SINS, WHO IS THE IMAGE OF THE INVISIBLE GOD"[1]

Image and *equality*[2] and *likeness* must be distinguished. For where there is an image, there is necessarily a likeness, but not necessarily an equality; where an equality, necessarily a likeness, but not necessarily an image; where a likeness, not necessarily an image and not necessarily an equality.

Where there is an image, there is necessarily a likeness, but not necessarily an equality. For example, there is in a mirror an image of a man. Because the image has been copied from him, there is also necessarily a likeness; but,

---

8 The Greek text of Phil 2.7 is *kai skhēmati heuretheis anthrōpos*.
9 Compare all the above discussion with Aristotle, *Categories* 15b17–33.

---

1 Col 1.14–15.
2 *aequalitas*. In this Q. *aequalitas* could sometimes better be translated "identity." However, "equality" makes better sense in most of the places in which *aequalitas* occurs, and hence the word has been uniformly translated "equality."

nonetheless, there is no equality, because there is absent from the image much that is present in that thing of which it is the copy.[3] Where there is an equality, there is necessarily a likeness, but not necessarily an image. For example, between two identical[4] eggs there is a likeness because there is an equality, for whatever belongs to one belongs also to the other. Still, there is no image, because neither one is a copy of the other. Where there is a likeness, there is not necessarily an image and not necessarily an equality. For every egg is like every other egg insofar as it is an egg; but a partridge egg, although like a chicken egg insofar as it is an egg, is, nonetheless, neither its image, because it is not a copy of that one, nor its equal, because it is smaller and of another species of living thing.

However, when saying "not necessarily," we clearly understand that the thing is sometimes possible. Therefore there can be some image in which there is also an equality. For example, in parents and children there would be found an image and an equality and a likeness if the age difference were lacking. For the child's likeness has been derived from the parent, so that the likeness may rightly be called an image. As well, the likeness can be so great that it may even rightly be called an equality, except that the parent has come earlier in time. For this reason we understand that sometimes equality has not only a likeness, but also an image, as is clear from the above example. It is also possible sometimes for there to be a likeness and an equality, although no image, as was said of the two identical eggs. It is also possible for there to be a likeness and an image, although not equality, as we have shown with the mirror. There can also be a likeness where there is an equality and an image, as we have mentioned in regard to children, if one disregards the precedence in time of the parents. Thus, in fact, do we say that one syllable is equal to another syllable, although the one precedes and the other follows.

3 Another possible translation here is: "For example, in a mirror there is an image of a man because the image has been copied from him. There is also . . . ."
4 *paribus*.

In God, however, the conditions of time do not obtain, for God cannot be thought of as having begotten in time the Son through whom he has created the times. Hence it follows that not only is [the Son] his image, because he is from [God], and the likeness, because the image,[5] but also the equality is so great that there is not even a temporal distinction standing in the way between them.

75. ON THE INHERITANCE OF GOD

(1) Inasmuch as the Apostle says to the Hebrews: "A testament becomes valid with the death of the one who made the testament,"[1] he therefore asserts that, with Christ's death for us, the New Testament has become valid. Its likeness was the Old Testament, in which the death of the testator was prefigured in the sacrificial victim. Therefore, if one should ask how it is that we, in the words of the same Apostle, are "coheirs with Christ, and sons and heirs of God,"[2] since of course the inheritance is made valid by the death of the deceased, and since an inheritance cannot be understood in any other way, the answer is this: he himself having in fact died, we have become heirs because we were also called his sons. "The sons of the bridegroom," he says, "do not fast while the bridegroom is with them."[3] Therefore we are called his heirs, for he has left the peace of the Church, a peace which we possess in this life, in our possession through faith in the divine plan of salvation [revealed in] time.[4] He has attested to this with these words: "My peace I give to you, peace I leave with you."[5] Moreover, we will become his coheirs when death will be swallowed up into

5 Col 1.15.

1 Heb 9.17.
2 Rom 8.17.
3 Mt 9.15.
4 *per fidem temporalis dispensationis.*
5 Jn 14.27.

victory at the end of the age,[6] for we will then be like him when we see him as he is.[7]

This inheritance is not one which we acquire by the death of his Father, who cannot die, since indeed [the Father] is himself our inheritance, as has been written: "The Lord is the portion of my inheritance."[8] Rather, since the divine mercy has reached even to our very lowly ways of thinking,[9] when we were called while yet children and less suited to contemplating spiritual things, in order that we might strive in some way or other to see what we could not clearly and distinctly see, then the very thing which we were seeing in an obscure [vision] will die when we have begun to see face to face. Accordingly it is to the point to say that what will be laid aside is going to die: "But when there comes what is perfect, what is partial will be laid aside."[10] Thus, for us and in a sense, the Father dies with the obscure [vision], and the very same becomes the inheritance when he is seen face to face, not because he himself dies, but because our imperfect vision of him is entirely done away with by the perfect vision. And yet, unless that earlier vision nourished us, we would not be made capable of the other vision, [which is] the fullest and clearest of all [visions].

(2) Furthermore, if in the case of the Lord Jesus Christ, not insofar as [he is] the Word in the beginning, God with God,[11] but insofar as [he was] a boy, a sound faith[12] admits that he grew in years and wisdom,[13] having preserved as his own that assumption of humanity which he does not hold in common with other men, then it is clear by whose death, as it were, he came to possess the inheritance.[14] For we cannot

---

6 1 Cor 15.54.
7 1 Jn 3.2.
8 Ps 15(16).5.
9 *cogitationes.*
10 1 Cor 13.10.
11 Jn 1.1.
12 *pius intellectus.*
13 Lk 2.40.
14 From these remarks it should be clear that, for St. Augustine, the Christ of Lk 2.40 becomes an heir through the same kind of "death" that makes us eligible for our inheritance which is the Father. That "death" is described in the preceding paragraph as the death of the Father as content of the *uisio in aenigmate* of 1 Cor 13.

ourselves be coheirs with him unless he himself is an heir too.

If, however, soundness of faith[15] does not allow that the Lord's Man[16] possessed first of all a partial vision, then a full vision (although he was said to have increased in wisdom), then he should be understood to be an heir in his body, i.e., the Church, of which we are coheirs, in the same way that we are said to be sons of this Mother, although we ourselves are its component parts.[17]

(3) But again it can be asked by whose death have even we ourselves become the inheritance of God, in accord with the verse: "I will give the nations to you as your inheritance."[18] Assuredly[19] it is [by the death] of this world, which first had possession of us as though it were [our] lord and master. Afterwards, however, when we say: "The world has been crucified to me, and I, to the world,"[20] then Christ possesses us, for that has died which used to possess us. Whenever we renounce it, we die to it, and it, to us.

76. ON THE CLAIM OF THE APOSTLE JAMES: "WOULD YOU LIKE TO KNOW, YOU EMPTY-HEADED MAN, THAT FAITH WITHOUT WORKS IS USELESS?"[1]

(1) The apostle Paul, in proclaiming that a man is justified by faith without works, was not properly understood by those who took this word in such a way that they considered, when once they had believed in Christ, that

---

15 *pietas.*
16 *homo Dominicus.* See above, Q. 36, n. 6.
17 My translation of this section of Q. 75 owes much to that of the French translation of Beckaert in BA 10, pp. 330 and 332.
18 Ps 2.8.
19 *nisi forte.* This expression regularly introduces "an objection or exception *ironically.*" See J. Allen and J. Greenough, *New Latin Grammar* (Boston 1931), p. 337.
20 Gal 6.14.

---

1 Jas 2.20.

they could be saved through faith, even though they carried on their wicked deeds and lived scandalously and dissolutely. For this reason, this passage in the letter before us explains how that particular thought of the apostle Paul is to be understood.[2]

Accordingly [James] prefers to use[3] the example of Abraham, that faith is barren if not accompanied by good works, because the apostle Paul also used the example of Abraham, [but] to prove that a man is justified by faith without the works of the Law.[4] For when the passage mentions the good works of Abraham which attended his faith, it shows adequately that the apostle Paul does not use Abraham to teach the following: that a man is justified by faith without works so that, if someone should believe, good works are not required of him. Rather, [he teaches] that no one should suppose that he has attained by the merit of previous works the gift of the justification which is in faith.

Indeed, in this respect the Jews wanted to vaunt themselves over the gentile believers in Christ, because they were saying that they had attained the grace of the gospel by the merits of the good works which are in the Law. Accordingly there were many Jewish believers who took offense at the grace of Christ being handed on to uncircumcised gentiles. For this reason the apostle Paul says that a man can be justified without works—preceding works. For, having been justified by faith, how can he in turn do anything but what is righteous, although, when earlier he did nothing righteous, he attained the justification of faith, not by the merit of good works, but by the grace of God, which cannot now be barren in him when now he does good works through love? But, should he depart this life soon after having believed, the justification of faith remains with him, though not because of preceding good works, since he attains justification by grace rather than by good works, and not because of subsequent good works, because he is not allowed to continue in this life.

2 Cf. Jas 2.14–26.
3 *magis . . . utitur.*
4 Cf. Rom 4.1–5.

Hence it is clear that the apostle Paul's claim, "For we consider a man to be justified by faith without works,"[5] must not be understood in such a way that we say that a man who has received faith and continues to live is righteous, even though he leads a wicked life.

Consequently the example of Abraham is used both by the apostle Paul, because Abraham was justified by faith without the works of the Law, which he had not received, and by James, because he demonstrates that good works followed on the faith of the same Abraham, [and thus] he shows how the preaching of the apostle Paul is to be understood.

(2) Now those who think that the apostle James's statement is contrary to that of the apostle Paul can consider even Paul himself to be inconsistent, because he says in another place: "For it is not the hearers of the Law who are righteous before God; rather, the doers of the Law will be justified."[6] And in another place [he says]: "but faith which is active through love."[7] And again [he says]: "For if you live according to the flesh, you will die; but if you by the spirit put to death the deeds of the flesh, you will live."[8] As for the deeds of the flesh which must be put to death by the works of the spirit, he shows what they are in another passage with these words: "Now the works of the flesh are obvious: they are acts of fornication, impure deeds, lewdness, idolatry, magic arts, enmities, acts of strife, outbreaks of jealously, angry quarrels, dissensions, factions, envyings, bouts of drunkeness, revellings, and things like these. In regard to these things I am warning you as I have warned you, that those who do such things will not inherit the kingdom of God."[9] And to the Corinthians he says: "Do not be mistaken! Neither fornicators, nor idolaters, nor adulterers, nor the effeminate, nor liers with men, nor thieves, nor the covetous, nor the drunken, nor the foul-mouthed, nor

---

5 Rom 3.28.
6 Rom 2.13.
7 Gal 2.6.
8 Rom 8.13.
9 Gal 5.19–21.

swindlers will inherit the kingdom of God. And such you indeed were; but you have been washed, but you have been made holy, but you have been justified in the name of our Lord Jesus Christ and in the Spirit of our God."[10] With these statements he teaches quite clearly that they have not attained through past good behavior the justification of faith nor through their merits this grace which has been given when he says: "And such you indeed were." However, when he says: "Those who do such things will not inherit the kingdom of God," he adequately shows that moral conduct is required of believers from the moment of their faith. James as well says this, and in all sorts of places the same apostle Paul, with sufficiency and candor, preaches to all believers in Christ the necessity of living aright in order to avoid coming to punishment. Even the Lord himself mentions this when he says: "Not everyone who says, 'Lord,' 'Lord,' will enter into the kingdom of heaven; rather, he who does the will of my Father who is in heaven, he it is who will enter into the kingdom of heaven."[11] And in another place [he says]: "Why do you say to me, 'Lord,' 'Lord,' and do not do what I tell you?"[12] Again [he says]: "As for everyone who hears these my words, I will liken him to a prudent man who built his house upon a rock . . . And as for him who hears these my words and does not act upon them, I will liken him to a foolish man who built his house upon sand."[13]

Wherefore the statements of the two apostles Paul and James are not contrary to one another when the one says that a man is justified by faith without works, and the other says that faith without works is vain. For the former is speaking of the works which precede faith, whereas the latter, of those which follow on faith, just as even Paul himself indicates in many places.

---

10 1 Cor 6.9–11.
11 Mt 7.21.
12 Lk 6.46.
13 Mt 7.24–27.

77. IS FEAR¹ A SIN?

"All emotion is passion;² all coveting is emotion; therefore all coveting is passion. Moreover, when any passion is present in us, we are in a passive state³ by virtue of that passion, and we are in a passive state to whatever extent there is a passion. Therefore when any coveting is present in us, we are in a passive state by virtue of the coveting, and we are in a passive state to whatever extent there is coveting. But, according as we are in a passive state because of passion, no passion is sin. Thus, likewise, if our experience of fear involves a passive state,⁴ it is not sin."

This is like one saying: "If it has two feet, it is not an animal." Therefore, if this does not follow for the reason that there are many two-footed animals, then the former likewise does not follow for the reason that there are many sins in which we are passive. For the objection is this: it does not follow that, if our experience of fear involves a passive state, there is accordingly no sin. But you say that it does follow that, if our experience of fear involves a passive state,

---

1 *Timore.* See above, Q. 33, "On Fear."
2 *passio.* Augustine here uses the word *passio* with a meaning which was nicely expressed by Aristotle in discussing the equivalent Greek term *pathos.* Aristotle says: "I mean by *passions* desire, anger, fear, confidence, envy, joy, affection, hate, distress, jealously, pity—in general, those [feelings] on which pleasure or pain follows" (*Nichomachean Ethics* 1105b21–23). A good English translation of the Greek *pathē* and the Latin *passiones* would be "emotions," which is a word that we have already preempted in Q. 77 for translating the word *perturbatio,* which bears aproximately the same meaning as *passio* in the above-mentioned sense.
3 *patimur.*
4 *patimur.*

it is not sin, although, nonetheless, you concede that there are some sins in which we are passive.[5]

78. ON THE BEAUTY OF PAGAN IDOLS[1]

That supreme art of the omnipotent God through which all things have been made from nothing, which is also called his Wisdom, also works through artists to produce things of beauty and proportion, although they do not produce from nothing, but from some material such as wood or marble or ivory or whatever other kind of material is supplied for the artist's hands. But these artists cannot make something from nothing because they work with existing matter.[2]

---

5 The first paragraph of this Q. contains an argument put forward, perhaps, by a member of St. Augustine's religious community at Hippo. The second paragraph contains Augustine's response. The argument that fear is not a sin has several implicit premises, and it turns on an equivocal use of *passio*. The implicit premises are: (1) no passive state is a sin, and (2) fear is an emotion and hence a passion. Moreover, there is an equivocal use of *passio* which allows the argument to move from the premise that every emotion is a passion to the conclusion that every emotion involves on our part a passive state. There are two senses of *passio* here. The first is discussed above in n. 2. The second is a classical philosophic sense which refers to "the fact or condition of being acted upon or affected by external agency; subjection to external force" (OED s.v. "passion"). With these things in the logical background, the arguer goes on to conclude, through the explicit premise that the experience of fear involves a passive state, that fear is not a sin.
   On the other hand, Augustine's response does not deal with the explicit features of the argument. Rather, he attacks the implicit general premise that no passive state is a sin by asserting that "there are many sins in which we are passive". However, he gives no examples of such sins, and then, in the last sentence of the Q., proceeds to deal with the issue of fear and sin in an *ad hominem* fashion by attacking the consistency of his opponent. All this, reflecting a lack of Augustine's usual care in these matters, might suggest that what we have in this Q. is a brief resume of a much longer discussion which, if handed down to us, would greatly illuminate and enhance an otherwise incomplete response.

---

1 *simulacrorum.*
2 *per corpus.*

Still, nonetheless, those numbers and the harmony of lines which they impress upon matter with material tools[3] are received in their minds from that supreme Wisdom, which has impressed the very numbers and harmony itself in a far more artistic way upon the whole physical universe,[4] which has been made from nothing. In this universe there are also the bodies of living beings which are fashioned from something, i.e., from the elements of the world, but in a manner far more powerful and excellent than when human artists copy the same physical shapes and forms in their own works. For not all the numerical harmony[5] of the human body is found in the statue; but nonetheless, whatever is found there is transferred by the artist's hand from that Wisdom which forms the human body itself by natural processes. Nonetheless, those who fashion or love[6] such works must not be held in high esteem, and for this reason: the soul, when intent on the lesser things which it makes by physical means through the body, clings less to the supreme Wisdom itself from which it derives these powers. The soul employs these powers improperly when it exercises them outside itself, for, by loving those things over which it exercises its powers, the soul neglects their inner, stable form and becomes vainer and weaker. But as for those who have even worshipped such works, the extent of their deviation from the truth can be understood from this: if they worshipped the very bodies of living things, which have been much more excellently fashioned, and of which those works are copies, what would we pronounce more wretched than they?

---

3 *quae per corpus corpori imprimunt.*
4 *uniuerso mundi corpori.*
5 *numerositas.*
6 *diligunt.* See above, Q. 35, n. 6.

79. WHY DID PHARAOH'S MAGICIANS PERFORM CERTAIN MIRACLES IN THE MANNER OF MOSES THE SERVANT OF GOD?[1]

(1) Every soul, to some degree, exercises an authority belonging to it in virtue of a certain private law, and, to some degree, is constrained and ruled by universal laws analogous to public laws.[2] Therefore, since each and every visible thing in this world has an angelic power set over it, as divine Scripture declares, in respect to that thing in its charge the angelic power acts in one way by a sort of private law and is compelled to act in another way before the public, as it were. For the whole is more powerful than the part, because what [the angelic power] does there privately, it is permitted to do only to the degree that the universal law permits.

But each and every soul is the purer in piety when, having received less pleasure in its own private domain, it contemplates all the more the universal law and obeys it willingly and devotedly, for the universal law is the divine Wisdom. But the more each soul finds enjoyment in its own private domain, and, by a disregard for the God who presides over all souls for their benefit and salvation, desires to "play God"[3] in respect to itself or others where possible, loving[4] its own power over itself or others rather than God's power over all, the more foul it is, and the more is it forced in punishment to be subject to the divine laws, as if to public

---

1 Ex 7–8. See Mutzenbecher, pp. xliv–xlvi, for a discussion of the authenticity of this Q. There are several problems about the Q., but Mutzenbecher argues conclusively that the Q. here translated is indeed Augustine's and that there is no convincing manuscript evidence that the length or the content of the Q. should be otherwise than it is here.

2 On "private law" and "public laws," see Berger, p. 532 (*ius priuatum*), and p. 546 (*leges publicae*). Augustine employs the analogy of private law and public law throughout this entire Q. Hence, while it is often tempting, for the sake of a bit more elegance and smoothness, to translate *priuatum* and *publicum* by "personal" and "universal" respectively, I have retained, with few exceptions, the words *private* and *public* in order to preserve the analogy as much as possible in translation.

3 *uult esse pro Deo.*

4 *diligens.* See above, Q. 35, n. 5.

laws. Accordingly, likewise, the more the human soul in its abandonment of God takes delight in self-esteeem or in its own power, the more is it subject to powers of the kind that find enjoyment in themselves and covet being honored as gods by men. To these powers the divine law often allows through that private law, for those who have deserved subservience to them, the performing of even miraculous feats—feats to be displayed among those things over which these powers have been appointed at the lowest level of authority, but nonetheless, a level subject to a high degree of order. But where the divine law commands in the manner of public law, it obviously prevails over private freedom, although even private freedom itself would be nothing apart from the permission of the universal divine power.

Consequently it happens that the holy servants of God, when it is useful for them to have this gift, in accord with the public and, as it were, imperial law, i.e., the power of the most high God, have command óver the lowest powers in order to perform certain visible miracles. For it is God himself who rules in them, whose temple they are, and whom they, having despised their own private power, love most fervently. However, in magical imprecation, in order to make the deception attractive so as to subjugate to themselves those [magicians] to whom they grant such things, [the lowest powers] give effect to their prayers and rituals, and they dispense through that private law what they are allowed to dispense to those who honor them and serve them and keep certain covenants with them in their mystery rites. And when the magicians appear to have command, they frighten their inferiors with the names of more elevated [powers], and exhibit to those looking on with wonder some visible effects which, due to the weakness of the flesh, seem momentous to men unable to behold eternal things which the true God offers through himself to those who love him. However, God permits these things through his righteous government of all things, in order that he may distribute to them the kinds of bondage or the kinds of freedom that are proportioned to their own desires and choices. And if they gain something for their own evil desires when they call upon the most high God, that is a punishment and not a kindness. Indeed not without reason does the Apostle say: "God has given them over to the desires of their hearts."[5] For the opportunity to commit certain sins is a punishment for other preceding sins.

(2) Now as for the Lord's saying: "Satan cannot drive out Satan,"[6] lest perhaps anyone using the name of some of the lowest powers when driving out a demon should think this opinion of the Lord's to be false, let him understand the point of the saying: although Satan does spare the body or the senses of the body, he does so for the purpose of dominating the will of the man in question, in a triumph of greater import, through the error of impiety. Moreover, Satan does not depart [from a man] in this way, but rather, he enters into the innermost part in order to work in him in the manner described by the Apostle: "according to the prince of the power of this air, who is now active in the sons of disobedience.'"[7] For [in this case] Satan was not troubling and tormenting the senses of their bodies, nor was he battering their bodies, but he was reigning in their wills, or better, in their covetousness.

(3) But as for the Lord's claim that false prophets will perform many signs and wonders so as to deceive, if possible, even the elect,[8] clearly he is urging us to understand that even wicked men do certain miracles of a kind which the saints cannot do. Still, they must not be thought to be in a better position with God on that account, for the magicians of the Egyptians were not more acceptable to God than were the Israelite people because the latter could not do what the magicians were doing, although Moses had been able to do greater things by the power of God.[9] However, the reason for not granting these miracles to all the saints is this: to prevent the weak from being deceived by a most pernicious error of supposing that there are greater gifts in such feats

5 Rom 1.26.
6 Mk 3.23.
7 Eph 2.2.
8 Cf. Mt 24.24.
9 Cf. Ex 7–12.

than in the works of righteousness whereby one obtains eternal life. Accordingly the Lord prohibits his disciples from rejoicing on this account when he says: "Do not rejoice in this, that the spirits are subject to you; rather, rejoice in this, that your names are written in heaven."[10]

(4) When, therefore, magicians do things of a kind which the saints sometimes do, indeed their deeds appear to the eye to be alike, but they are done both for a different purpose and under a different law. For the former act seeking their own glory; the latter, the glory of God. Again, the former act through certain things granted to the powers in their own sphere, as if through business arrangements and magic arts[11] of a private nature; but the latter, by a public administration at the command of him to whom the entire creation is subject. For it is one thing for an owner to be compelled to give his horse to a soldier, it is another thing for him to hand it over to a buyer, or to give or lend it to someone. And just as a great many evil soldiers, whom imperial discipline condemns, terrify some owners with the ensigns of their commander and extort from them something which is not in accord with public law, so evil Christians, or schismatics, or heretics sometimes exact through the name of Christ or Christian words or sacraments something from the powers who have been enjoined to defer to the honor of Christ. However, when the powers submit to the bidding of evil men, they do so willingly in order to seduce men, in whose error they rejoice. Consequently it is one thing for magicians to perform miracles, another for good Christians, and another for evil Christians. Magicians do so through private contracts, good Christians through a public righteousness,[12] and evil Christians through the "ensigns" or symbols[13] of this public righteousness.

---

10 Lk 10.20.
11 *ueneficia.* A number of manuscripts read *beneficia,* a reading which would easily fit into the context. The sentence would then be translated: "as if through business arrangements and services of a private nature."
12 *per publicam iustitiam.*
13 The phrase *ensigns or symbols* represents an attempt to capture in translation at least two of the nuances of the single Latin word *signa.* A

Moreover, it is no wonder that these "ensigns" are efficacious when put to use by these. Even at the time when they are unlawfully appropriated by strangers who have not enlisted at all in this army, nonetheless they are efficacious because of the repute of [its] most distinguished commander. Such a stranger was that one of whom the disciples told the Lord that he was casting out demons in his name, although he was not following him along with them.[14] But when such [demonic] powers do not defer to these "ensigns," God himself intervenes[15] in hidden ways when he judges it to be just and useful. Indeed none of the spirits dares in any way to despise these symbols, for they tremble in fear at them, wherever they observe them. Rather, although men do not understand, God commands otherwise either in order to throw the wicked into confusion when such a thing is necessary, as we read in the Acts of the Apostles concerning Sceva's sons, to whom the unclean spirit says: "Jesus I know, and Paul I am acquainted with; but as for all of you, who are you?";[16] or [he does so] in order to admonish the good to advance in faith and to exercise this power, not in a boastful way, but in a way that will bring benefit; or [he does so] to discern the gifts of the members of the Church, as the Apostle says: "Not all are workers of miracles, are they? Not all have the gifts of healing, do they?"[17] Consequently these are the most common reasons, as was said, for the divine command, unknown to men, that such spirits refrain from obeying the will of men when these symbols are employed.

---

few sentences above the term means military "ensigns," i.e., the standards which identified each Roman legion. Here the term is better translated "symbols," "signs," "marks," "tokens," or some such thing. The *signa* in question are clearly the *signa* mentioned a few lines earlier, viz., the "name of Christ" and "Christian words and sacraments." However, since Augustine still seems to have the military metaphor in mind, and since he will again pick up that metaphor explicitly in the very next paragraph, it seems best to translate *signa* at this point by the disjunctive phrase *ensigns or symbols*.

14 Lk 9.49.
15 *prohibet.*
16 Acts 19.14–15.
17 1 Cor 12.30.

(5) However, for the wicked to inflict harm on the good in this present time,[18] as they often do, they receive[19] power over them, [but a power which works] to the greater advantage of the good due to the exercise of patience. Accordingly the Christian soul is ever watchful in its tribulations to follow the will of its Lord, lest it secure for itself, by resisting the decree of God, a more severe judgement. For the Lord himself, living as a man, said something to Pontius Pilate that Job as well could have said to the devil: "You would have no power over me except it had been given you from above."[20] Therefore, not the will of him whose power for evil over the good is a derived power, but the will of him from whom this power is derived ought to be most precious to us: "because tribulation produces patience, and patience, what is tested and tried.[21] But what is tested and tried [produces] hope, and hope does not put to shame, because the love of God is poured out in our hearts through the Holy Spirit who has been given to us."[22]

---

18 *temporaliter*.
19 *accipiunt*. The sentence in which this word occurs is very difficult, more from the point of view of its teaching rather than its syntax. *Accipere* can be translated "to take" or "to receive." The use of either possible translation gives a decidedly different flavor to the sentence. Taken by itself, it would be difficult to know how to translate the sentence. However, the context of the sentence appears to settle the question in favor of "to receive."
20 Jn 19.11.
21 *probationem*.
22 Rom 5.3-5.

80. *AGAINST THE APOLLINARIANS*[1]

(1) The heretics who are said to have been called Apollinarians after a certain Apollinaris,[2] who was their founder, maintained that our Lord Jesus Christ, insofar as he deigned to become man, did not have a human mind. Some, clinging to them and hearing them with eagerness, have indeed taken delight in that perversity whereby [Apollinaris] diminished the human nature[3] in God by saying that he did not have a

---

1 See above, Q. 36, n. 6.
2 Apollinaris of Laodicea (ca. 310–ca. 390). For several discussions which, taken together, give a view of his life, works, and teachings, see A. Harnack, *History of Dogma*, vol. 4 (New York 1961), pp. 149–63; Quasten, 3.377–73; and H. Wolfson, *The Philosophy of the Church Fathers*, vol. 1, *Faith, Trinity and Incarnation* (Cambridge, Mass. 1956), pp. 433–44.

    Quasten describes Apollinaris as "the author of the first great Christological heresy" (Quasten, 3.377). Apollinaris denied that Christ had assumed a human mind *(nous)* or rational soul *(psykhē logikē),* although he affirmed that he did assume a body possessed of its own distinct animating principle or animal soul *(psykhē alogos* or *psykhē sarkikē).* (But see Wolfson, pp. 433–44). For Apollinaris, the place and function of the absent human *nous* in Christ were taken over by the *Logos* himself, who became "the principle of self-consciousness and self-determination . . . in this *sarx*" (Harnack, p. 151). This denial of the full humanity of Christ was founded upon a number of arguments. The most recurrent theological argument appears to have been the following. Arguing, apparently, from two assumptions: (1) that God, and only God, can save, and (2) that God saves only that which he assumes (the famous principle of the Latin theologians, *quod non est assumptum, non est sanatum),* Apollinaris concluded that Christ could not save us if he were, in addition to being divine, a *complete* man with a rational soul. For if it is the addition of mind which, with the body and its animal soul, produces the concrete, individual, complete human person, and if the man thus understood cannot be divine because fully man, then the *Logos* could not have become fully man without at the same time losing the wherewithal to save man. For what the *Logos* assumes must become divine in order to be the instrument of salvation. But a *complete* man cannot, in the assumption, become divine without ceasing to be a complete man and without thus jeopardizing our opportunity for salvation.
3 *hominem.*

mind, i.e., a rational soul, which, as intellect,[4] distinguishes man from the animals. But upon realizing that it was necessary, if this is so, to agree to the supposition that the only begotten Son of God, the Wisdom and Word of the Father through whom all things were made, had assumed in the form of a human body only that part of man which is had in common with the animals,[5] they were then uneasy with themselves. Nonetheless [their displeasure was] not to the point of correction so as to return to the way of truth and to confess that man in his entirety was assumed by the Wisdom of God with no diminution of nature. Rather, having exercised a greater insolence by depriving him of even the very soul[6] of man and all that is proper to man, they have said that he had assumed only human flesh. Making use even of the witness of the gospel—or better yet, by not understanding its meaning—they presume in their perverseness to contend against Catholic truth by referring to the Scripture passage: "The Word became flesh and lived among us."[7] For, under the influence of this passage, they think that the Word has been joined to and compounded with the flesh in such a way that there is nothing there, whether the mind or even the human soul, which stands between them.

(2) In answering them, it is first of all necessary to say that the passage in question was set down in the gospel in the way in which it was because that assumption of human nature by the Lord extended even to the visible flesh, and in the entire unity [resulting from] the assumption, the Word is the principal element, but the flesh, last and farthest removed. Accordingly, wishing for our sake to commend the

---

4 *animum*. St. Augustine, in this Q., uses several terms to denote what is variously called *nous, pneuma,* or *psykhē logikē* by the Apollinarians. Augustine speaks of *mens* ("mind"), *anima rationalis* ("rational soul"), and *animus* ("mind" or "intellect"). In a number of places he also speaks simply of *anima,* but he clearly means *anima rationalis. Anima* in this case is not equivalent to *psykhē alogos* or *psykhē sarkikē,* notions to which Augustine assigns the name *bellua* (literally, "beast," "brute," "lower animal"). See below, n. 5.

5 *belluam* ("that part of man which is had in common with the animals").

6 *animam*.

7 Jn 1.14.

abject humility of God who humbled himself, and expressing the depth to which his humility extended, the evangelist
spoke of the Word and flesh, while passing over the nature of
the soul, which is inferior to the Word, but more excellent
than the flesh. For he commends the humility in a greater
way by saying, "The Word became flesh," than by saying,
"The Word became man." For if these words are given ex-
cessive consideration, someone else no less perverse can so
misrepresent our faith with these words that he might say
that the Word himself was transformed and changed into
flesh and that the Word ceased to be, because the Scripture
says: "The Word became flesh." Analogously, human
flesh, when it becomes ash, it not flesh and ash, but ash
resulting from flesh. Moreover, according to a manner of
speaking and rather widespread usage, whatever becomes
what it was not ceases to be what it was.

Nonetheless, we do not understand these words in this
way. Rather, even [the Apollinarians] themselves, along
with us, so understand them that, the Word remaining what
he is, the Scriptural affirmation that "the Word became
flesh" derives from his assumption of the form of a slave[8]
and not from his transformation into that form by way of
some alteration. Finally, wherever the flesh is mentioned
and the soul not mentioned, if the passage must be
understood in such a way that one not suppose a soul to be
there, neither will those have souls of whom it was said:
"And all flesh will see the salvation of God",[9] and of whom
it was said in the Psalm: "Hear my prayers, all flesh will
come to you";[10] and of whom it was said in the gospel:
"Even as you have given him power over all flesh, in order
that everything which you have given him might not perish,
but have eternal life."[11] From this one perceives that men
are usually signified simply by the name *flesh*. As a consequence, in accord with this manner of speaking, even the
passage, "The Word became flesh," can be understood as

---

8 Cf. Phil 2.7.
9 Is 40.5; Lk 3.6.
10 Ps 64(65).3.
11 Jn 17.2.

saying nothing else but, "The Word became man." For one commonly understands man (the whole) when only the soul (the part) is named, as in the verse: "Such and such a number of souls went down into Egypt."[12] Likewise again, in terms of the part-whole relationship, man (the whole) is understood when even the flesh (the part) is named, as in the cases cited.

(3) Hence we respond to this objection of theirs, which they propose from the gospel, in a way which allows no man to be so lacking in understanding that he thinks that we are compelled by this text to believe and confess that the mediator between God and men, the man Christ Jesus,[13] did not have a human soul. In the same way I inquire how they respond to objections so palpable as ours, whereby we show through countless places in the gospel writings what was narrated of him by the evangelists, viz., that he was found with feelings which are impossible without a soul. Indeed I do not bring forward those things which, so many in number, the Lord himself mentions: "My soul is dejected to the point of death";[14] and: "I have the power to lay down my soul and to take it back again";[15] and: "There is no greater love than the love of him who lays down his soul for his friends,"[16] which one who stubbornly contradicts me can claim were said in a figurative way by the Lord, just as, manifestly, he has said many things in parables. For, even if this is not so, nonetheless, there is no need to act contentiously where we have the gospel writers' historical accounts through which we learn of his birth from the Virgin Mary, and his arrest by the Jews, and his beating, and his crucifixion and death, and his burial in the tomb—all facts which are unintelligible without a body. Nor would anyone, even the most foolish, say that these things are to be taken in a fictitious or figurative sense, since these things have been related by those who have narrated the events as they

---

12 Gn 46.22, 27.
13 Cf. 1 Tm 2.5.
14 Mt 26.38.
15 Jn 10.18.
16 Jn 15.13.

remembered them. Therefore, just as those events give witness that he had a body, so those feelings, which cannot exist in anything but a soul, indicate that he had a soul. Nonetheless, we read about these feelings in the reports of the same evangelists: Jesus was astonished,[17] was angered,[18] sorry,[19] was gladdened,[20] and many such things without number. Likewise, as well, the joint functions of the body and the soul make [this point] clear. For instance, he was hungry;[21] he slept;[22] tired from his journey, he sat down;[23] and other such things.

Indeed they cannot say [in response] that even the Old Testament mentions the wrath and the joy of God and several emotions of this kind, and that, nonetheless, it does not follow on that account that one must believe God to have had a soul. For those things were said by way of prophetic imagery, not by way of historical presentation. For God is also said to have members: hands, feet, eyes, a face, and similar things; and just as these do not indicate that he has a body, so neither do the former, a soul. Moreover, just as the historical accounts mention Christ's hands and head and other things which indicate his body, so likewise what is reported of the feelings of a soul by the same narrative content makes known his soul. But it is foolish to believe the evangelist's account that he ate and not to believe the account that he was hungry. For [granted,] it does not follow that everyone who eats is hungry (for we read that even an angel ate,[24] but we do not read that he was hungry), nor that everyone who is hungry eats (if he either restrains himself due to some obligation or lacks food and the means to eat). Nevertheless, when the gospel writer records both occurrences,[25] one must believe that the two [happened], because,

---

17 Cf. Mt 8.10.
18 Cf. Mk 3.5.
19 Cf. *ibid.*
20 Cf. Jn 11.15.
21 Cf. Mt. 4.2.
22 Cf. Mt. 8.24.
23 Cf. Jn 4.6.
24 Gn. 18.8; Tb 12.19.
25 Cf. Mt 4.2, 9.11.

as a witness to the events, [the writer] has selected two which actually took place. Now, just as the fact that he ate is unintelligible without a body, so the fact that he went hungry was impossible without a soul.

(4) Furthermore, that empty and absurd pretence does not frighten us—that pretence whereby, in their invidious resistance, they make this claim: therefore [the Lord] was subjected to necessity if he experienced these genuine feelings of the soul.[26] We have, to be sure, an easy response: therefore he was subjected to necessity because he was arrested, beaten, crucified, and then died! As a consequence, if they wish, let them finally understand, without obstinacy, that he freely[27] assumed by providential choice[28] the passions[29] of the soul,[30] i.e., feelings, but genuine feelings for all that. [And let them understand that he did so] in the same manner as he assumed by providential choice, without any necessity, the passive character[31] of the body. Just as we ourselves do not die by choice,[32] so also are we not born by choice. However, he effected[33] both by choice, as was fitting, and, nonetheless, he did so in a completely genuine manner. Therefore, just as no one uses the term *necessity* to part either us or [the Apollinarians] from belief in a completely genuine passivity through which his body is manifested, so also no one deters us with the same term *necessity* from believing in a completely genuine, affective nature[34] through which we recognize his soul. Nor should [this term] deter [the

---

26 The theological difficulty here is this. Necessity (or compulsion) go hand in hand, as do freedom and activity. God is active and free; but if he subjects himself in the incarnation to the passivity of affective (feeling) states by assuming a human soul, then he who is free has destroyed his own freedom—an unacceptable notion for the Apollinarians.
27 *ut placuit.*
28 *uoluntate dispensationis.* See the entry for *dispensatio* in A. Souter, *a Glossary of Later Latin to 600 A.D.* (Oxford, 1957), p. 108.
29 *passiones.* See above, Q. 77, n. 2.
30 *animi.*
31 *passiones.* See above, Q. 77, n. 5.
32 *uoluntate.*
33 *exhibuit.*
34 *affectiones.*

Apollinarians] from consenting to Catholic faith, provided they are not deterred by the deadly disgrace of an opinion in need of change which, in spite of its falsity, has been long and rashy defended.

81. ON QUADRAGESIMA AND QUINQUAGESIMA[1]

(1) All instruction in wisdom, the purpose of which is the education of men, is for distinguishing the creator and the creature, and worshipping the one as Lord and confessing the other as subject. And the creator is God, from whom are all things, through whom are all things, and in whom are all things,[2] and he is threfore a trinity—Father, Son, and Holy Spirit. The creature, however, as soul, is partly invisible; as body, partly visible. To the invisible the number 3 is assigned. For this reason, we are commanded to love God in a three-fold way: "with the whole heart, with the whole soul, and with the whole mind."[3] To the body the number 4 is assigned on account of its clearly evident make-up,[4] which consists of the hot and the cold, the moist and the dry. Consequently the number 7 is assigned to the creature taken as a whole. Wherefore all instruction which distinguishes and separates the creator and the creature is suggested by the number 10.

This instruction, inasmuch as it is expressed through the movements of bodies in time, rests upon believing, and it nourishes its little children by an authoritative record[5] of transient events, as if by milk, so that it might ready them for the contemplation which does not come and go, but which remains ever the same. With this [instruction], and possessed of the record of the things carried out by God in time for the salvation of men (or to be carried out and now proclaimed as future), each one, if he has persevered in the faith and trusted in the promises, and if he has taken care to

1 Cf. Q. 57.
2 Rom 11.36.
3 Mt 22.37.
4 *naturam.*
5 *auctoritate* (i.e., the Bible).

fulfill with an indefatigable love what divine authority commands, will conduct his life, subject to necessity and time, uprightly. This life is designated by the number 40, since the number 10, which suggests the whole body of instruction, taken four times, i.e., multiplied by the number which is assigned to the body (because through the movement of material bodies is carried out the providential course of events[6] on which faith rests, as was said a moment ago), produces the number 40. Thus [this instruction] brings about a stable wisdom independent of time. This wisdom is designated by the number 10, in order that 10 may be added to 40, because the whole factors of the number 40, added together, produce 50. Moreover, the number 40 has these whole factors: first, *1* times 40, then *2* times 20, *4* times 10, *5* times 8, *8* times 5, *10* times 4, and *20* times 2. Therefore the sum of 1 + 2 + 4 + 5 + 8 + 10 + 20 is 50.[7] Consequently, just as the number 40, when its whole factors are added together, generates an additional 10 and becomes 50, so the time of faith in what has been done and will be done for our salvation, when lived with wholeness of life,[8] brings about an intellectual grasp of immutable wisdom, so that instruction [in wisdom] may be supported not only by belief, but also by understanding.

(2) For this reason, although we are the sons of God, nonetheless, that which is now the Church, prior to the appearance of what we will be, lives in toils and afflictions, and in her the just man lives by faith.[9] For, "except you believe," it is said, "you will not understand."[10] And this is the time wherein we groan and suffer pain, awaiting the redemption of our bodies,[11] which is celebrated at Quadragesima.[12] "However, we know that when it appears,

---

6 *administratio geritur.*

7 See above, Q. 57, n. 9.

8 *cum aequitate uitae.* Note that Augustine's term for "whole factors" is *partes aequales.*

9 Rom 1.17.

10 Is 7.9 (according to the Septuagint).

11 Rom 8.23.

12 *Quadragesima,* meaning "fortieth [day]," is the traditional name for the forty-day Lenten period.

we will be like him, because we will see him as he is,"[13]
when 10 will be added to 40 so that we merit not only believing those things which belong to faith, but also understanding
truth in its transparency. Such a Church, in which there will
be no mourning, no commingling of evil men, no iniquity,
but rather, gladness, peace, and joy, is prefigured by the
observance of Quinquagesima.[14] Consequently, after our
Lord arose from the dead, and after a period of forty days
with his disciples, a period whose number suggests the very
same plan of salvation in time which is the sphere of faith, he
ascended into heaven,[15] and after another ten days had
elapsed, he sent the Holy Spirit.[16] The purpose of this was
the addition of 10 to 40, not for the beholding of the human
and temporal, but for the beholding of the divine and eternal
by a sort of breathing forth[17] and kindling of love and charity. And therefore now must we mark this total, i.e., the
number of the fifty days, by a celebration of gladness.

(3) Moreover, our Lord also signified these two times,
i.e., the one of toil and care, the other of joy and security, by
the nets cast into the sea. For, before his passion, there is the
story of the net cast into the sea. They took so many fish that
they could scarcely haul them to shore, and the nets broke.[18]
In fact, the nets were not cast to the right-hand side, for the
Church has many wicked men in the present time, nor to the
left-hand side, for she has good men as well, but in every
direction, to signify the commingling of the good and the
wicked. As for the nets having been broken, that signifies
that many heresies have sprung up because of the violation
of charity. After the resurrection, however, when he wanted
to give a preview of the Church which is to be, where all are
going to be perfect and holy, he commanded the nets to be
cast to the right-hand side. They caught one hundred and

13 1 Jn 3.2.
14 *Quinguagesima,* meaning "fiftieth [day]," is a traditional name for the
period extending from Easter to Pentecost.
15 Acts 1.1-9.
16 Acts 2.1-4.
17 *spiramento.* Note that the word *spiritus,* used of the Holy Spirit, also
means "breath."
18 Lk 5.6-7.

fifty-three huge fish, [and] the disciples were astonished that, although the fish were so large, the nets did not break.[19] The great size of the fish signifies the greatness of wisdom and righteousness. However, their number [signifies] the very instruction which, we said, is designated by the number 50 and is brought to perfection both by the divine plan of salvation in time and by rebirth in eternity. For [in eternity], since there will be no need for physical supports, both faith and wisdom will be possessed[20] by the mind. Since we have said that the number 3 is assigned to the mind,[21] then we take 50 three times and get 150, to which 3, a trinity, is added, because [the number 3], in all its perfection, has been hallowed by the name of the Father and the Son and the Holy Spirit. The result is 153, which is the number of fish found on the right-hand side of the fishermen.

82. ON THE SCRIPTURE: "FOR WHOM THE LORD LOVES, HE REBUKES, AND HE SCOURGES EVERY SON WHOM HE RECEIVES"[1]

(1) Many who murmur under the discipline[2] of God raise a question when they see the righteous often experiencing serious difficulties in this life. [They murmur] as if no benefit comes to the righteous for serving God, because either they suffer the common hardships—hardships involving indiscriminately [their] bodies and injuries and insults and all other things which mortals consider evil—or they suffer even greater hardships than others on account of the word of God and righteousness. [The latter, being] irksome to sinners, stirs up tumultuous outbreaks or plots or enmities against its proclaimers.

---

19 Jn 21.6–11.
20 *continebitur.*
21 *animo* (the dative singular form of *animus*). Earlier (p. 212) it was to the *anima* that Augustine assigned the number 3.

---

1 Heb 12.6. Cf. Prv 3.12.
2 *Disciplina.* This word is the same as the one translated "instruction" in Q. 81 above.

The answer to this objection is that if this life were all that men had, then it would seem, not altogether absurdly, that the righteous life is of no benefit or that it is positively harmful. However, there has been no lack of those who weighed the sweetness of righteousness and its inner joy against all the physical hardships and troubles which the human race suffers because of this mortal state—even against all those things which, on account of righteousness itself, are most unjustly imagined against those who live righteously. [They have done so, and,] the hope of a future life having been laid aside, they [nonetheless] experienced torment out of a love for truth with more delight and more gladness than banquet the wanton out of a passion for drunkenness.

(2) Nonetheless, however, there is a reply to those who think God unjust when they see the righteous in pain and toil. And if they dare not call God unjust, certainly they consider him either to be without concern for the affairs of men, or to have determined once for all the destinies of the fates,[3] to which not even he himself does anything contrary lest he be supposed to distrub through capriciousness the order arranged by himself or they are of some other opinion, that God, because impotent in some respect, cannot prevent these evils from happening to the righteous. To these it must be said that there would have been no possibility for righteousness among men if God had no concern for the affairs of men. For none of this righteousness [realized by] men, righteousness which the human soul can possess by doing good and lose by sinning, would be impressed upon the soul unless there were some immutable righteousness, which would be found undiminished by the righteous when they turned themselves toward it, and would be left undiminished by sinners when they turned themselves from its light. The unchangeable righteousness is obviously of God, nor would he direct it to the illumination of those converted to himself if he had no concern for the affairs of men. However, if he allowed the righteous to endure harsh things for the reason that he did not wish to go against the order of things deter-

---

3 *necessitates fatorum.*

mined by himself, not even he himself would be just—not because he wishes to preserve his decreed order, but because he has so determined the order of things that the righteous are afflicted with undeserved punishments. But whoever holds the opinion that God is in some respect incapable of repelling the evils which the righteous suffer, he is therefore foolish, because he does not understand that, just as it is impious to say that God is unjust, so is it impious to deny that he is all-powerful.

(3) Having established in the brief period of time allotted to the question posed that it belongs to the most pernicious iniquity to doubt that even God himself is just as well as omnipotent, no more probable reason occurs why righteous men so often suffer hardships in this life unless that it be to their advantage. For there is one righteousness, the present righteousness of men, which is directed to receiving eternal salvation; there is another righteousness, the past righteousness of man situated in paradise, which ought to have been directed to keeping and not losing the same eternal salvation. For just as the righteousness of God consists in prescribing what is beneficial and in distributing punishments to the disobedient and rewards to the obedient, so the righteousness of man consists in obeying these beneficial prescriptions. However, since happiness is in the soul in the same way that health is in the body, just as in the body itself one medicine is prescribed to prevent the loss of good health, but another, to recover lost health, so, in regard to the whole condition of man, one set of prescriptions was previously given to prevent the loss of immortality, and another is now prescribed for getting it back.

Continuing the analogy of the body's health, if someone should fall ill by not complying with the doctor's prescriptions, which are meant for the preservation of the same good health, he then takes other prescriptions so that he can get well. These are often not sufficient, if the illness is of a certain character, unless the doctor should employ certain aids causing, very frequently, rude and painful effects, which aids, nonetheless, are efficacious in the recovery of health. The result is that a man, although now obeying the doctor, nonetheless still suffers pains, not only from the unhealed ailment itself, but also from the medicinal aid. Likewise man, having fallen through sin into the diseased and un-happy mortality of this life because he did not want to com-ply with the first prescription for preserving and holding onto eternal salvation, has taken in his diseased condition the second set of prescriptions. If he complies with these, indeed not absurdly is he now said to live righteously, but nonetheless, [there are] annoyances which he suffers, [and they] are the result of either the illness itself, not yet healed, or the medicinal aid. This aid is indicated in our text: "For whom the Lord loves, he rebukes, and he scourges every son whom he receives."

However, those who live unjustly by not complying with the prescriptions most suited to salvation are repeatedly aggravating their illnesses. Either they suffer even in this life, due to the illnesses, the countless hardships and pains of [their] afflictions, or, through punishments used to touch and bring pain to the unhealthy part in which the sickness resides, they are admonished in mercy to become whole through the grace of God by turning to the healing remedy. If they despise all these things, i.e., the prescriptions of words and pains, then they will merit after this life a just [and] eternal damnation. Accordingly that person can say that these things happen unfairly who, thinking that this life is the only life, does not believe that the things foretold by God are going to be and [thus] will pay more severe penalties for his persistence in his sins and unbelief.

83. ON MARRIAGE, IN THE LIGHT OF THE LORD'S CLAIM: "IF ANYONE SHOULD DIVORCE HIS WIFE, EXCEPT FOR REASON OF FORNICATION"[1]

If the Lord admits fornication as the only grounds for divorce in marriage, and if he does not forbid divorce in pagan marriages, then it follows that paganism should be

---

1 Mt 5.32.

considered fornication. Moreover, it is clear that the Lord, when speaking in the gospel of the dissolution of marriage, makes an exception only for the grounds of fornication. However, divorce in pagan marriages is not forbidden, because when the Apostle advised in respect to this matter that the believer not divorce the unbelieving spouse who wanted to stay with him, he said: "I myself speak, not the Lord."[2] The purpose for this was to understand that the Lord does not indeed command divorce, lest the Apostle's advice seem contrary to his commandment, but that he does, nonetheless, permit it, so that no one is bound by the compulsion[3] of a commandment in that matter, but may act freely in accord with the plan of [his] choosing.[4]

However, if anyone should assert that the Lord admits as a reason for leaving one's spouse only that fornication which is commonly called fornication, i.e., what is perpetrated through illicit intercourse, one can affirm that the Lord, when talking about this matter, had spoken of both a believing husband and a believing wife. Hence, if both are believers, then neither one is permitted to leave the other, except for reason of fornication, which cannot be understood to be paganism, because both spouses are believers. Indeed the Apostle seems to make this same distinction when he says: "But to these who are married, I command—not I, but the Lord—that the wife not leave the husband. But if she does leave, let her remain unmarried or be reconciled to her husband."[5] Here it is likewise understood that if the wife has left the husband for that one reason which alone permits separation from the spouse, she ought to abide strictly in the unmarried state. But if she does not remain continent, [she ought] to be reconciled to her husband, either after he has been straightened out or when she can at least put up with him, rather than marry another. Moreover, he follows this up and says: "and the husband should not divorce his

---

2 1 Cor 7.12.
3 *necessitate.*
4 *consilii uoluntate.*
5 1 Cor 7.10–11.

wife,"[6] declaring in brief the same pattern for the man
which he was prescribing for the woman. Having recommended these things on the basis of the Lord's commandment, he concludes: "But to the others I myself speak, not
the Lord. If any brother has an unbelieving wife, and she
agrees to live with him, he should not divorce her; and if a
woman has an unbelieving husband, and he agrees to live
with her, she should not divorce the husband."[7] We are here
given to understand that the Lord's comment about these
means that neither spouse may divorce the other if they
should both be believers.

6 1 Cor 7.11.
7 1 Cor 7.12–13.

INDICES

A page number followed by "n." refers to a footnote on the page in question. A page number followed by "(n.)" refers to both the text and to a note on the page in question. For example, "7 n." refers to a note on p. 7, while "7(n.)" refers both to the text and to a note on p. 7.

Aaron, 119

Abel, his murder by Cain fore-shadows Christ's death at the hands of Jews, 104

Abraham, 105, 106, 119, 176, 177; his two sons allegorically repre-sent the two Covenants, 104-5, 136; father of the people of faith, 118; the use of his example by the apostles James and Paul, 194-95

Abraham's Bosom, 154, 157

Academics, 30 n.

Achab (Ahab), deceived by the false prediction of false prophets, 92(n.)

Action, it is thoughtless without knowledge, 106

Adam, 90, 105, 106, 136, 137, 145, 163 n., 168; his fall possibly resulted in his losing the image and likeness of God, 85; as the "inner man" and the "outer man," 85; the first or "earthly" man, 85; did not merit death ex-cept by sinning, 146

Adoption, by it do we become sons of God, 151, 156

Advent, of the Lord, 75, 106, 107, 128; see also Second Coming

Aeuum, it is unchangeable, 185-86

Africa, 2, 11, 14, 16, 17

Age(s), the Lord's advent was in the period of mankind's youth, 75(n.); the Lord's advent was in the sixth age of mankind, 75(n.),

105, 128; the Old and New Test-ament economies were adapted and suited to the ages of the human race, 90; parallel be-tween the ages of an individual and those of the entire human race, 90, 105; the six ages of the human race, 105-6, 128; man-kind's first age is dominated by the five bodily senses, 132-33; mankind's old age is character-ized by an obscured vision of soul, 162; see also Period(s)

Alexander of Aphrodisias, 8(n.)

Alfaric, P., 31 n.

Allen, J., 193 n.

Ambrosiaster, 9(n.)

Angel(s), the composition of their bodies, 82(n.); the highest live by spirit but the lowest by soul, 152(n.), 154; their freedom from pain, 156-57; an angelic power is set over each and every visible thing in this world, 200

Animal(s), those without reason cannot be happy, 39; in what sense they have soul, 40; man's superiority to, 43-44; can "en-joy" but not "use" anything, 56

Animal Man, he who is carried along by the dissolute lascivi-ousness of his soul, 153-54

Anna, 126

Anti-Pelagian Writings, 24(n.)

Appelles, 9(n.)

Apollinarians, the heresy of, 206-7;

Create, God has created all things in accord with the ideas, 80-81(n.); individual things are created in accord with ideas or reasons unique to themselves, 81; by his supreme Art has God created all things from nothing, 198; *see also* Created, Creator, and Creature

Created, on God and the, 47; nothing created is eternal, 47; no created thing animated by a soul is immortal, much less eternal, 47; *see also* Create, Creator, and Creature

Creation, see Create, Created, Creator, and Creature

Creator, in his mind exist the ideas of all created things, 80-81(n.); is God, from whom, through whom, and in whom are all things, 212; is a trinity, 212; *see also* Create, Created, and Creature

Creature, his deliverance from the bondage to sin, 149-57; the ambiguity of the term, 149 n., cf. 157 n.; refers to whatever has been created by the Father through the Son in the unity of the Holy Spirit, 150; is whatever in us suffers pain and anguish in the travail of this life, 150; expectantly awaits the revelation of the sons of God, 150-51; its subjection to vanity and sin, 152; every crature is recapitulated in man, 153-54; spiritual creatures are not subject to pain and misery but are perfectly happy, 157; its number is 7, p. 212; *see also*

Create, Created, and Creator
Cross of Christ, 51
Cyprian, 125 n.

Damnation, in the absence of God's mercy we as sinners deserve nothing other than eternal damnation, 161; awaits those who despise the healing remedy offered by God's grace, 218

David, 105, 106, 126; and the prophet Nathan, 116 n., 118-19; his place in Christ's genealogy, 118-19

Davies, P., 7 n.

Death, neither it nor any manner of dying is to be feared by the man of good and upright life, 51; the symbolic meaning of the day of John the Baptist's death, 104; the symbolic meaning of the day of Christ's death, 104; its destruction, 172; signifies a carnal habit which resists the good will through a delighting in temporal pleasures, 178; and delight and pleasure, 178-79; its sting is sin, 179; in what sense the Father dies so that we might obtain the inheritance, 192; of this world, 193

Deception, the highest virture is to deceive no one, and the worst vice is to deceive everyone, 90; God has sometimes permitted it, 91-95

Deer, their example in bearing one another's burdens, 180

Delight, and love, 146; and the sting of death, 179; through sin has come about a delight which resists the good will and is kept back only with pain, 179; carnal and spiritual, 179; *see also* Pleasure

Deliverance, of mankind, 42; from the bondage of sin, 149-57

Demons, their power, 200-202; covet being honored as gods by men, 201; how their power is exercised through magicians, 201-2; God permits the evil exercise of their power for worthy ends, 201; *see also* Devil, Satan, Spirits, and Wicked Spirit

Denarius, and the number 10, pp. 99, 102

Desire, love is a kind of, 66; its accord with mind and reason brings peace to the soul, 66

Devil, 205; *see also* Demons, Satan, Spirits, and Wicked Spirit

Dialectic, what it is for Augustine, 26 n.

Divine Ideas, see Ideas

Divorce, and fornication, 218-19; in pagan marriages it is not forbidden, 218-20; among believers it is permitted only by reason of fornication, 219

Docetism, 44 n.

Duty, it arises from natural law, 58; its definition, 58

Education, the progressive education of mankind, 75, 84, 90-95

Edwards, P., 30 n.

Egypt, 117, 209

Egyptians, why they were robbed by the Israelites, 93; why their magicians were able to perform certain miracles, 200-205

Eight (8), signifies earthly and corruptible things, 97

Eighty (80), its symbolic meaning in Cant (Song) 6.7, p. 97

Eighty-three Different Questions, when, why, how, and for whom written, 1-3; literary form, 2-13; chronology, 13-20; doctrinal content, 21-34; principal features of the work, 25-26; dialectical character, 26-27; reliance on authority of Scripture, 27-28; its Pythagoreanism, 28-29; Platonic and Neoplatonic character, 29-32; optimism about man, 32-34

Elements, the four elements, 99, 137, 212

Elijah (Elias), looked for as the precursor of the Lord's second coming, 107; in his spirit and power is John the Baptist the precursor of Christ, 107-8; *see also* John the Baptist

Elizabeth, birth of John the Baptist, 107; visited by Mary, 107-8; was of the priestly tribe, 118; filled with the Holy Spirit, 126

Enjoy, animals can "enjoy" but not "use" anything, 56; *see also* Enjoyable

Enjoyable, definition and relation to the honorable and the useful, 55-57

Equal, why God has not made all things equal, 74; God has begotten the Son as his equal, 84; in what sense the Son is and is not equal to the Father, 166-68

Equality, its relationship to image and likeness, 189-91

Equity, is a part of customary law, 59; its definition, 59

Erasmus, 9 n.

Esau, 164(n.); signifies the people of Old Testament faith, 105

Eternal Life, is the happy life, 66; comes through the soul's spiritual embrace of the Word, 133

Eternity, and sempiternity, 45 n.; and immortality, 47; and change, 47; and time, 47

Eusebius of Caesarea, 9(n.)

Evil, in what sense absolute evil does not exit, 39, 48; absolute evil is the absence of all good, 39, 48; absolute evil is the privation of all form, 39, 48; God is not its author, 48(n.)

Evil Desire, was forbidden by the Law and grew in the absence of faith, 141; *see also* Covetousness and Passions

Evil Spirits, see Demons

Faith, living water was the reward for the Samaritan woman's faith, 130; and the Law, 140; and grace, 140, 161; and grace and merit, 161; and the calling of God, 164 n.; its relationship to works according to the apostles James and Paul, 193-96

Fall, the, 57

False, among sense impressions the true cannot be distinguished from it, 41

Farges, J., 105 n.

Father, the, it is in God's very nature to be the eternal Father, 45; how the Son is the Father's likeness, 50; and Son are one

substance, 50; has begotten the Son as his equal, 84, 166-69, 191; by him has everything been created through the Son in the Holy Spirit, 150, 212, cf. 167; an objection to the Son's equality with the Father, 166; in what sense the Son is and is not equal to him, 166-68; the Son is his image, but he is not the image of the Son, 167; begets while the Son is begotten, 167; is himself our inheritance as sons of God, 192; in what sense he dies so that we might obtain the inheritance, 192; *see also* God

Fear, whether one can fear losing freedom from fear, 62; its nature, source, and control, 62-63; whether freedom from it is the only thing to be loved and desired, 62-63; and covetousness, 62-63, 68; a life without it ought to be loved and desired, 64; its role in one's moral and spiritual life, 68-69; of God, 68-71; characterized obedience under the Old Testament, 179; whether or not it is a sin, 197-98; and passion, 197-98

Fetus, the stages of its development, 98

Fifty (50), and the cleansed and perfected Church, 101, cf. 214 and Quinquagesima, 214

Firstfruit, our spirit as a firstfruit offering to God, 155(n.)

Fish, the meaning of the one hundred and fifty-three fish, 102-3, 214-15; the meaning of the two fish with which the Lord fed the

templation of them, 80-81; in accord with them has God created
all things, 80-81(n.); there are
ideas or reasons unique to individual created things, 81; the
vision of them brings the soul full
blessedness, 81

Idolatry, in the Scriptures it is often
represented by Samaria, 129; it
is often signified by adultery in
the Scriptures, 133(n.)

Idols, the worship of them, 121,
129, 199; their beauty, 198-99

Illumination, and the achievement
of true wisdom, 76, 86; and the
ideas, 80-81; of souls by God, 93

Image, on man made in God's image and likeness, 84-88, 87 n.;
the distinction between "in the
image" and "in the likeness,"
87-88; of God was lost on account of sin, 152(n.); the Son is
the image of the Father, but not
the Father of the Son, 167; its
relationship to equality and
likeness, 189-91

Immortality, and eternity, 47; and
change, 47; its loss and recovery,
218

Incarnation, through it has the
Wisdom of God declared
mankind's deliverance, 42, 137;
the Wisdom of God became man
in order to show us how to live
virtuously by conquering the
fear of death, 51; the Son of God
became man in order to show us
a pattern for living, 74; Christ
came as a teacher to direct
mankind to the best morals, 75;
Truth has assumed humanity in

order that man might become
wise, 76; and the Lord's humbl-
ing of himself, 129, 174-76; the
character of the Lord's reign
during the period of his incarnation and passion, 174-76; its purpose is to subject all worldly
pride to Christ in his humility
and lowliness, 175; refutation of
the Apollinarian view of, 207-9;
see also Assumption

Influence, a kind of virtue, 60

Inheritance, of God, 191-93; the
Father is himself the inheritance
of the sons of God, 192; in what
sense we ourselves are the inheritance of God, 193

Injustice, why it is experienced by
the righteous and just, 217-18

Intellect, is limited in respect to
itself, 44; loves itself, 44; *see also*
Intelligence, Mind, and Understanding

Intelligence (as a quality), a part of
prudence, 58; its definition, 58

Intelligence (as a faculty), the
highest part of the soul and that
wherein lies its excellence, 80; *see
also* Intellect, Mind, Reason,
and Understanding

Intelligible World, Augustine's regret at using this phrase, 81 n.;
and the kingdom of heaven, 81
n.; Plato was not mistaken in
asserting its existence, 81 n.

Isaac, the prophetic meaning of his
near-sacrifice, 104

Israelites, why they performed
animal sacrifice, 84; their
despoiling of the Egyptians, 93

Italy, 2

as good as God, 37; the cause of
his perversity, 38; the more honorable sex, 42; his superiority to
animals, 44; for his use have all
things been created, 55-57; before and after the Fall, 57; the
old man and the new, 69, 84, 85,
105, 128; the inner man and the
outer, 69, 84-87, 105, 128-29;
the earthly man and the heavenly, 69, 85; his progressive education over several periods or ages
of time, 74-75, 84, 90-95; Christ
came in the time of his youth,
75(n.); grows from infancy to old
age in the manner of an individual human being, 75; made
in God's image and likeness,
84-88; nothing is more closely
united to God than man, 86; in
what sense even his body has
been created in the image and
likeness of God, 87; a corpse is
not rightly termed a man,
87(n.); made in the image and
likeness of God in contrast to the
Son, who is the image and likeness of God, 87(n.), cf. 191; his
threefold division into Jews,
Gentiles, and carnal Christians,
101; the six ages of, 105, 128;
Christ came in the time of his old
age, 107, cf. 75 n.; the four
periods in his redemptive history, 123, 141; his spirit is, in a
way, the husband of the soul and
thus rules its dispositions, 133;
lives under the Law as long as he
lives in sin, 138; prior to the
Law, 141, 142, 149; under the
Law, 141, 142-45, 149; under

grace, 141, 142, 145-48, 149; in
the peace which follows the
resurrection, 141, 142, 148, 149;
lost the image of God on account
of sin, 152(n.); in him is every
creature recapitulated, 153, 154;
carnal or animal man, 153-54;
carnal man and spiritual,
153-54; the apostle Paul prohibits the carnal, but not the
spiritual, man from inquiring into the mind of God, 159-60; his
nature sinned in paradise, 161

Mani (or Manes), 15 n.

Manichaeism, 157 n., 158 n.; the
anti-Manichaean QQ., 14-16;
what it is, 15 n.; its denial of the
reality of Christ's body, 44 n.

Marcion, 9 nn.

Marcus, R., 9 n.

Markus, R., 26 n., 30 n.

Marriage, a wife is bound to her
husband while he is alive, but
she is free to marry another
when he dies, 138; and divorce,
218-20

Marrou, H., 20 n., 26 n., 28 n., 33
nn.

Martha, 137

Mary, 176, 209; her visit with
Elizabeth, 107-8; was descended
from both a royal and a priestly
tribe, 118

Massa, the mass of sins, 141, 163;
of sin, 161; sinners constitute a
single mass on account of the sin
of Adam, 163; in the single mass
of sinners there are deeply hidden merits which render some
worthy of righteousness, 163

Mathematicians, the term desig-

Philo of Alexandria, 9(n.)

Place, the soul's movement is not from place to place, 40; what is contained in it is body, 47; God does not occupy a place, 47-48, 126; in what sense the temple of God can be called the place of God, 48

Plato, 29, 30(nn.), 81, 83 n.; did not discover the Ideas but is the one who first gave them their name, 79; his doctrine of the two worlds, 81 n.; is not mistaken in saying that the intelligible world exists, 81 n.

Platonism, its influence on Augustine, 29-32

Platonists, 30 n., 81 n.

Pleasure(s), of the world and the periods of the redemptive history of man, 149; and the sting of death, 179; *see also* Delight

Plotinus, 30 n.

Plutarch, 7(n.), 8(n.)

Pontius Pilate, 205

Porphyry, 30 n.

Possidius, 4(nn.), 5, 15 n., 71 n.; his catalogue of Augustine's writings, 4-5

Power of God, is Wisdom and therefore the second person of the Trinity, 42

Predestination, of our calling is in secret, 136

Pride, in what it consists, 57; one must avoid it, 71; fear of God is necessary for avoiding it, 71; and the incarnation, 174-77; on ridding oneself of it, 182-83

Princeps, 92(n.)

Privation, of all form is absolute evil, 39; and the knowledge of sins, 144(nn.)

Prophecy, is embodied in John the Baptist, 103; prophetic meaning of Old Testament symbolism, 104-5

Providence, governs all things, 50-51, 52-3, 68, 73-74; and free will, 50-51, 52-53; its administration, 52-53, 94; is also called usefulness, 56; and the fear of God, 68; in its private and public administration, 75-76, 200-205; and the spiritual perfection of humanity, 84; works sometimes in secret and sometimes openly through visible created things, 126; and the suffering of the righteous, 217-18

Prudence, one of the four parts of virtue, 58; its definition and parts, 58; one of the four virtues of the soul, 121

Prying, the meaning of the apostle Paul's rebuke of prying, 158-59

Punishment, of the wicked is an evil to them but is counted among the good works of God, 48 n.; opportunity to commit sins is sometimes a punishment for other, preceding sins, 202

Pythagoreanism, its influence on Augustine, 28-29

Quadragesima, its symbolic meaning, 213-14

Quasten, J., 9 nn., 71 n., 206 n.

Queens, in Cant (Song) 6.7 it refers to souls ruling in the intelligible and spiritual realm, 97

Quinquagesima, its symbolic meaning, 214

INDEX OF HOLY SCRIPTURE

For an explanation of the page references, see the explanatory note prefaced to the General Index.

(Books of the Old Testament)

Genesis
  1.27: 106
  1.31:86
  2.2: 103
  3.9: 136
  3.19: 137, 152, 160
  4.8: 104
  6.6: 88
  7.1 ff.: 104
  14.18: 117
  18.8: 210
  22.3-13: 104
  25.23:105
  37.41:105
  41: 165
  46.22: 209
  46.27: 209

Exodus
  3.22: 90, 93
  4.21: 163
  5.14: 165
  7.8: 200
  7.12: 202
  12.35: 90
  32.6: 121

Deuteronomy
  13.3: 114

2 Kings (2 Samuel)
  12.1-13: 119

3 Kings (1 Kings)
  22.20-23: 92

Tobit:
  12.19: 210

Psalms (LXX numbers first)
  2.8: 193
  8.8: 169 n., 172
  15(16).5: 192
  18(19).13: 145
  38(39).7: 152 n.
  44(45).8: 110
  50(51).13: 126
  50(51).19(17): 52
  62(63).9: 77, 139
  64(65).3: 208
  67(68).19 = Eph 4.8: 131
  72(73).28: 95, 97
  95(96).10: 174(n.)
  100(101).1: 165
  109(110).1: 169 n.
  109(110).4 = Heb 5.6: 117
  117(118).8-9: 170
  122(123).2: 171
  140(141).5:112

Proverbs
  3.12: 215
  5.19: 180
  8.35: 164 n.
  16.2: 88
  20.9: 111

Ecclesiastes
  1.2-3: 152

Canticle (Song)
  6.7: 97

251

THE FATHERS
OF THE CHURCH

(A series of approximately 100 volumes when completed)

translated by L. Schopp
The Magnitude of the Soul
    translated by J. McMahon
On Music
    translated by R. Taliaferro
The Advantage of Believing
    translated by L. Meagher
On Faith in Things Unseen
    translated by R. Deferrari, M–F. McDonald

OCLC 856032

Volume 5:   SAINT AUGUSTINE   (1948)
The Happy Life
    translated by L. Schopp
Answer to Skeptics *(Contra Academicos)*
    translated by D. Kavanagh
Divine Providence and the Problem of Evil
    translated by R. Russell
The Soliloquies
    translated by T. Gilligan

OCLC 728405

Volume 6:   WRITINGS OF SAINT JUSTIN MARTYR   (1948)
The First Apology
The Second Apology
The Dialogue with Trypho
Exhortation to the Greeks
Discourse to the Greeks
The Monarchy or Rule of God
    translated by T. Falls

OCLC 807077

Volume 7:   NICETA OF REMESIANA   (1949)
Writings of Niceta of Remesiana
    translated by G. Walsh
Prosper of Aquitaine: Grace and Free Will
    translated by J. O'Donnell
Writings of Sulpicius Severus
    translated by B. Peebles
Vincent of Lerins: The Commonitories
    translated by R. Morris

OCLC 807068

Volume 8:   SAINT AUGUSTINE   (1950)

The City of God (books 1–7)
    translated by D. Zema, G. Walsh

OCLC 807084

Volume 9:   **SAINT BASIL ASCETICAL WORKS**   (1950)
    translated by M. Wagner

OCLC 856020

Volume 10:   **TERTULLIAN APOLOGETICAL WORKS**   (1950)
Tertullian Apology
    translated by E–J. Daly
On the Soul
    translated by E. Quain
The Testimony of the Soul
To Scapula
    translated by R. Arbesmann
Minucius Felix: Octavius
    translated by R. Arbesmann

OCLC 1037264

Volume 11:   **SAINT AUGUSTINE**   (1957)
Commentary on the Lord's Sermon on the Mount
Selected Sermons (17)
    translated by D. Kavanagh

OCLC 2210742

Volume 12:   **SAINT AUGUSTINE**   (1951)
Letters (1–82)
    translated by W. Parsons

OCLC 807061

Volume 13:   **SAINT BASIL**   (1951)
Letters (1–185)
    translated by A–C. Way

OCLC 2276183

Volume 14:   **SAINT AUGUSTINE**   (1952)
The City of God (books 8–16)
    translated by G. Walsh, G. Monahan

OCLC 807084

Volume 15:   **EARLY CHRISTIAN BIOGRAPHIES**   (1952)
Life of St. Ambrose by Paulinus
    translated by J. Lacy
Life of St. Augustine by Bishop Possidius

Life of St. Cyprian by Pontius
translated by M. M. Mueller, R. Deferrari
Life of St. Epiphanius by Ennodius
translated by G. Cook
Life of St. Paul the First Hermit
Life of St. Hilarion by St. Jerome
Life of Malchus by St. Jerome
translated by L. Ewald
Life of St. Anthony by St. Athanasius
translated by E. Keenan
A Sermon on the Life of St. Honoratus by St. Hilary
translated by R. Deferrari

OCLC 806775

Volume 16:   SAINT AUGUSTINE   (1952)
The Christian Life
Lying
The Work of Monks
The Usefulness of Fasting
translated by S. Muldowney
Against Lying
translated by H. Jaffe
Continence
translated by M–F. McDonald
Patience
translated by L. Meagher
The Excellence of Widowhood
translated by C. Eagan
The Eight Questions of Dulcitius
translated by M. Deferrari

OCLC 806731

Volume 17:   SAINT PETER CHRYSOLOGUS   (1953)
Selected Sermons
Letter to Eutyches
               SAINT VALERIAN
Homilies
Letter to the Monks
translated by G. Ganss

OCLC 806783

Volume 18:   SAINT AUGUSTINE   (1953)

262

Letters (83–130)
  translated by W. Parsons

OCLC 807061

Volume 19:   EUSEBIUS PAMPHILI (1953)
Ecclesiastical History (books 1–5)
  translated by R. Deferrari

OCLC 708651

Volume 20:   SAINT AUGUSTINE (1953)
Letters (131–164)
  translated by W. Parsons

OCLC 807061

Volume 21:   SAINT AUGUSTINE (1953)
Confessions
  translated by V. Bourke

OCLC 2210845

Volume 22:   FUNERAL ORATIONS (1953)
Saint Gregory Nazianzen: Four Funeral Orations
  translated by L. McCauley
Saint Ambrose: On the Death of His Brother Satyrus I & II
  translated by J. Sullivan, M. McGuire
Saint Ambrose: Consolation on the Death of Emperor
  Valentinian
  Funeral Oration on the Death of Emperor Theodosius
  translated by R. Deferrari

OCLC 806797

Volume 23:   CLEMENT OF ALEXANDRIA (1954)
Christ the Educator
  translated by S. Wood

OCLC 2200024

Volume 24:   SAINT AUGUSTINE (1954)
The City of God (books 17-22)
  translated by G. Walsh, D. Honan

OCLC 807084

Volume 25:   SAINT HILARY OF POITIERS (1954)
The Trinity
  translated by S. McKenna

OCLC 806781

Volume 26:   SAINT AMBROSE (1954)

Letters (204–270)
    translated by W. Parsons

                                        OCLC 807061

Volume 33:   SAINT JOHN CHRYSOSTOM   (1957)
        Commentary on St. John The Apostle and Evangelist
        Homilies (1–47)
            translated by T. Goggin

                                        OCLC 2210926

Volume 34:   SAINT LEO THE GREAT   (1957)
        Letters
            translated by E. Hunt

                                        OCLC 825765

Volume 35:   SAINT AUGUSTINE   (1957)
        Against Julian
            translated by M. Schumacher

                                        OCLC 3255620

Volume 36:   SAINT CYPRIAN   (1958)
        To Donatus
        The Lapsed
        The Unity of the Church
        The Lord's Prayer
        To Demetrian
        Mortality
        Works and Almsgiving
        Jealousy and Envy
        Exhortation to Martyrdom to Fortunatus
        That Idols Are Not Gods
            translated by R. Deferrari
        The Dress of Virgins
            translated by A. Keenan
        The Good of Patience
            translated by G. Conway

                                        OCLC 3894637
Volume 37:   SAINT JOHN OF DAMASCUS   (1958)
        The Fount of Knowledge
        On Heresies
        The Orthodox Faith (4 books)
            translated by F. Chase, Jr.

                                        OCLC 810002

                    265

The Sacrament of the Incarnation of Our Lord
The Sacraments
translated by R. Deferrari

OCLC 2316634

Volume 45:   SAINT AUGUSTINE   (1963)
The Trinity
translated by S. McKenna

OCLC 784847

Volume 46:   SAINT BASIL   (1963)
Exegetic Homilies
translated by A–C. Way

OCLC 806743

Volume 47:   SAINT CAESARIUS OF ARLES II   (1963)
Sermons (81–186)
translated by M. M. Mueller

OCLC 2494636

Volume 48:   THE HOMILIES OF SAINT JEROME   (1964)
Homilies 1–59
translated by L. Ewald

OCLC 412009

Volume 49:   LACTANTIUS   (1964)
The Divine Institutes
translated by M–F. McDonald

OCLC 711211

Volume 50:   PAULUS OROSIUS   (1964)
The Seven Books of History Against the Pagans
translated by R. Deferrari

OCLC 711212

Volume 51:   SAINT CYPRIAN   (1964)
Letters (1–81)
translated by R. Donna

OCLC 806738

Volume 52:   THE POEMS OF PRUDENTIUS   (1965)
The Divinity of Christ
The Origin of Sin
The Spiritual Combat
Against Symmachus (two books)
Scenes from Sacred History Or Twofold Nourishment
translated by C. Eagan

268

Volume 59:   SAINT AUGUSTINE   (1968)
          The Teacher
          The Free Choice of the Will
          Grace and Free Will
                    translated by R. Russell

                                        OCLC 712674

Volume 60:   SAINT AUGUSTINE   (1968)
          The Retractations
                    translated by I. Bogan

                                        OCLC 712676

Volume 61: THE WORKS OF SAINT CYRIL OF JERUSALEM I (1969)
          Procatechesis
                    translated by A. Stephenson
          Lenten Lectures 1–12 (Catecheses)
                    translated by L. McCauley

                                        OCLC 21885

Volume 62:   IBERIAN FATHERS I   (1969)
          Writings of Martin of Braga
                    Sayings of the Egyptian Fathers
                    Driving Away Vanity
                    Exhortation to Humility
                    Anger
                    Reforming the Rustics
                    Rules For An Honest Life
                    Triple Immersion
                    Easter
          Paschasius of Dumium
                    Questions and Answers of the Greek Fathers
          Writings of Leander of Seville
                    The Training of Nuns and the Contempt of the World
                    Sermon on the Triumph of the Church for the Conver-
                    sion of the Goths
                    translated by C. Barlow

                                        OCLC 718095

Volume 63:   IBERIAN FATHERS II   (1969)
          Braulio of Saragossa
                    Letters of Braulio
                    Life of St. Emilian
                    List of the Books of Isidore of Seville
          Writings of Fructuosus of Braga

Rule for the Monastery of Compludo
General Rule for Monasteries
Pact
Monastic Agreement
translated by C. Barlow

OCLC 718095

Volume 64:   THE WORKS OF SAINT CYRIL   (1970)
                     OF JERUSALEM II
Lenten Lectures (Catcheses) 13–18
    translated by L. McCauley
The Mystagogical Lectures
Sermon on the Paralytic
Letter to Constantius
    translated by A. Stephenson

OCLC 21885

Volume 65   SAINT AMBROSE   (1972)
Seven Exegetical Works
    Isaac or the Soul
    Death as a Good
    Jacob and the Happy Life
    Joseph
    The Patriarchs
    Flight from the World
    The Prayer of Job and David
    translated by M. McHugh

OCLC 314148

Volume 66:   SAINT CAESARIUS OF ARLES III   (1973)
    Sermons 187–238
        translated by M. M. Mueller

OCLC 1035149; 2494636

Volume 67:   NOVATIAN   (1974)
    The Trinity
    The Spectacles
    Jewish Foods
    In Praise of Purity
    Letters
        translated by R. DeSimone

OCLC 662181